cooperation in mobilizing resources and inventing transnational structures, as well as the strategies and prospects for transforming human behavior so as to strengthen national capabilities to safeguard the biosphere. Each measure that he recommends has its basis in action or organization now underway. Although the task is enormous and difficult, the nucleus of necessary organization and policy now exist. All persons concerned about public policy toward the environment will find the book interesting, impelling, and rewarding.

Lynton K. Caldwell,
Arthur F. Bentley Professor of Political Science at Indiana University, has served with the Council of State Governments, the Agency for International Development, and the United Nations and has been consultant to numerous educational and research institutions and public agencies. His books include *Environment: A Challenge to Modern Society,* selected by the Indiana Writers Conference as one of the outstanding books of 1970, and *Man and Environment: Public Policy and Administration.*

In Defense of Earth

In Defense of Earth:

International Protection of the Biosphere

LYNTON K. CALDWELL

INDIANA UNIVERSITY PRESS

Bloomington / London

DEDICATION

*To the men and women in many countries and
in many organizations who must succeed
in their efforts to obtain a sustainable
relationship between man and Earth if the
human experiment is to continue.*

CONTENTS

vii

CONTENTS

ACKNOWLEDGMENTS

MANY PERSONS IN MANY WAYS CONTRIBUTED TO THE shaping of this book. But the author's indebtedness is so varied and extensive that only a part of it can be acknowledged here.

Financial assistance was received from the Conservation Foundation, the Conservation and Research Foundation, and the Research Committee of Indiana University.

The Conservation and Research Foundation, which provided the greater part of the financial aid, has since 1953 assisted a variety of efforts to preserve the quality of the natural environment. It has supported the Nature Conservancy in that organization's programs of land acquisition for scientific, educational and aesthetic purposes. It sponsored the pioneering Conference on Law and the Environment, and more recently has helped in the initial funding of the Institute of Ecology. The author especially appreciates the interest shown in this book by Dr. Richard H. Goodwin, President of The Conservation and Research Foundation, and the members of its Board of Trustees.

Information, ideas, criticism, and interchange of experience and observations were derived from a wide variety of associations and from individual and institutional generosity. Of particular benefit to the author has been his association with the Committee on International Environmental Programs of the National Academy of Sciences, its chairman, Thomas Malone, and its executive director, Henry S. Kellermann; with the International Union for Conservation of Nature and Natural Resources; with the Woodrow Wilson International Center for Scholars; with the Conference on International Organization and the Human Environment cosponsored by the Institute on Man and Science, and the Aspen Institute on Humanistic Studies organized by Richard N. Gardner; and with the Public Administration Division of the United Nations Secretariate, particularly with its deputy-director, Emil J. Sady.

For assistance at Indiana University, thanks are owed to Dorothy Dooren, Michael Gill, Nicholas Henry, Toufiq Siddiqi, and May Lee, Jan Lundy, and Mary Sinnock. A debt of gratitude is owed to the staffs of the university libraries, and especially to the government documents and reference sections. I also would like to thank the editors and production staff of the Indiana University Press, who have helped greatly to put the manuscript in final form.

For assistance in Washington, personal appreciation must be expressed to Richard Carpenter and Wallace Bowman of the Environmental Policy Division of the Congressional Research Service, to Adele N. Wilson of the Department of the Interior, and to John P. Milton of the Conservation Foundation.

It is the author's hope that the book will merit the interest and effort that these and other contributors directly and indirectly have made to its production.

LYNTON K. CALDWELL

In Defense of Earth

INTRODUCTION

Why This Book?

THIS BOOK IS INTENDED TO HELP PEOPLE UNDERSTAND one of the significant developments of our times: the movement to bring man's relationships with the planet Earth under some form of rational control. This effort has enlisted the participation of people in nearly every part of the world and from all segments of society. It has become an international movement, not only in the formal and official sense of action by governments and international organizations, but also because it has involved people-to-people interaction across national boundaries. The focal point of this movement is now the United Nations Conference on the Human Environment in Stockholm in June 1972. This book should, therefore, be helpful to persons who want to understand the background of the conference, the reasons for its occurrence at this time, and its outcomes and implications for the future.

Almost nowhere has the movement on behalf of the human environment originated within governments. Particularly in the more highly developed nations, concern for the environment has been thrust upon often reluctant governments by popular demand. The movement was largely unforeseen and unpredicted even by those whose business it has been to study social trends. In this, and certain other respects, its development parallels the course of sociopolitical revolutions; and it may be said of this movement, as Alexis de Tocqueville wrote of the coming of the French

3

Revolution, "Never were there events more important, longer in ripening, more fully prepared, or less foreseen."

The movement to protect the planetary environment is both national and international, but it is most significantly international because its concepts and propositions have come from many different countries and cultures. For example, the fundamental concept of the biosphere appears to have originated with the French naturalist Jean Baptiste Lamarck, was first used by the Austrian geologist Edward Suess, was developed into substantially its present form by the Russian minerologist V. I. Vernadsky, was popularized in the writings of the French priest and paleontologist Pierre Teilhard de Chardin, became a subject for official international attention in the Biosphere Conference of 1968 sponsored by UNESCO with the cooperation of other international organizations, and was incorporated in the text of the United States National Environmental Policy Act of 1969.

The movement offers some striking analogies and contrasts to the major international political movement of the past century, Marxism. The environmental protection movement is an action-oriented philosophy. Like Marxism, it claims (but with more demonstrable validity) a base in science; it has developed a set of propositions regarding man's relationship to his history and to the existential world, and it leads to a specific course of action. It shares with Marxism a moral imperative to reshape the behavior of society and to direct the course of history. And this imperative may assume the quality of religious conviction, the elements of which have been described by René Dubos in "A Theology of the Earth."

Unlike Marxism, the movement for environmental protection is not at war with a social class, nor is it guided by a specific dialectic or dogma. It is a movement for the defense of the Earth against the unwise and improvident behavior of man himself. It is not inherently divisive although it opposes certain forms of human behavior that impair the beauty, variety, stability, or viability of the Earth. The abuses it attacks have not been unique to any social or political system. They have been most pronounced in industrialized societies and are found in both socialist and private enterprise systems. The propositions of the environmental protection movement are based upon scientific investigation that

4

may be tested and modified by scientists everywhere. The effects of CO_2 in the atmosphere, or oil pollution in the oceans, are objectively demonstrable. Nations may differ over the importance of these effects, but the effects themselves cannot be changed by political interpretations.

For these reasons, the defense of the Earth against misuse by man could become a powerful unifying force in a world of nations. It has already enlisted the cooperation of scientists and public officials in every part of the world. There are, as yet, marked differences among nations as to the urgency of protective action and the extent to which traditional attitudes and contemporary ambitions must be modified to safeguard environmental values. Nevertheless, awareness of the threat to the Earth and man's future is spreading, and the time is approaching when the global environment will become an explicit object of international public policy.

The growth of all great social movements has been marked at certain critical points by catalyzing or consolidating events. The United Nations Conference on the Human Environment is such an event. Even if the actual 1972 meeting did not occur, Resolution 2398 (23) of the United Nations, adopted on December 3, 1968, represents a milestone in the recognition by nations of a common danger in the threat to the viability of the Earth. The call for the conference set in motion preparations throughout the world that have already influenced public policies and enlarged public awareness of the issues at stake. Preparations for Stockholm have been unique in the history of international conferences in the extent and focusing of the preconference work. And while the outcome of the sessions at Stockholm cannot be foreseen, nor fully evaluated immediately, it seems safe to say that this conference will prove to be one of the more significant events of the twentieth century.

There is today among many thoughtful observers a belief that the modern age is drawing to a close, that the sequence of events that began around the year 1500 has nearly run its course. This belief is based, in part, upon the evident impossibility of extending many of the dominant modern trends indefinitely into the future. It is not revelation but the exponential curve that leads to this conclusion. The operating assumptions of the modern

5

world have been based upon tacit expectations of infinity—of infinite horizons, abundance, adaptability, and time to correct mistakes. But the limitations have been there none the less.

The legend of Faust epitomizes the ambition of modern man to master the world without first mastering his behavior in relation to it. He has employed science and technology to serve his desires without troubling greatly about the consequences and ultimate costs of his actions. The environmental crisis is thus an outward manifestation of a crisis of mind and spirit. There could be no greater misconception of its meaning than to believe it to be concerned only with endangered wild-life, man-made ugliness, and environmental pollution. Those are part of it, but more importantly, the crisis is concerned with the kind of creature that man is and with what he must become in order to survive. And what man can become must not only be individually motivated—it needs also to be socially assisted.

Inevitably, the movement to protect the biosphere and defend the Earth is concerned with institutions as well as with behavior, because through institutions human effort is guided and social goals attained. The transformation of institutional structure is in fact the transformation of society. Obviously there is much more to be said about the nature and probabilities of institutional change than can be said here. All modern institutions are to some degree involved, but this book is largely concerned with changes in the institutions of government and international action.

The emphasis of the book is historical. It endeavors to help people understand a little more clearly how modern society has arrived at its present critical juncture. It tries to help the reader orient himself on the trajectory of history and see that where modern society has been exerts a powerful influence in determining the direction that it must go. If the book does this, it will, hopefully, help people make the conceptual and ethical adjustments that may be required in the rapidly approaching future when, in the words of Nicholas Berdyaev, "the fate of man in the modern world" will be decided.

1

An Unecological Animal:

MUST HUMAN BEHAVIOR

ENDANGER THE BASIS OF LIFE?

IT HAS BECOME COMMONPLACE TO HEAR THAT MAN-
kind is facing the greatest crisis in its history—and that the cause
of the crisis is man himself. The crisis is the growing threat
posed by the activities of man to the planetary life-support systems of air, water, soil, and living organisms. The reality of the
threat is widely acknowledged among informed people. That the
threat is a crisis is less generally accepted. Skeptics argue that
man has always been confronted by environmental challenges
which he has somehow met. Dissenters contend that ecological
developments taking place over decades or even centuries ought
not to be lumped together and called a crisis. But there is a
logical justification for calling the present state of man's environmental relationships critical.

First, the word "crisis" implies a culmination of events. It
suggests a stage in development at which a fundamental change
of state or direction occurs.

Second, it is the decisive nature of events and not their
duration that constitutes a crisis. The modern news media has
persuaded some people that no event lasting much beyond a
weekend could be a crisis. In fact, most of the coups, confronta-
tions, and summit conferences to which the label "crisis" is
applied have not been crises at all, merely dangerous or portentous events or pseudo-events. It will not do to use modern

man's political stopwatch to measure ecological trends. A critical stage in the transformation of ecological systems may last for decades by human timekeeping, and yet be a mere tick of the clock of geochronology.

Third, a human passion for simple explanations obscures the complex and convergent character of the ecological crisis. It is hard for most people to understand how circumstances with which man has lived for generations can suddenly become critical. Yet the ecological crisis of our times is the culmination of separate events, often long-maturing, that have converged in the mid-twentieth century to threaten the continued existence of life upon Earth.

The premise of this book is that mankind is in fact confronted by a convergence of developments in his relationship to the Earth that can properly be called critical, by a crisis of crises.[1] The ecological crisis of our times may be the most severe test of his capability that man has undergone. Our focus, therefore, will not be on the facts of ecology, which have been detailed in other places, but rather upon the behavior that has brought on the crisis, and upon the means by which man, an "unecological" animal, may cope with it—and himself.

Evolutionary Factors in Human Behavior

THE LIVES OF individual prehistoric or primitive men may have been more precarious than those of their present day descendants; but early man, as a species, was less vulnerable to extermination. Until modern times, communities of men were widely scattered around the Earth, isolated from one another by distance and geophysical barriers. They were thus buffered to some extent from contagious disease and from the aggressive tendencies of other men. There was room to run away and there were places to hide. Human technology was not yet able to produce rapid and irreversible global effects.

Such relative safety was destroyed by the ingenuity that developed intercontinental ballistic missiles, DDT, the internal combustion engine, and telecommunications. Man's security now depends less upon individual initiative than upon the social competence of the race; and if past experience indicates future prospects, the outlook is discouraging. More than ever before, the future of mankind depends upon the creation and administration of institutions to guide and regulate human behavior. These institutions are largely those of science and education, and especially of domestic and international public administration. And these agencies of society, upon which man must rely to surmount his environmental crisis, have hitherto contributed to the very injuries that they are now called upon to cure.

Civilized human society has reached a point at which it must change its habits if it is to survive. Otherwise, man's future may be brief or, if extended, may decline to an irretrievable state of technological barbarism and environmental degradation.

A practical response to this necessity would be to enlarge and strengthen the art of self-government and to improve institutions and procedures through which knowledge may be organized and applied to man's real needs and higher values, and to counteract his more dangerous weaknesses and tendencies.

Unfortunately the human animal is too much a part of his own experience to see it clearly in historical perspective. Historians share the human inconvenience of a life too short to compare directly sequential changes in social systems. The disintegration of societies and the decline and fall of civilizations are no better understood than are the causes of biological old age and death. Symptoms can be described and immediate causes analyzed—but the causes of the causes are seldom understood.

To cope with his present and future as best he may, man must estimate where he is on the trajectory of history and learn better to forecast the future, or alternative possible futures.[2] He must develop at least a minimal understanding of how human society has become its own worst danger. Many *whys* may long remain unanswered, but one need not always know the *why* of something in order to bring it under control. Knowledge of *how* a process works may be sufficient to control or arrest a trend. A large part of successful medicine relies on such limited understanding. The *how* of human experience is obviously more accessible to description and analysis than the *why* and, to this extent, the anthropologist and the historian may help society to understand how it has jeopardized its future. This understanding

9

does not guarantee remedial action; but knowledge is necessary to reason, and human rationality is our best hope for bringing ecological wisdom to bear on man's present and future behavior.

Some may object to the description of man as an unecological animal. It may be argued that through culture and technology man has emancipated himself from the ecological imperatives. Natural populations of animals rarely eat themselves out of their food supply or breed beyond the carrying capacities of their ecological niches.[3] The human animal has obviously enlarged his niche or habitat through artificial means and has, through agriculture and urban technologies, amended the ground rules of nature regarding numbers and food supply. But it does not follow that the ecological ground rules governing the fate of species have been repealed by mankind. Man's modifications of natural conditions contain their own parameters and constraints, and the long-range consequences of man's supposed improvements upon nature are not fully evident. By the geobiological clock of nature, it is much too early to pronounce the human species more than a temporary success.

Human behavior has been unecological in the sense that it appears to be deficient in certain instinctual safeguards possessed by most animals. While the human animal, as a species, is highly aggressive, human aggression has not been in itself an unecological trait. But armed by evolving technology, man has become progressively more dangerous to all forms of life, including his own. Evidence of homicide and of cannibalism have been found among the remains of Pleistocene man.

Konrad Lorenz[4] attributes this behavior to a genetic circumstance, a relatively weak inhibition of intraspecific aggression. Animals of great physical strength, equipped with death-dealing teeth and claws, have evolved with strong inhibitions against murderous attack upon their own species and normally resolve conflicts over mating and territory by submission or flight. In a wholly natural state, men, doves, and rabbits cannot easily destroy their own kind, and evolved no inhibitions. But, so this reasoning goes, man devised weapons more formidable than the tiger's without acquiring the tiger's innate inhibitions regarding their use.

Evidence of human inhibition toward homicide is conflicting. It appears strongest toward the family and familiar individuals and weakest toward strangers and persons differing markedly in appearance or behavior. Yet crimes of violence in modern countries occur frequently among relatives and within families.[5] Human societies have attempted to cope with this behavioral deficiency through cultural means. They have attempted, so to speak, to substitute ethics for ethology, law for instinct. Nevertheless in almost every society permissible behaviors to strangers and foreigners differ from those expected to friends and compatriots. The weakness of human inhibition toward killing is most strikingly evident in war, where man has not hesitated to destroy not only his human enemy, but all forms of life associated with the enemy or upon which the enemy might in any respect depend.

Man's relatively weak inhibition against attacking other species may indeed be merely a special manifestation of a highly aggressive disposition toward the world generally. Mankind has shown little restraint in wresting whatever it could get from both animate and inanimate nature. For prehistoric man, this tendency must have had a survival value, but it may not even then have been an unequivocal good. There is strong evidence that prehistoric man hastened the extinction of large mammals in the Northern Hemisphere at the end of the last great Ice Age by overkill.[6]

In the post-Pleistocene period, extinction of species has proceeded so far that today virtually all wildlife above the microorganic exists by human sufferance. Prospects for the survival of all larger birds, reptiles, and mammals are poor. Primitive human societies are being destroyed by acculturation or economic pressure, and by paternalistic policies that destroy their structure, self-respect, and means of livelihood. The contemptuous posture of modern societies in relation to the natural world is dangerous because it opens the way toward the inadvertent destruction of the basis of life itself. Cynics rightly say that the world could struggle along without the pelican or the whooping crane; they do not often note that it could as easily do without man. Quite possibly the unecological tendencies of *homo sapiens* may already have marked him for the extinction he has so freely meted out to other species.

In their introduction to a published symposium on *Man the Hunter*,[7] Richard B. Lee and Irven DeVore observe that during 99 per cent of the million years man has occupied the Earth he has been a hunter-gatherer. Living in small mobile bands normally well within the carrying capacity of their territories and frequently employing deliberate population controls, hunters maintained long-term man–environment equilibriums that contrast strongly with the instabilities of the modern world. "To date," they write, "the hunting way of life has been the most successful and persistent adaptation man has ever achieved." [8]

To recapture the ecological advantages of this condition without losing the advantages of advanced technology, Nigel Calder has suggested the return of large areas of the Earth to wilderness, with urban man concentrated on artificial islands on the continental shelves.[9] Modern man could then live alternatively in two worlds—the world of nature to which he has been biologically adapted and the world of high civilization which his intelligence has created. Even if man's ecological difficulties seem unlikely to be overcome by such simple though radical expedients, some means must be found to correct or to compensate for man's unecological tendencies if humanity and the biosphere are to survive.

Lee and DeVore conclude that:

> It is still an open question whether man will be able to survive the exceedingly complex and unstable ecological conditions he has created for himself. If he fails in this task, interplanetary archeologists of the future will classify our planet as one in which a very long and stable period of small-scale hunting and gathering was followed by an apparently instantaneous efflorescence of technology and society leading rapidly to extinction. . . .[10]

Can this threatening denouement be averted? It is as rational to assume that remedial action is possible as to assume that nothing can be done. It is possible to describe an ecologically stable environment and to prescribe human behavior patterns that could avoid many ecological abuses. The problem lies less in what should be done, which is often known, than in how to do it, which is often difficult. Natural catastrophes and many forms of disease would continue to trouble man even if he learned to be less trouble to himself, but man's effectiveness in coping with natural events could be enhanced were he freed from the burdens of his own ecological errors. Is human intelligence equal to the task of liberation?

A Peculiar Species

THE HISTORICAL RECORD of rational control over human affairs is discouraging. Trial efforts to establish self-maintaining societies have ultimately ended in error. Inquiring men have searched for the causes of their mistakes in the belief that the *how* of guided behavioral change cannot be discovered without knowledge of the *why* of human behavior.[11] The observed discrepancies between human ideals and behaviors, between knowledge and action, have suggested to some a basic discontinuity in human personality—a fundamental imperfection in the human brain. For example, Arthur Koestler hypothesizes a genetically based lack of coordination between the neocortex of the brain (the seat of rationality) and the hypothalamus, or seat of emotionally-generated behavior:

> The neurophysiological evidence indicates, as we have seen, a dissonance between the reactions of the neocortex and limbic system. Instead of functioning as integral parts in a hierarchic order, they lead a kind of agonised coexistence. To revert to an earlier metaphor: the rider has never gained complete control of the horse, and the horse asserts its whims in the most objectionable ways. We have also seen that the horse—the limbic system—has direct access to the emotion-generating, viscerally orientated centres in the hypothalamus; but the rider has no direct access to them.[12]

Reasoning that evolution has left mankind in this dangerous schizoid state, Koestler suggests that inadequate coordination between the newer and older parts of the brain may possibly be remedied by chemical agents where centuries of moralizing and indoctrination have failed.[13]

Perhaps Koestler is right that, should the biological factors in man's unecological behavior come to be fully understood, a safe and reliable means of altering that behavior might be discovered. But until very recently, men generally have resisted the idea that a large part of human conduct was biologically determined. A deterministic view of behavior, exemplified by the work of Watson, Hull, and Skinner, has now won partial acceptance throughout modern society.[14] Psychological theory has yet to trace a satisfactory linkage between the behavior of individuals and of societies, between reactive and purposive behavior.

Among attempts to discover such a linkage are the organismic theories of society. These theories range from crude and simplistic attempts to describe direct analogies between the form and functions of the individual human organism and the structure and processes of societies, to efforts to discover principles or "laws" common to all complex organic structures.[15]

An example of the latter is the book *BioPolitics* by Morley Roberts, an English novelist with profound interest in the interconnections between pathology, social behavior, and evolution.[16] Perhaps because he was a generalist in an age of specialists and held no formal scientific credentials, his book has not received the attention that it deserves. The value of *BioPolitics* lies in its provocative analysis of social behavior which fuses social science and biomedical theory.

Morley Roberts believed that only through understanding the physico-biological dynamics of society could men assert any effective control over human behavior. He did not argue that human social behavior was inexorably deterministic. Events tended to occur as if predetermined in large part because of the perverse and sometimes self-imposed blindness of men, who refused to see that basic causes must be reckoned with if behavior is to be guided or significantly changed. He compared the present state of large-scale organized societies to relatively rudimentary invertebrate organisms capable of gross responses to stimuli but in which ability to act upon rational foresight has not yet evolved. The basic error of governments and rulers was to act upon premises contrary to natural circumstances, or, as he might have said, contrary to organic reality.

Man's study of nature has not revealed an infinite number of methods by which natural systems work. All natural systems, physical and biological, appear to operate consistently with known physicochemical uniformities.[17] Nothing that man does or builds has departed from these principles, unless it belongs to the supernatural and so lies beyond science or human understanding. Implicit in Roberts' approach to social behavior is the proposition that biological and cultural evolution are not separate and distinct processes, as contemporary man generally prefers to believe. The principles of organic evolution extend into so-called superorganic or cultural evolution, and the latter cannot be adequately understood without recourse to the former—sociologists must study biology.[18]

Theodosius Dobzhansky states the scientific position incisively:

> . . . the superorganic has not annulled the organic–biological heredity, which is the basis of biological evolution, does not transmit cultural, or for that matter physical, traits ready-made; what it does is determine the response of the developing organism to the environment in which development takes place. . . . Man is a part of his own environment. . . .[19]

The popular thesis that biological evolution has come to an end and man now evolves wholly through cultural change is based on the narrow time span of man's self-observed history. There is insufficient evidence for unguarded assertions regarding the present status or future course of biological evolution.

Perhaps the most accurate statement of man's unecological tendencies would be to say that human evolution has permitted man to develop cultures, altering the nature of his relationship to the natural world and permitting him at least in the short run to separate himself psychologically and economically from it. Thus, as in the conclusions of Konrad Lorenz concerning human aggression, it may be the absence rather than the presence of genetic factors that explain man's unecological behavior. This is supported by observation of so-called primitive or pre-technological societies which appear to have maintained a more harmonious and balanced relationship with their ecosystems than has civilized man. James V. Neel, professor of human genetics at the University of Michigan Medical School, has observed, "Primitive man seems to have curbed his intrinsic fertility to a greater extent than has the civilized world in recent centuries. Exactly how those curbs were relaxed with the advent of civilization is unclear, but the agricultural revolution undoubtedly played a part." [20]

On the other hand, the possibility should not be discounted that the genetic constitutions of the dominant populations of the modern world have a positively exploitive and destructive tendency in relation to the environment. In the absence of genetic and cultural inhibitions, innate tendencies, not in themselves destructive, might operate to that effect. We cannot yet rule out the possibility that man's aggressive tendencies are too strong to be contained by culture. If that were true, efforts to protect the human environment from human abuse would at best be an uphill struggle.

Science has been slowly discovering the mechanism of man's self-destructive tendencies, but the painful reality was recognized in man's earliest poetic expression of human tragedy. But the extent of man's ability to guide his future biological and cultural evolution in order to extricate himself remains to be discovered.

Perhaps most importantly, present knowledge of man's evolutionary past indicates that effective control of human behavior for survival can be achieved only through valid understanding of man as he is—not as theoreticians think he ought to be. Valid knowledge of human biology, not only in relation to individuals but also in relation to progressively larger aggregations and ultimately in relation to the human species, will enable us to develop effective belief systems, behavior patterns, and public policies for correcting man's ecological deficiencies. Man has been moved to great achievements by beliefs that had no basis in truth, and great discoveries have not always been followed by action. To overcome man's unecological behavior patterns knowledge and belief must reinforce each other.

Cultural Roots of Environmental Dereliction

THERE IS GENERAL AGREEMENT then that genetic tendencies are supplemented or mediated by culturally-conditioned behavior patterns. These behavior patterns are formalized in institutions which, through customs, legal procedures, and structured relationships, govern, contain, or displace genetic tendencies that might otherwise destroy social cohesion. Some institutions may exacerbate possible genetic tendencies, however, and implement them in highly destructive forms. War is a notorious example. But all institutions are manifestations of culture, and cultures are expressions of human imagination and aspiration. Cultural tests of truth and reality are not necessarily those of science, although science is, of course, a cultural invention. Culture-based beliefs and practices may, therefore, have no relationship whatever to existential reality, nor to the ecological parameters of human welfare.

Were proceeding upon false premises always to bring swift and obvious punishment, cybernetic or feedback processes would have long ago corrected at least some of man's ecological errors. But the slow attrition of the environment may not easily be perceived by peoples lacking science or ways to measure and monitor environmental change. That large areas of the Earth have suffered impoverishment and reduced viability during the past five to ten thousand years has been established through paleo-ecological research.[21] Profiles of resource and species depletion have been established through core samples in the beds of old lakes, through the sifting of kitchen middens, and through recorded descriptions of ancient environments, confirmed by archaeology.

Ecological degradation has almost always been followed by economic decline and cultural decay. The alleged progress of modern industrial societies may be cited as exceptions. The industrial, technological, and economic strength of the United States, for example, has grown roughly in proportion to the destruction of the natural environment and the pollution of its soils and waters. But this relationship does not take full account of the time lag in ecological and cultural change. The enormously productive capabilities of the American economy do not unequivocally result in human happiness, health, or security. More significantly civic disintegration in American society has been in process for at least several decades and appears to be proceeding more swiftly as the aggregate of conditions in the environment also worsens.[22]

Despite the advance and diffusion of ecological knowledge during the past half-century, much of man's culturally-induced ecological error may still be caused by ignorance. Ecological feedback, unlike the effects of leaps from tall buildings, is seldom swift and simple enough to be self-evident. The extinction of a "useless" bird or the drying up of a pasture spring may indicate a threatening trend. But such information is fed back irregularly and in small bits, and its relevance to larger matters may go unperceived. Nevertheless, cultural man has often permitted his actions to be guided by monumental superstitions while simultaneously failing to see (or rejecting) reliable indicators of the sequence of natural events.

It cannot be established that there is less actual superstition in the world today than in ancient or medieval times. Modern superstitions are merely more sophisticated. They come dressed in pseudoscientific language, buttressed with statistics, and untainted by any tinge of the supernatural. Most modern political ideologies, many economic doctrines, and nearly all social theories are heavily freighted with beliefs that may fairly be called superstitions—having much the same relationship to reality as belief in witchcraft. For example, beliefs that the Gross National Product is an index of economic health, or that there are *inherent* social or political "rights" are as rational as the belief that bleeding will reduce fevers. The difficulty in correcting social error is that, unlike the individual, a society seldom dies and submits to an autopsy. Society's difficulties, when apparent to everyone, may still be explained by guesswork and untestable theories.

Unlike ancient superstitions, modern beliefs have the dangerous potential of being implemented through science-based technology. Moreover, the rejection of supernatural forces and the supposed objectivity of science has reinforced modern beliefs with an arrogance or hubris that could not as easily be supported when man's ability to manipulate nature was limited to the technological levels of pre-scientific ages. Throughout much of the ancient world, environmental deterioration seems to have occurred despite, and not because of, what men believed. The ancient religious systems of Greece and China emphasized harmony between man and nature. Divine forces resided in the natural environment and a presumption to dominate nature was inconsistent with the prevailing assumptions of the culture.[23]

The destructive effects of culture on man's environment

have been increased coincident with, but not necessarily because of, the separation of God and man from the normal processes of nature. This separation was most marked in religions arising in Western Asia, and especially in the closely related triology of Judaism, Christianity, and Islam. That Western Asia has been one of the most disastrously ecologically impoverished areas of the Earth may be merely coincidental. The Middle Eastern transcendental religions have avoided consideration of the biological nature of man and his relationship to the natural world, developing instead a concept of man as a uniquely privileged being created by Divine Will.

Hinduism and its derivative systems of belief interrelate the lives of men and other animals, but preserve a distinction between them.[24] Judaism and its derivatives separate man from nature more decisively. Jewish and Islamic theologians appear not to have been greatly concerned with the man–nature relationship. In Christianity, however, the relation of man to nature has been a source of speculation and controversy.[25] The historically dominant doctrine placed man outside of nature: man was merely a transient visitor, and eternal life was not of this world. The world was made for man's convenience; for its future he need have no concern. If God willed the world to be saved, He would save it. Meanwhile, man had dominion over every living thing—or so the Scriptures declared. To this doctrine of the supernatural origin and destiny of man, some scholars trace the historical roots of the ecological crisis of modern society. This sort of Judeo-Christian cosmology has nourished unecological interpretations of man and nature, but at least two considerations prevent us from holding historical religions wholly accountable for man's ecological crisis.

The first consideration is the many-channeled course of Christian evolution. Lynn White observes that the teachings of St. Francis of Assisi are a countercurrent to the main stream of religious orthodoxy.[26] In modern times, the Franciscan ethic has won adherents among clergy and laity, and it has become a dominant theme in the reformed theologies of many modern churches. If the Neo-Franciscanism of contemporary Christianity has a very limited influence, religion in general seems ineffective when it opposes the social and economic expediencies of modern men. Nevertheless, a religious imperative latent in Western culture has been gaining strength, reinforced by convergent concepts in literature and science.[27] Albert Schweitzer's "reverence for life" is its most direct expression,[28] but the ethic of respect for the natural world is evident in more sophisticated theologies, such as that of Paul Tillich.[29]

The second consideration is that, although the religions of southern and eastern Asia never wholly separated man from nature, nature has nevertheless suffered at the hands of Hindus, Taoists, and Buddhists. Acculturation by Western ideas and technologies may, in part, account for the attrition of the natural environment in India and the Far East. Nevertheless, the traditional religions did not prevent their societies from inadvertently destroying the quality of their environments through overpopulation and through migratory expansions of peoples and their agriculture, or from destroying the habitats of other living things. One need not kill animals or plants to cause their extinction; preempting their territory and breeding areas will do as well.

The basis and actual state of man–environment relationships are not, therefore, directly reflected in artistic, literary, or religious expressions within a culture. The despoilers of environments seldom write books or concern themselves greatly with ethics or esthetics. Awareness of the significance of man–environment relations has been confirmed to a minority of perceptive individuals and, of these, a smaller number has communicated environmental values. But this minority has gained influence as existential circumstances arouse public apprehension, and as the worst environmental dereliction begins to affect the lives of individuals directly. The gap between science and religion has been a major "conditioning" factor in the destructive impact of modern man on his environment, but there are indications that this gap may be closing.[30]

Unecological Systems in Technological Societies

WHAT ARE THE PROPERTIES of a system that would suggest the qualifying adjective "unecological"? Perhaps the most significant single property of an ecosystem is its relative internal stability. Living systems are dynamic, but their changes mostly occur in orderly sequences, interactions tending to be mutually consistent and containing. Thus, the ecosystem, although it may evolve, preserves over periods of time a recognizable form and composition. Its continuity is preserved by negative feedback or damping of oscillations or perturbations within the system. The ecosystem is, therefore, self-renewing. It does not run down, and its natural transformations normally occur over centuries or millennia.[31]

Those human institutions with the longest record of continuity and stability have continued to evolve over extended periods of time, and have been adapted to changing conditions. Some of these institutions, however, appear to have a biological or innately behavioral base—the human family, with its many variations, being an example. Some more exclusively cultural institutions have internal mechanisms to accommodate external or internal stress. Modern industrial organizations, however, are obviously artificial in origin and structure and tend to be unsettled by oscillations and perturbations in their environments since they are deficient in self-sustaining or self-renewing abilities. Technological systems are thus artificial in that they have been created by man for some specific purpose, and they must be nourished and managed throughout their entire existence by human effort.[32]

Instability, latent or potential, characterizes nearly all large modern organizations. Whether this condition is a corollary or a cause of the instability of modern society is a chicken–egg question. The aggregate instability of social institutions culminates in an unstable society; but, as social instability increases, formerly stable organizations, such as churches and universities, become unsettled. As industrial technology becomes more elaborate and interlocking, it becomes more vulnerable to disruption. Oscillations set in motion tend to reverberate throughout the system and, through positive feedback, to grow rather than to be damped. Nevertheless, the technological systems of modern society are subject to some controls, the origins of which are external to the systems themselves. These controls, expressed through police powers or other governmental measures, are born out of human dependence upon the systems for such necessities as potable water, food, heat, transportation, and protection from natural disasters and human violence.

Among the more unecological characteristics of modern technological organizations is their disjunctive or incomplete structure. Although these organizations form a matrix of inter-dependencies in the production-distribution-consumption systems of modern societies, neither they nor their aggregate political economy are ecologically complete. Unlike the world of nature, the technological world has not biodegraded or recycled its residual or waste products. It has assumed that natural systems could perform this ecological function, but contemporary industrial man has overtaxed the biosphere's capacity to absorb an ever-mounting volume of wastes. The consequence has been environmental pollution.[33]

The science of economics has only very belatedly begun to remedy its deficiencies in dealing with waste and residuals. The modern economist has tended to manipulate abstract symbols rather than to investigate material things. Abstractions like the Cost of Living Index and the Gross National Product became economically more real than material reality itself. Pragmatically focused upon the monetarily measurable production-distribution-consumption processes of society, most economists ignored the material products of industrial society when they ceased to have a positive monetary value. Only when real costs in degraded environments, in impaired and destroyed ecosystems, or in esthetic values, began to be charged to the economy in the form of taxes, fines, operating expenses, and political embarrassments did the economists begin to look beyond their self-imposed boundaries and to reinterpret economic processes to correspond to ecological realities. This reinterpretation of economics has only recently begun.[34] It has not yet become the prevailing economics, and has not yet reshaped popular understanding of how the total economy works. The consequences of this conceptual lag have been injury to the welfare of society and to the well-being of natural systems.

Before considering some examples, the major complication of excessive population should be mentioned. Throughout previous history, concentrated populations were generally able to obtain subsistence without extensively impairing basic processes. Beyond their immediate hinterland, cities indirectly modified but seldom disrupted the capacity of natural environments for self-renewal. The growth of cities required a supporting agricultural economy, along with the construction of aqueducts, wells, reservoirs, roads, canals, and sewers. Most of these artificial life-support systems were simple to construct and to manage; some continue usable after centuries of indifferent maintenance. In the great river valleys of the East, however, were engineered the first great technological systems requiring unremitting attention and continuing management. Large-scale irrigation and flood control works in China, the Indian subcontinent, Mesopotamia, and Egypt facilitated the growth of populous societies which were dependent on such works for survival. The absolute dependence of the people on the operation of their hydraulic systems led, in the view of the historian Karl A. Wittfogel, to a form of social control that he has called "oriental despotism." [35]

The particular forms of despotic government that arose in the hydraulic societies of the Orient may not have inevitably followed the dependence of populations on an artificial system requiring expert management. But some form of authoritative control was, and is, an unavoidable price that men must pay for living far beyond the limits of the natural life-support system. How high a price strongly depends on the vulnerability of the system and the degree of control necessary to its uninterrupted operation. When death is the alternative to discipline, men's resistance to regimentation is weakened.

The need to feed a multiplying population impels men to create a technological system, and to maintain and enlarge systems already in effect. To destroy the technological system which supports a society is to destroy that society. Mongol destruction of irrigation systems in the Middle East has been held to be a major factor in the disappearance of the old Persian culture. But possibly, there may also have been deterioration in Middle Eastern agriculture. Siltation, waterlogging of soils, and salinity have come to hamper irrigated agriculture over many other areas of the Earth, notably today in Pakistan.[36] Neglect or mismanagement of artificial systems of food production could bring malnutrition or starvation to millions of persons where population has met or passed the capacity of the system to support.

Dependence on continuing artificial life-support systems

becomes increasingly an interdependence among people. The interlocking complexities of modern industrial society require people to cooperate, regardless of mutual antipathies. Thus, a network of antagonistic symbioses arises. People who do not like one another must nevertheless work together to keep in operation the machinery on which they all depend, especially in great urban centers. The forces that promote and undermine stability maintain a precarious balance in modern societies. The many variables involved sharply qualify any confidence that we can predict the future of man's ecosystem.

Consequences of a Distorted World View

A MAN WHO MISREADS his surroundings and his relationship to them is in a very real sense lost. Failure to properly evaluate his relationship to his life-support system, natural or artificial, can have serious consequences for his welfare and survival. It matters little that his erroneous assumptions may have been arrived at honestly, or that they have been tacit rather than explicit. Man's destructive exploitation of his environment has been a consequence of unthinking, undiscerning, day-to-day routine responses to the need for food, clothing, and shelter rather than a consequence of any formalized concept of man–nature relationships. Man's natural behavior has been that of an unecological animal. Throughout history man has repeatedly "eaten himself out of house and home." His technological ingenuity and the size of the Earth have permitted him, for the time being, to escape the worst consequences. But a fundamental change has occurred in man's environmental situation, making past history a poor guide to future prospects.

Evidence from anthropology indicates that, whereas man the species has behaved in an unecological manner, certain subgroups of men have, over long periods of time, maintained an ecological balance with their environments. Examples known to us have been confined to so-called primitive peoples—who should more properly be described as peoples at relatively primitive states of culture or technology—among whom are found patterns of behavior which show a higher degree of ecological sensitivity than those prevailing in high-level technologically advanced societies.

Should advanced technological societies end in self-destruction through war, civil disintegration, or ecological suicide, such peoples might become the ancestral stock for future men—if they haven't been acculturated or developed out of existence in the meantime.

The historical change which has so greatly increased the danger of man's unecological tendencies is, of course, his ability to alter his environment through science-based technologies. From the time man was able, consciously and deliberately, to manipulate his environment rapidly on a massive scale, his formalized systems of belief regarding his relationship to the environment gained greatly in importance. The interconnection between the professed beliefs and the actual behaviors of men are not well understood and do not appear consistent among aggregations of men. The human animal exhibits a wide range of variability, both genetically and culturally. Generalizations regarding human behavior ought, therefore, to be regarded only as statements of trends to which significant exceptions can be found.

But trends that are far from universal may nevertheless be important if they have critical impact on human welfare or viability of the environment. For example, the influence of the managers of the policy-shaping and technological apparatus of modern industrial society greatly outweighs that of their less strategically placed fellows. In a technological society (managed through statistical projections, computers, company policies, public laws, treaties, and contracts), formalized beliefs, assumptions, theories, and concepts can be put into practice with an effectiveness and efficiency hardly possible in technologically underdeveloped societies. Science has too often been used to implement human desires and ambitions, unexamined as to the probable range of their effects, alternative means to their attainment, and the full range of costs attached to each alternative. The means may be products of rational thought but, like the mass diffusion of DDT in the biosphere, the unevaluated ends can be called rational only within a distorted view of the real world.

While ignorance and shortsightedness may have been the principal historical causes of ecological impoverishment and environmental decay, the modern causes are, paradoxically, quite the opposite. Scientific knowledge and a future-oriented outlook have been major contributors to the rapid ecological deterioration of the modern world. Under the slogans "progress," "development," and "economic growth," the policymakers of modern times have proceeded to reshape the world with only the slightest regard for the ultimate consequences of their actions. And, when confronted by the evidence of damage to the life-supporting base of modern society, a large and influential number reject the data as emotionally biased, exaggerated, or insignificant. But, if such skeptics are ill-informed or opinionated, they are not illogical. Their rejection of an ecological outlook is a defense of their way of life, of their economic habits and interests, of their personal values and self-esteem.

The misconceptions of intelligent and scientifically learned people are not easily corrected, especially when integrated in a matrix of beliefs that comprise the individual personality.[37] When the unecological man is asked to adopt an ecological view of life, he is in effect, being asked to break and reset his personality.[38] The truly "radical" character of the ecological movement lies primarily in this necessity. If the critical threat to the viability of the world environment is to be overcome, the policymakers of the world, in and out of government, either must undergo fundamental personality change, or they must be replaced by others whose total personal makeup is consistent with ecological realities. Experience suggests that few men will change themselves. Few are willing, and even fewer are able; but some have changed and others will make the transition. They will be a minority, but an exceedingly important minority if they are major influencers and shapers of public policy. New attitudes in high places are greatly needed now. As converts from unecological ways, they may understand the previous errors with sufficient clarity to persuade others of the need for change.

But for the most part the ecological integrity of the Earth must depend on new and younger men and women for the leadership required. Formal public education must help produce a new leadership that is ecologically oriented, for, in a techno-scientific age, young fogies are even more dangerous than old ones. They are more vigorous and they may be ambitious.

Critics argue that the assumptions of the ecology movement are not well-founded and often reflect an anti-rational negativism. The more confident among the anti-ecologists have a high regard for human ingenuity and are unimpressed by the processes of nature. Nature is regarded as inefficient and generally inimical to human welfare.[39] Human history, at best, is seen as the story of man's struggle against the brutal indifference of the natural world. Almost anything that nature does man can, or one day may, do better, including perhaps the recreation of extinct animals and creation of new species. Nature lovers and "ecologizers" are misguided romantics who would, in effect, return mankind to the caves and expose the human species to the natural ravages of famine, disease, floods, and drought.

Human overpopulation is, to the anti-ecologists, not a problem of numbers; but a pseudo-problem resulting from inefficient production and allocation, resolvable through social engineering. Conceding a theoretical limit to the number of individuals that a finite globe can hold, they nevertheless contend that through effective use of science and technology the population of Earth may greatly exceed its present densities. Moreover, with more people there will be more men of genius to enable man to solve his problems independent of uncontrolled Nature.

Earth as a spaceship is not a valid analogy to the anti-ecologist because it fails, he says, to account for that unique property of man—his creativity. Moreover, the spaceship suggests a very limited stock of resources, whereas the Earth still holds vast stores of natural wealth under the sea, in the polar regions, and deep beneath the surface. Resource economists have demonstrated—to the satisfaction of optimists who do not closely follow their reasoning and reservations—that modern society is not about to run out of basic raw materials.[40] The supply of easily accessible resources may diminish, but the real problem is with efficient use. There is a short-range reason for conserving potentially exhaustible resources, such as fossil fuels, because satisfactory substitutes of unlimited availability have not yet, in all cases, been developed.

2 7

This line of reasoning is wrongheaded not so much in specific allegations (some of which are demonstrably correct and some plausible) but wrongheaded principally in what it fails to take into account. Against the charge that the pro-ecologist is a modern Druid or nature worshipper, the ecologically-oriented may truthfully reply that the anti-ecologist has become his own god. Man worship has become the tacit modern religion, and dogmatic Marxists and rugged individualists may be seen as separate sects of a common cult. If there were a maxim for this unacknowledged theology, it would be the assertion attributed to Protagoras, "Man is the measure of all things." Plato suggested (Theaetatus, Sec. 152A), that the statement meant that each man sees the world in his own way. But in modern times, it has more often been taken to mean that all things are to be evaluated by their effects upon abstract and isolated "man." It has, paradoxically, brought man back into the center of the universe from which Galileo and Copernicus had removed him, but without taking into account man's interdependencies with the world.

The optimism of the unecological attitude rests upon assumptions unsupported either by folk wisdom or the findings of science. Scientific knowledge of human potentiality is, as yet, fragmentary and imperfect. The anti-ecological argument asks for an act of faith in possibilities which historical evidence renders dubious. There are two great risks in the anti-ecological propositions: first, the human animal may not safely adapt to the conditions and requirements of ecumenopolis [41]—to a totally urbanized high-density, highly-interdependent world; and, second, human society may be unable to control its behavior sufficiently to avoid fatal disruptions of its artificial systems.[42]

Although unproved, "salvation through technology" is perhaps possible. Yet one may ask, "Are the risks wise and are they necessary?" Man is demonstrably a highly adaptable animal; René Dubos suggests that his adaptability may be his undoing.[43] Modern man could adapt himself progressively into a state of existence from which he could not retreat and in which he could not survive. In claiming the indefinite feasibility of a world populated by tens of billions of people, the anti-ecologists assume a perfection of mechanisms of social coordination and control beyond any a society has yet developed. The possibility of a world-city is supported by suggestions that human personality can be modified by chemotherapy or habituation through training, but such concepts raise more questions than they answer.

The true measure of things, if this phrase has meaning, cannot be in man's own wholly subjective evaluations. Men can discover the dimensions of reality through science, broadly construed. Through knowledge of cause–effect relationships and of the interactions of natural systems, men can correct and refine their own values. But *self*-knowledge has long been held to be the prerequisite to wisdom, and man has far too little understanding of his own potentialities and limitations at present to attempt a totally man-made world. Given the inevitable distortion in both ecological and technological concepts, the former are the safer. The ecologist may lead man toward a more restrained existence, but he will not lead him to self-destruction or to a precarious existence wherein a total social effort is needed to keep man's artificial systems operating because the Nature that once freely nourished him is no longer able to do so.

Must Men Destroy the Earth?

THE BEHAVIORAL SCIENCES at present do not tell us how far, or even whether, the human race is capable of collective self-control. Experimental neurophysiology has shown that individual human behavior can sometimes be artificially manipulated, but the techniques used are not presently applicable to the behavior of society. Moreover, they hold no evident promise for strengthening the moral or rational aspects of behavior upon which depends man's ability to control his behavior toward his environment. Until the social and behavioral sciences equip us to deal more reliably with behavioral problems, we must do what we can with the knowledge we have. We must also be cautious about acting beyond the limits of that knowledge.

Hope for mankind's future lies in the possibility that realization of the danger of his unecological tendencies, whatever their origin or explanation, will induce him to take remedial measures. It is widely agreed that human amibition and ingenuity have outrun moral growth, and that human experience and philosophic interpretations of it are only now beginning to catch up with the tremendous changes in man's relation to his world resulting from the exponential growth of science and its applications through technology. The hypertrophic society—a society committed to endless indiscriminate growth—thus seems an accident of the discontinuity between man's ability to act and his ability to understand the consequences of his action.[44] Societal hypertrophy is not inherently inevitable, incurable, or irreversible. The decision of the Ninety-second Congress to discontinue governmental support of the development of the supersonic transport is an encouraging indication that technological progress is, in fact, subject to rational human control.

The philosophic position most appropriate to our times is, therefore, a hopeful pessimism. Pessimism, because environmental degradation is moving swiftly and massively across the face of the Earth, apparently beyond the ready power of man to stem or reverse. This course if unchecked would surely end in destruction of the biosphere and ultimately of human society itself. But hope is also indicated, for we cannot be sure that man is incapable of rising to the challenge of his predicament. If there is a chance that man can control his behavior toward the Earth, it would seem that the attempt should be made to persuade him to do so. We must act as if man is capable of defending the Earth, and will do so when he understands the alternatives that confront him. Surely the essence of human dignity, for the individual and for society alike, is to live so that if the Earth should be destroyed and mankind with it, the disaster will have been uninvited and undeserved. We must act, therefore, upon a hope rooted in pessimism but not in despair: "And if it is nothingness that awaits us, let us so act that it shall be an unjust fate."[45]

2

Discovering the Biosphere:

CONDITIONS FOR SURVIVAL

IN A FINITE WORLD

THE ROUGHLY FIVE HUNDRED YEARS BETWEEN THE
discovery of America in 1492 and the landing of the Apollo XI
astronauts upon the Moon will surely appear in retrospect as a
distinct and decisive era in the history of man and the Earth. In
our times, this half-millennium is called *modern*—whatever
name future eras may give it. The Earth can never again be what
it was when the era began, nor can prospects for the era to come
be forecast by precedents that have given reliable predictions in
the past.[1]

"In the twentieth century, man, for the first time in the
history of the Earth, knew and embraced the whole biosphere,
completing the geographic map of the planet Earth, and colo-
nized its whole surface. *Mankind became a single totality in the
life of the Earth.*"[2] Thus the Russian scientist V. I. Vernadsky
in 1938 summarized the end of a process of discovery which
began at least five thousand years earlier when man began to
leave behind records of his impressions and descriptions of the
natural world.

At the beginning of modern times, large areas of the world
had no permanent human settlements. The major areas of human
habitation were isolated and had developed distinctive cultures.
Farming and herding relied largely upon the natural operations
of natural systems, modified only marginally by public works for

water supply, flood control and irrigation. Today large urban concentrations of man are absolutely dependent for survival on the continuous operation of artificial systems. Without a steady flow of electricity and fossil fuels, millions of men would die. As population has grown, the world's peoples have become increasingly homogenized physically and culturally. All major premodern cultures have been extinguished or acculturated by the dominant civilization.

The modern age has been characterized not only by an explosive increase in human population but also of knowledge, especially in technology. Through technology, the impact per human individual upon the biosphere has increased exponentially, accelerating toward the end of our century. Distinctive among the many forms of human dominion, the nation-state has been the characteristic structure for extending human preemption of the Earth. It was developed in Europe and accompanied the expansion of the European peoples into the Americas, into South Africa and Australia, and across northern Asia to the Pacific Ocean.

The unifying and distinguishing work of this era has been the human preemption and discovery of the biosphere. This is a simple way of stating a complex paradox: the biosphere was occupied and its exploitation well advanced before its true nature—vulnerable and finite—was even vaguely perceived. Before A.D. 1500 man's knowledge of the nature of the Earth or its relationship to the rest of the universe was very limited, and much of what he believed was wrong. By the end of the era, man had won an experiential knowledge of the Earth and its place in space, and had gathered many clues as to its evolution in time.

The discovery of the biosphere in the latter half of the twentieth century has come none too soon for the survival of man. By the late 1960s, it was becoming evident that the uncontrolled impact of human activity upon the biosphere could not long continue without endangering the basis of life itself. However opinions differed about the imminence of danger and the prospects for avoiding it, few who read the evidence could discount the potential catastrophe pointed to by existing trends.

To understand the changes in attitudes and institutions

required for the defense of Earth, it may be useful to trace the discovery of the biosphere as an evolved living system with tolerances and limitations that human exactions cannot exceed without risking or, in some cases, causing disaster.

Locating and Measuring the Earth

To THE BEST OF OUR KNOWLEDGE, man alone among the animals is aware of himself in relation to his environment and able to make objective observations to discover his place in it. The search to locate himself and guide his journeys has been a major factor in the development of many of man's sciences and technologies. The list includes astronomy, geography, geology, navigation, astronautics, cartography, and surveying.

The first records of man's extending knowledge of his environment are his maps. The oldest ones known were found on Sumerian and Babylonian clay tablets in the Tigris-Euphrates Valley.[3] The Greeks seem to have been the earliest to try to ascertain the shape of the world: they first thought the Earth was circular and, subsequently, an elliptical plane. Pythagoras (c. 532 B.C.) and Aristotle (384–322 B.C.) appear to have believed that the Earth was a sphere, but the first globe that we know of appears to have been made by a Greek named Crates of Mallus about 145 B.C. The science of geodesy may be said to have been founded by Eratosthenes of Alexandria (c. 276–194 B.C.), the first man known to have measured the size of the Earth. Relatively accurate measurements were also made by the Arabs, but Eratosthenes' calculations were not substantially improved upon until A.D. 1615 when the Dutch scientist Willebrord Snell measured the Earth by triangulation.

The ancient geographer, Ptolemy of Alexandria, author of a geography in eight books (c. A.D. 150), established the concepts of the world that prevailed into early modern times. Maps of the fifteenth and sixteenth centuries generally followed the Ptolemaic projections, and, in 1492 in Nuremberg, Martin Behaim constructed one of the first modern globes following the Ptolemaic concepts.

Toward the end of the Middle Ages, collections and translations of the astronomical and geographical works of Greek and Arab scholars were made available through the *Sphaeramundi* by an Englishman named John of Holywood, writing under the name of Sacrobosca (c. 1250); and by the eighteen *Libros del Saber de Astronomia* compiled under the direction of the Spanish King, Alfonso X, el Sabio (c. 1284), an enormous work containing the translation into Spanish of all the contemporary theoretical knowledge of astronomy and descriptions of such scientific instruments as astrolabes, quadrants, armils, and clocks.[4]

The great European voyages of discovery during the latter half of the fifteenth century and after spurred the development of techniques of location and measurement. Successful navigation on the high seas depended on them, and between 1500 and 1600 the sciences of astronomical navigation and cartography developed rapidly. In 1569 the Flemish cosmographer Gerard Mercator published his famous projection, which was further refined by the English mathematician Edward Wright in 1599; it is still today "the most useful map of the world in the practice of navigation."[5] The problem of maritime navigation became so great that in 1713 the English government appointed a special Commission for the Discovery of Longitude at Sea and offered substantial rewards for useful inventions. The invention of the marine chronometer by John Harrison followed in 1735, and he was eventually (1773) awarded the equivalent of one hundred thousand dollars for his instrument.

The extended voyages of Christopher Columbus, Vasco Da Gama, and Ferdinand Magellan began a process of discovering, describing, and mapping the surface of the Earth that continued to the end of the nineteenth century. In 1891 a Geographical Conference in Berne received a proposal to construct an accurate map of the world on a uniform scale. A committee was appointed to pursue the project, and it reported consecutively to Geographical Congresses held in London in 1895, in Berlin in 1899, and in Washington in 1904. Finally a special conference convened in London in November 1909 managed to develop proposed standards for the map and rules to govern its production. These proposals were accepted by the Geographical Congress meeting in 1913. A general international conference, at which thirty-four nations were represented, was held in

Paris of that year and accepted the project of the *Carte du Monde au Millionième* on a scale of approximately 1 inch to 15.8 miles.[6]

Exploration of the sea floors required further technology and instrumentation; the scientific voyage of H.M.S. *Challenger* around the world (1872–1876) provided the first comprehensive survey of the physical and biological conditions of the oceans.[7] The laying of submarine telegraph cables required accurate measurements of the ocean depths and added to knowledge of submarine conditions.

The discovery, description, and measurement of the surface of the Earth were matched by advances in knowledge of the relationship of the Earth to the cosmos. Modern astronomy began with the theories of Nicolaus Copernicus (1473–1543), who held that the planets together with the Earth revolved in circular orbits around the sun. Advanced by the work of Galileo, Huygens, and Kepler among others, the dynamics of the universe were first satisfactorily formulated by Isaac Newton (1642–1727) in his *Philosophiae Naturalis Principia Mathematica* (1687). Terrestrial mechanics as formulated by Newton and modified and refined by his successors remained a dominant explanation of the behavior of the universe until Albert Einstein advanced his theories of relativity in the early twentieth century. In the twentieth century, the measurement and description of the universe was extended to the galaxy which encompasses the solar system to which the Earth belongs. But the scope of twentieth century astronomy rapidly transcended the limits of our immediate galaxy to a presently incalculable, but seemingly immense, number of external galaxies or island universes, extending indefinitely into space. Exploration of deep space was advanced by the discovery of K. Jansky in 1931 that radio waves, apparently from the farthest reaches of the universe, can be received, and interpreted upon the Earth. Giant radio telescopes are now augmenting our knowledge of the universe.

Thus, by the latter third of the twentieth century, man was not only able to locate himself at whatever point he might happen to be on the surface of the Earth, but also to a degree undreamt of at the beginning of the modern era, he was able to locate his planet with some accuracy in the nearer regions of a universe of incomprehensible size. This process of discovery involved the interaction of virtually all sciences, discovery in any one of which was contingent upon discovery in others.

Before the mid-twentieth century, different geodetic systems were in use in a number of different countries. A world system of control points and coordinates was devised with the assistance of the International Union of Geodesy and Geophysics and the United Nations. A major step toward understanding the physical Earth was the International Geophysical Year (IGY), 1957–58, sponsored by the International Council of Scientific Unions and the World Meteorological Organization.[8] One consequence of the IGY was the Antarctic Treaty of 1959 which established the Antarctic continent as the world's first international scientific reserve and set a precedent for the UN Treaty on the Peaceful Uses of Outer Space.[9] Scientific exploration of the Earth was greatly advanced by innovations in instrumentation, such as radar, sonar, and remote sensing by satellite, and the development of new methods of photogrammetry which enormously increased the speed and accuracy of determining the configuration and topographical properties of the physical world, of its climate and oceanographic conditions, and of the extent and condition of its vegetation.

Indeed, in recent years instrumentation of all kinds, essential to obtaining an accurate picture of the Earth in context has increased extraordinarily. Telescopes, refracting, reflecting, and radio; microscopes of several varieties, including the electronic microscope; cyclotrons and other accelerators in high-energy physics; chromatographs for the analysis of chemical substances; the instrumentation for space exploration—the list of scientific and technical developments could fill many pages. The very mass of the material and its frequently specialized character have made difficult its synthesis into any coherent picture, especially for laymen. It has facilitated man's exploitation of parts of Earth's resources, but has kept fragmented knowledge that might have enabled man to act prudently towards Earth seen as a whole. Further, before 1950 science had dealt chiefly with descriptions of physical matter. With respect to the living world, and especially to those aspects of it having to do with interrelationships and social behavior, man's knowledge was much less satisfactory.

Interdependencies of the Living World

IN 1807 THE NATURALIST Alexander von Humboldt wrote, "In the great chain of causes and effects no thing and no activity should be regarded in isolation." [10] This interconnectedness of the living world had been recognized over the centuries, but not until the twentieth century did the terminology to designate the specific, systematic interconnections of the natural world come into general use. In 1867 Ernst Haeckel had put forward the word "ecology" to designate the study of living systems in relation to their environment, but, like "biosphere," it was slow to find common usage. [11] The term "ecosystem" does not appear to have been used commonly before an essay by A. G. Tansley published in 1935 in the journal *Ecology*. [12] The ecosystem has also been known by other names, notably, "biogeocoenose," especially in the Russian literature. [13] It means a definable or bounded system of complex and dynamic biological and physical relationships that vary greatly in size and complexity from the minute or simple to the very large and infinitely complex. The term "ecosphere" has been used to summarize the totality of living systems that envelop the Earth and is synonymous with "biosphere." [14]

In the course of discovering the interdependencies of the living world, the organisms of which it was comprised were located and described. Taxonomy and systematics, description and classification of species, were thus major concerns of biological science in the eighteenth and greater part of the nineteenth centuries, a work particularly associated with the name of the Swedish botanist, Carl von Linné (Linnaeus, 1707–78). Exploration of the continents and the seas and the collection of plant and animal specimens laid foundations for the geography of plants and animals and for more sophisticated understandings of habitat requirements and competition among species. [15]

The distribution of plants and animals was discovered to be neither random nor static. The reasons that a particular species was found to be where it was proved often to be complex. Spatial locations were found frequently to be related to biological dependencies of which symbiosis, parasitism, and territoriality represented special cases. At any given time the network of interdependencies in the living world was found to be in a state of approximate, although dynamic, equilibrium. This homeostatic state was subject to change through forces acting, not only in the physical environment external to organisms, but through genetic changes in the organisms themselves. The consequences of this process of change were discovered to result in the evolution of the species, and theoretical mechanics of this process were described by Charles Darwin in 1859 in *The Origin of Species*, by Alfred Russell Wallace in 1870 in *Contributions to A Theory of Natural Selection*, and by the science of genetics after 1900.

The transplanting of species into areas in which they had not naturally occurred, if it did not fail, frequently had disruptive and calamitous results. The homogenizing and impoverishing of the ecosystems of the Earth was an easily measurable consequence of human interference with natural interdependencies. At almost no time and place in the expansion of populations, and especially of European populations in modern times, did an ecological awareness or an ecologically-oriented policy guide the behavior of the explorers and settlers. By mid-twentieth century, however, the disastrous record of untested and unguided human intervention had been well documented, and there was a growing popular awareness of the dangers of uninformed disruptions of natural systems. Nevertheless, individual and institutionalized human behavior was slow to catch up with human understanding.

Less readily understood than the interconnectedness of things in space was their interconnectedness in time. The theory of evolution dealt with intervals of time far greater than the experience of any human individual and beyond the comprehension of most of them. Yet, in part because of the work of Albert Einstein (1879–1955) showing the relativity of time and space, the significance of time in human affairs was changing. Past expectations in relation to time were becoming less and less reliable as guides for expectations in the future. Cultural change, based heavily upon innovation in science and technology, was accelerating throughout the nineteenth and twentieth centuries. This artificial speeding up of history not only contributed to man's disruptive impact upon the natural world, but also created tensions and discontinuities in his personal life and in society.[16]

The biological and behavioral sciences identified chronological sequences, periodicities, and interdependencies among organisms that must be respected to avoid harmful consequences. For example, because of an almost universal failure to appreciate the significance of the processes of exponential growth, societies failed to take timely action to prevent the catastrophic explosion of human population in the last half of the twentieth century. The necessities for lead time, the inevitability of ramifications, and the effects of time lag had become concepts essential to managing man's behavior in relation to the biosphere.

The lesson that future constraints and opportunities depend upon what is done in the present is as old as the fable of the ant and the grasshopper, but before the mid-twentieth century this counsel of foresight and prudence was not generally applied to the irreversible processes of life in all of its many aspects, but merely to the relatively narrow confines of economic policy. Similarly, the truism that the world is so made that no act occurs in isolation has only slowly influenced the behavior of individuals or of societies. In 1969 it was still necessary for Garrett Hardin to reiterate the aphorism, "You can't do just one thing." [17]

The discovery of the interdependencies of the living world revealed, in ever-sharpening profile, how anthropocentric and unecological modern behavior has been. There was a tacit assumption that culture had repealed biology, and that human history was totally disassociated from the evolution of the species. Such notions were challenged by writers like Morley Roberts (*Biopolitics*, 1938), and Robert Ardrey, whose book, *The Territorial Imperative* (1966), suggested that the principle of dominance of territory, widely established among other living species, was also a powerful force in human affairs, even though disguised by cultural rationalization.

There had been less reluctance to recognize relationships between the development of civilization and the climate, land forms, and resources of the physical world.[18] Environmental theories of history and human development figured prominently among historians and geographers, and indeed often had been pushed beyond the bounds of demonstrable evidence.[19] Reaction against such overenthusiastic environmentalism often led others to unduly depreciate the influences of the physical environment. The result was a lack of attention to the undercutting of the human life support system by an expanding commercial and industrial civilization.

Curiously, the pinnacle of technological effort, space exploration, led in the 1960s to a new appreciation of the interdependencies of the biosphere. Space travel required man to devise a minimum personal artificial ecosystem, the spaceship, and to do this he was required to learn how he must accommodate to those interdependencies which he could not change. The effort to discover, through space biology and medicine, what was required for human survival beyond the limits of the Earth's biosphere, inevitably clarified and emphasized the conditions necessary to life on Earth. So the voyages into space had an effect similar to that of the sea voyages of preceding centuries—they added cumulatively to the process of discovering the true nature of the Earth.

The discovery of the biosphere inevitably involved man in a process of self-discovery. As man's profound and often destructive impact upon the Earth became more obvious, the need to know more about man became ever more evident. The seeming growth of aberrant behavior among individuals and societies strongly suggested that the human adjustments required by man-made changes in the modern world might be exceeding the ability of many individuals to accommodate them.[20]

A variety of physiologically and sociologically harmful phenomena that resulted from the increasingly rapid changes have been summarized by Alvin Toffler in the term "future shock."[21] The factors that cause future shock also often seemed to be upon examination factors in environmental degradation and pollution, and in the impairment of human health through environmental stress and the contamination of the atmosphere, water, and food chains. The acceleration of history which was altering the face of the earth and the human condition was also bringing man face to face with the parameters of his own existence and the question of the survival of the natural world.

Limitations of the Living World

IN 1913 A HARVARD UNIVERSITY BIOCHEMIST, Lawrence J. Henderson, published a book, *The Fitness of the Environment*,[22] which undertook to explore the full range of physicochemical conditions under which living matter could exist. It examined the inorganic basis of life and the planetary conditions permitting genesis of life. Henderson showed that the requirements of living matter are conversely, its limitations. Some of Henderson's analysis has been modified as a result of advances in physical chemistry, but the book did give a concise and systematic formulation to an old and continuing question. In the concluding chapter Henderson observed:

A half century has passed since Darwin wrote "The Origin of the Species," and once again, but with a new aspect, the relation between life and the environment presents itself as an unexplained phenomenon. The problem is now far different from what it was before, for adaptation has won a secure position among the greatest of natural processes, a position from which we may suppose it is certainly never to be dislodged; natural selection is its instrument, even if, as many think, not the only one. Yet natural selection does not mold the organism; the environment it changes only secondarily, without truly altering the primary quality of environmental fitness. This latter component of fitness, antecedent to adaptations, a natural result of the properties of matter and the characteristics of energy in the course of cosmic evolution, is as yet no wise accounted for. . . .

There is, in truth, not one chance in countless millions of millions that the many unique properties of carbon, hydrogen, and oxygen, and especially of their stable compounds water and carbonic acid, which chiefly make up the atmosphere of a new planet, should simultaneously occur in the three elements otherwise than through the operation of a natural law which somehow connects them together. There is no greater probability that these unique properties should be without due cause uniquely favorable to the organic mechanism. There are no mere accidents; an explanation is to seek. It must be admitted, however, that no explanation is at hand.[23]

Henderson's studies pushed him toward a philosophical conclusion very similar to the later evolutionary interpretation by Pierre Teilhard de Chardin in *The Phenomena of Man* (1955).[24] In the concluding paragraph of his study Henderson wrote, "The properties of matter and the course of cosmic evolution are now seen to be intimately related to the structure of the living being and to its activities; they become, therefore, far more important in biology than has been previously suspected. For the whole evolutionary process, both cosmic and organic, is a unity and the biologist may now rightly regard the universe in its very essence as biocentric." [25] Is it also teleological, does it evolve toward some predictable state, as Teilhard appears to have believed? Prevailing opinion in the sciences does not accept a teleological explanation of evolution as necessary or demonstrable. Nevertheless, there are aspects of evolution and ecology that strongly suggest purposiveness. Perhaps our concepts are as yet insufficiently refined to handle the question of teleology in biological processes.[26]

Thirty-five years after first publication of *The Fitness of the Environment*, Harold S. Blum explored the relationships between the second law of thermodynamics and organic evolution in *Time's Arrow and Evolution* (1951),[27] drawing heavily upon Henderson's thesis. In his concluding observations Blum reaffirmed in general Henderson's position that the evolution and present condition of life as it has developed on the earth is an extremely improbable phenomenon although the enormous size of the universe permits the statistical probability of other planets capable of sustaining life. Blum concluded, "If we think, however, of the delicate balance of conditions our earth enjoys, and to what extent chance has entered repeatedly into biological evolution, it seems that the probability of evolving a series of living organisms closely resembling those we know on earth may be a relatively small number. This becomes poignantly evident when we think of all the chance events concerning the evolution of the human brain—which occurred only once on our planet." [28]

Even more true today than when it was written is Blum's observation:

And perhaps for this reason alone, this life-stuff is something to be cherished as our proper heritage. To be guarded from destruction by, say the activity of man, a species of living system that has risen to power and dominance through the development of a certain special property, intelligence. Such a development—vastly exceeding that of any other species—has apparently given this particular system the ability to determine its own destiny to a certain extent. Yet at the moment there are all too many signs that man lacks the ability to exercise the control over his own activities that may be necessary for survival.[29]

The very success of modern society in modifying natural environments, in rearranging and augmenting them for human purposes, has encouraged the euphoric assumption that there are no insurmountable barriers to man's ability to transcend the limits of his environment. But because what appeared to be obvious has been sometimes found to be untrue, it does not follow that the apparently obvious may not also be inexorable.

In his book, *The Human Use of the Earth*, Philip L. Wagner observes, "There are necessary natural limitations to the security, stability, and success of artificial environments." The survival of all artificial systems depends upon the stability and the reliability of the biosphere. But as Wagner observes, "Societal limitations likewise assert themselves." [30] Human disruptions of artificial systems can be as destructive to human life and welfare as natural hazards. Economic depressions, epidemic diseases, and political revolutions can impede essential operations of an artificial system and thus endanger the welfare and survival of a city, a nation, or indeed of humanity. Finally, Wagner points to technical limitations on man's systems.

Modern industrial societies, for example, are heavily dependent upon a continuing supply of electrical energy and of water. Disruption of the man-made and maintained systems not only stops the functioning of the systems as a whole, but indirectly affects all other systems upon which the continuing supply of water or electrical energy depends. No great concentrations of population in modern cities could long survive the breakdown of their basic life-support systems. Thus the need to maintain the artificial systems imposes a rigorous limitation on the priorities and actions of governments and peoples for whose support natural systems, of water for example, are no longer adequate. This constraining necessity now includes the overwhelming majority of people in the industrialized countries of the modern world.

Thus, as we have seen, the requirements of the living world are a reverse way of expressing the limitations of the living world. There are limits beyond which man cannot go in altering his relationships with the natural world. But in many areas of life the location of the limits is uncertain. Controversies over the use of nuclear energy, of the supersonic transport, or of genetic fertilizers and pesticides to enlarge farm crops illustrate a very large number of public questions in which contention over public policy has developed because the outcome of the proposed actions is not certain. Where irreversible consequences are involved or where the costs of reversibility are so great that it is doubtful that society will pay the price, the course of wisdom would appear to be one of great caution and the exploration of alternatives.

Arthur C. Clarke's precepts for ecological prudence are of continuing relevance.[31] They are: (1) Do not attempt the unforeseeable and, (2) Do not commit the irrevocable. Regard for the parameters of human existence has never been strong in the dominating philosophies of Western society. If the West along with all the peoples and nations of the earth are to take effective measures to preserve man's life-support base in the biosphere, some means must be found to include the concept of limitations among the assumptions, attitudes, and institutions of modern people. Far from restraining human energy and creativity, the development of a realistic assessment of the costs and dangers of transgressing the limitations of the living world would further advance applied science and technology toward improving human health, welfare, and happiness.

The Biosphere: Object of Policy

AWARENESS OF THE NEED for a public policy toward the biosphere has grown gradually as the concept of the biosphere itself has been built up by successive enlargements of scientific knowledge.[32] Edward Suess (1831–1914), an Austrian geologist has been credited with first use of the term in the concluding chapter of a small book entitled *Die Entstehung der Alpen* (1875); there he introduced the "biosphere" in a description of the concentric layers enveloping the Earth. The development of the term in modern scientific thought is particularly associated with the work of the Russian mineralogist and forerunner of modern biogeochemistry, V. I. Vernadsky (1863–1945). Although Vernadsky attributed the concept to the French scientist Lamarck (1744–1829), the term gained currency through the publication of Vernadsky's book, *Biosfera*, in Leningrad in 1926; and a French edition, *La Biosphère*, published in Paris in 1929.[33]

Vernadsky's ideas appear to have grown out of his study of biogeochemical phenomena, maturing during the period of World War I and first outlined in 1922–23 in lectures at the Sorbonne in Paris. The essential elements of Vernadsky's concept of the biosphere have been stated in an abstract of a paper published in translation in 1945 in the *American Scientist*.[34] Vernadsky distinguished the biosphere as the area or domain of life, a region where the prevailing conditions are such that incoming solar radiation can produce the geochemical changes necessary for life to occur. The biosphere includes the whole atmospheric troposphere, the hydrosphere or oceans, and the lithosphere—a thin layer in the continental regions extending three kilometers or more below the surface of the Earth.

Vernadsky identified sixteen propositions distinguishing living from inert material. Among them are the following observations. The processes of living natural bodies are not reversible in time, and the vast majority of living organisms change their forms in the process of evolution. The processes of changing growth in living matter tend to increase the free energy of the biosphere, and the number of chemical compounds produced by living organisms probably reaches many millions, whereas the number of different kinds of chemical compounds in inert bodies is limited to a few thousand. New living natural bodies are born only from preexisting ones, and have a common nature in their cellular morphology, substance, and reproductive capacity. All living matter is, therefore, ultimately genetically connected throughout the course of geologic time. Living organisms arise and exist only in the biosphere, and only as discrete bodies; no entry of life into the biosphere from cosmic space has ever been observed.

These propositions were not novel, but upon them Vernadsky based a summation which had never before been so concisely and pointedly stated:

> In everyday life one used to speak of man as an individual, living and moving freely about our planet, freely building up his history. Until recently the historians and the students of the humanities, and to a certain extent even the biologists, consciously failed to reckon with the natural laws of the biosphere, the only terrestrial envelope where life can exist. Basically man cannot be separated from it; it is only now that this indissolubility begins to appear clearly and in precise terms before us. He is geologically connected with its material and energetic structure. Actually no living organism exists on earth in a state of freedom. All organisms are connected indissolubly and uninterruptedly, first of all through nutrition and respiration, with the circumambient material and energetic medium. Outside it they cannot exist in a natural condition.[35]

Apparently influenced by the French mathematician and Bergsonian philosopher Édouard LeRoy (1870–1954) and the French Jesuit, geologist, and paleontologist Pierre Teilhard de Chardin (1881–1955), Vernadsky adopted the concept of the noösphere as the state toward which the biosphere is now evoling geologically. The noösphere, or realm of thought, declared Vernadsky, "is a new geological phenomenon on our planet. In it for the first time man becomes *a large-scale geologic force*. He can and must rebuild the providence of his life by his work and thought, rebuild it radically in comparison with the past."[36]

As man propagates the noösphere, he extends and transforms the biosphere. Vernadsky observed prophetically that:

> Chemically, the face of our planet, the biosphere, is being sharply changed by man, consciously, and even more so, unconsciously. The aerial envelope of the land as well as all its natural waters are changed both physically and chemically by man. In the twentieth

century, as a result of the growth of human civilization, the seas and the parts of the oceans closest to shore become changed more and more markedly. Man now must take more and more measures to preserve for future generations the wealth of the seas which so far have belonged to nobody. Besides this, new species and races of animals and plants are being created by man. Fairy tale dreams appear possible in the future: man is striving to emerge beyond the boundaries of his planet into cosmic space. And he probably will do so.[37]

Vernadsky followed his colleague the geologist A. P. Pavlov (1854–1929) in saying that we had entered the *anthropogenic era of geologic time*, "that man, under our very eyes, is becoming a mighty and ever-growing geological force." Nevertheless, man was bound by a seemingly infinite number of ties to the biosphere and was, except as his existence was modifiable and modified by his thought and effort, subject to its physical limitations. Within the parameters of the natural world, man's mere presence, as well as his deliberate and inadvertent impact, transforms its properties and conditions. There thus arises, as Vernadsky concluded, ". . . the problem of the *reconstruction of the biosphere in the interest of freely thinking humanity as a single totality*." The problem was how to adapt the biosphere to man's needs and desires without impairing its viability. In discovering the nature of the biosphere man was creating and simultaneously discovering the noösphere, which, declared Vernadsky, is "this new state of the biosphere, which we approach without our noticing it." [38]

Although Vernadsky developed the scientific concept of the biosphere, and posed the problem which makes it an object of policy, popular awareness of the biosphere may owe more to the writings of Pierre Teilhard de Chardin, whose principal work, *Le Phénomène Humain* (*The Phenomenon of Man*, 1938), took a poetic and metaphysical approach to the concept of the biosphere, which is evident in the following passage describing the fundamental unity of living matter:

> However tenuous it was, the first veil of organised matter spread over the earth could neither have established nor maintained itself without some network of influences and exchanges

which made it a biologically *cohesive* whole. From its origin, the cellular nebula necessarily represented, despite its internal multiplicity, a sort of diffuse super-organism. Not merely a *foam of lives* but, to a certain extent, itself a *living film*. A simple reappearance, after all, in more advanced form and on a higher level of those much older conditions which we have already seen presiding over the birth and equilibrium of the first polymerised substances on the surface of the early earth. A simple prelude, too, to the much more advanced evolutionary solidarity, so marked in the higher forms of life, whose existence obliges us increasingly to admit the strictly organic nature of the links which unite them in a single whole at the heart of the biosphere.[39]

To resolve the problem that Vernadsky posed regarding man's transformation of the biosphere, the biosphere must first become a subject of social concern and then an object of public policy. First recognition of the biosphere as an object of international policy came with the resolution adopted in November 1966 by the General Conference of UNESCO at its fourteenth session. Pursuant to this resolution, an Inter-governmental Conference of Experts on the Scientific Basis for Rational Use and Conservation of the Resources of the Biosphere was convened in Paris, September 4–13, 1968. This gathering, known for convenience as the Biosphere Conference, was organized by UNESCO with assistance from the United Nations, the Food and Agriculture Organization, the World Health Organization, the International Union for the Conservation of Nature and Natural Resources and the International Biological Programme. The significance of this conference and its recommendations for institutional development will be considered in subsequent chapters of this volume. Here the conference is mentioned as evidence of an awareness of the loss of environmental quality that had been occurring throughout the world.

In summarizing recurring themes which had emerged during the conference, the final report declared, "Although some of the changes in the environment have been taking place for decades or longer, they seem to have reached a threshold of criticalness, as in the case of air, soil and water pollution in industrial countries; these problems are now producing concern and a popular demand for correction." "Parallel with this concern," the report continued, "is the realization that ways of developing and using natural resources must be changed from single purpose efforts, both public and private, with little regard for attendant consequences, to other uses of resources and wider social goals." The report emphasized that human exploitation of the Earth "must give way to recognition that the biosphere is a system all of which is widely affected by action on any part of it." The problem was not one for science alone. A further consequence of a "new awareness that man is a key factor in the biosphere," the report declared, was "that natural science and technology alone are inadequate for modern solutions to resource management problems; one must also consider social sciences in particular, politics and public administration, economics, law, sociology and psychology, for, after all, it is resources as considered by man with which we are concerned." [40]

From 1968 onward, the concept of the biosphere as an evolved, integrated planetary life-supporting system was implicit even when not explicitly stated in declarations of international environmental policy, such as that issued by the United Nations Associations of the Nordic Countries in December 1969, and the "Declaration on the Management of the Natural Environment of Europe" by the European Conservation Conference in 1970. On January 1, 1970, the term "biosphere" was incorporated into the public laws of the United States in the Preamble of the National Environmental Policy Act of 1969 (PL 91–190), which declared that it is a part of national policy to "promote efforts which will prevent or eliminate damage to the environment and the biosphere. . . ."

In an article summarizing the findings of the Biosphere Conference, René Dubos epitomized the role of man in reshaping the biosphere in the following sentences:

> Planning the future demands an ecological attitude based on the assumption that man will continuously bring about evolutionary changes through his creative potentialities. The constant interaction between man and the environment inevitably implies continuous alterations of both—alterations which should always

49

remain within the constraints imposed by the laws of Nature and by the unchangable biological and mental characteristics of man's nature.[41]

Concluding Summary

WE HAVE SEEN that the discovery of the biosphere was a process of conceptual growth. Throughout the first five thousand years of human history man's knowledge of where he was in the cosmos and the true nature of his relationships with his environment remained substantially unchanged. There were, of course, instances of perceptive insight by philosophers and a remarkably accurate measurement of the circumference of the earth by Eratosthenes. Yet at the time of the discovery of America man's knowledge of the physical world had advanced little beyond that extant at the time of the Alexandrian mathematician and geographer, Ptolemy.

As Buckminster Fuller has pointed out,[42] the discovery of the true nature of the existential world has been a product of physical exploration and scientific investigation, of the mapping of the land masses, and of navigation on the sea, in the air, and finally of outer space beyond the Earth. The great age of discovery has lasted nearly five hundred years and may be nearing its close.[43] There is much yet to be learned about the Earth, but that knowledge would appear to be largely incremental to what is already known. It is possible that through unmanned spacecraft the mysteries of the other planets may be probed; but what will be learned is unlikely fundamentally to change man's present understanding of his relationship to the biosphere.

Man's knowledge of the biophysical world must ultimately be tested, confirmed, and systematized through science. The electron microscope, the seismograph, the spectroscope, the radiotelescope, the gas chromatograph, and many other instruments have supplemented man's direct observation in discovering the natural parameters of human existence. Yet this age of discovery and of science has thus far occupied less than ten percent of a human history that extends backward in time for at least five millennia. Man's ethical systems, his religions, his political ideas were born and developed in this prescientific age. The rich heritage of his past has been carried into the modern era, but like all wealth, this legacy which we call civilization brings with it burdens. Among the burdens of the past are those ways of perceiving and dealing with the natural world that are fundamentally inconsistent with the possibility of sustaining long term relationships with it.

It may seem strange that so radical a departure from historical views of man–environment relationships as are implicit in our present knowledge of the biosphere should not have had more profound effects upon human attitudes and institutions. Perhaps it is man's long and intimate association with the physical world that has caused him to be contemptuous of it or negligent toward it. The growth of knowledge concerning the biosphere has been slow, even in modern times, and has been the product of findings and theories in nearly every science. Scientific theories regarding the biosphere, supported by sufficient evidence, may in time be accepted as conventional wisdom and thereafter be taken for granted. But the discovery of the biosphere, unlike the splitting of the atom, has not been a dramatic event which can be located precisely in time. Perhaps that is why many intelligent individuals cannot understand how the incremental accumulation of knowledge about the biosphere may add up to an interpretation of man's environment relationships that holds absolutely fundamental and revolutionary implications for the future of human behavior patterns and institutions. Some critics found nothing new in Henderson's *The Fitness of the Environment*, seeing in it only platitudes. The unexceptional nature of Henderson's conclusions appears to have been a barrier to their acceptance.

As one may not see a forest for the trees, very large ideas may be lost in the specific arguments of which they are composed. The human mind, moreover, tends to see what it wants to see or what it has been trained to see. The notion of inexorable limitations has not been congenial to modern men. Even when the finiteness of the world is admitted intellectually, the concept will often be rejected emotionally. The traditionalist will feel that God will intervene somehow, and the unimpressed scientist deep in his own specialty, will merely ask, "So what?"

But as more is learned about the grand-scale cycles of energy and chemical processes that sustain the biosphere, processes that man can disrupt but not control, fewer skeptical questions are voiced. A more pertinent question has been asked by George Woodwell "How much of the energy that runs the biosphere can be diverted to the support of a single species: man?" [44] The answer to that question will be found, with or without searching for it, in the years ahead. But it is not sufficient that scientists alone understand the requirements of a self-regenerative biosphere—there must be a general recognition that there are requirements which man cannot modify.

Man's beliefs and attitudes are in some measure the product of his experience. If his behavior and institutions are to be reorganized consistent with the requirements of the biosphere, his life experience must somehow be modified to make those requirements a part of his operating assumptions. Something must be added to his experience that did not exist in the prescientific past and is consistent with what he knows today about the natural world, something that confirms this knowledge with great emotional power. Knowledge to support such a change of attitude exists and is growing, but a dramatic event may be needed to symbolize the new concept.

Such an event may well have already occurred. The astronauts of Apollo were the first men to ever see the Earth whole. The emotional impact of their photographs of the blue Earth, alone in the blackness of space, was obviously very great and was shared by millions throughout the world. How this view of the Earth from outer space, like a fragile glass sphere, will affect the future behavior of peoples and governments is uncertain, but it represents a powerful and moving event that had not occurred before in all human experience. The symbolic power of the image is suggested by its extensive use on the covers of books, on posters, in advertising, and on postage stamps.

When one considers that it is only in the present generation that men have seen the biosphere objectified in space, and that a body of knowledge and ideas has been brought together in its name, we may have some hope that human beings will behave differently towards it in the future than they have in the past. Upon the fulfillment of this hope, the future of man and perhaps of life itself depends.

3

International Conservation Efforts:

COOPERATION TO PROTECT

ENDANGERED SPECIES

AND ENVIRONMENTS

WE HAVE SEEN THAT MAN DID NOT PERCEIVE A THREAT to the viability of the Earth until he had conceived the idea of the biosphere. But the historical roots of the effort to defend the Earth reach back to a time long before men could imagine a need to conserve living species and natural habitat.

The scanty evidence available to us indicates that even when he sensed the distinctive qualities of his particular environment, early man accepted it as given. There was little he could do about the environment as a whole other than to adapt to it or leave it. His interest and curiosity was concentrated upon its parts, upon its salient geographical features—mountains, rivers, lakes, and forests—and upon the plants and animals with which he shared the Earth.

Beyond the practical necessity of obtaining his livelihood from it, man's initial reaction to his environment appears to have been to capture its more interesting features, particularly those wild animals and plants that seemed to him marvelous or edible, or otherwise useful. Thus science, conservation, and environmental protection efforts have roots in man's inquiring nature and, paradoxically, in his possessive tendencies which have

perhaps more often worked to the destruction of nature than to
its preservation.

Conservation, Ecology, and the Environment

BEFORE REVIEWING early international conservation measures to protect the environment, it may be useful to note the
distinctions involved in the words "conservation," "ecology,"
and "the environment." Simplifying, we may identify conservation as a political movement, ecology as a field of scientific
study, and environment as the context of an object, or as a focus
or object of study. None of these terms is precise, and the meanings of all of them have changed over the years.[1]

In all cases clarity requires that we distinguish between
study of the thing these terms represent and the actual phenomena themselves. Thus the study of the conservation movement
should be distinguished from the actual practice of conservation; the study of ecology should be distinguished from the
actual interrelationship of organisms and ecosystems; and
environmental studies or environmental science should be distinguished from the actual environmental context of any organic
or inorganic object. Environmental studies are not necessarily
the same as ecology, although there is a popular tendency today
to confuse the two. There are, of course, denominators and
linkages common to all three terms. All, for example, have to
do with man's relationship with the natural world.

There are also causal linkages. For example, efforts to
conserve specific species and resources began before anyone
thought of a general movement to protect nature and natural
resources, but efforts to protect and preserve seem to have been
one of the factors in the birth of the science of ecology. The
roots of ecology, as noted in Chapter 2, also are in the sciences
of taxonomy and systematics, the study of why animals and
plants are distributed as they are within the varied context of
the environment. Growth of taxonomic studies pushed the
search for new plant and animal species that might help to clarify
the course of evolution, a search which concomitantly stimulated efforts to conserve species and natural habitats so that they
might remain available for future study.

The growth of the conservation movement and of the science of ecology made it increasingly difficult for informed persons to take any environment for granted. Environmental influences drew attention as soon as investigations into the causes of species differentiation and evolution began. The growing science of ecology became indispensable in the conservation of the environment. Even before it could make accurate predictions, ecology provided a cautionary restraint on a human weakness for oversimplified solutions to environmental problems.

For example, absolute protection of forests from fire, an objective of the early conservation movement in the United States, has been found to be unwise. Fire has its ecological functions, among them, controlling the growth of certain vegetation, preserving the habitats of birds like the Kirtland's Warbler, and helping to germinate the seeds of some conifers—without fire, the pine forests of the southern states would be replaced by hardwoods.[2] Similarly, early efforts to preserve certain species of plants and animals by moving them out of a threatened or disappearing habitat frequently failed when the new habitat proved to be unsuitable. Thus the growth of the science of ecology increasingly tempered the enthusiasms of the conservation movement and provided a means for analyzing the character of an environment, particularly its resilience or fragility and the probable consequences of man's interference.[3]

Conservation Efforts Cross National Boundaries

THE PHENOMENON OF LIFE is dynamic, and populations of plants and animals have distributed themselves throughout the biosphere since living organisms first appeared.[4] The survival of the species has depended heavily upon their adaptability to their environmental circumstances. By far the greater number of species that have appeared during the course of evolution have become extinct—most of them through natural processes. As noted in chapter one, however, man himself played a role in the elimination of species, possibly having hunted many of the larger mammals of the Pleistocene into extinction. Vastly expanded and mobile human populations with sophisticated technology have speeded the process of extermination, as much through the elimination of habitats and environmental pollution as by direct killing.

Yet if some men have wantonly or inadvertently destroyed life, others have sought to protect it. In many instances, the motivation has been largely economic, but curiosity, aesthetic satisfaction, and even ethical conviction have inspired protective efforts. Since the beginning of history, some men have sought to surround themselves with unfamiliar plants and animals that they have found interesting and attractive. Collections of plants and animals have been recorded from Egypt, Babylonia, China, and Rome. Exotic species were especially valued and, at a very early period, man became an agent for redistribution of plants and animals.

In modern times, international conservation began with the establishment of botanical and zoological gardens, the scientific collection of rare and endangered species, and efforts to enlarge the genetic stock through controlled breeding and propagation. In many early efforts, governments were not involved and projects were international only in the sense that national boundaries were crossed. With the establishment of national scientific institutions, however, governments soon did become parties to the international movement of plants and animals.

Relative ease of transport and their value for agricultural and medicinal purposes made plants an early object of international exchange.[5] Botanical gardens were established in Italy by the middle of the sixteenth century, and the Museum National d'Histoire Naturelle was established by the French government in Paris in 1635. The Royal Botanic Garden at Kew in England was established in 1759. A century later the Missouri Botanical Garden, now the oldest in North America, was founded in St. Louis by Henry Shaw. The Arnold Arboretum of Harvard University was founded in 1872, the New York Botanical Garden in 1895, and the Brooklyn Botanical Garden in 1910. Important botanical collections and arboretums were established in tropical countries, among them those at Bogor in Java, at Georgetown in Guiana, and at Singapore.

Plant hunting and exploratory expeditions began in the eighteenth century. One of the first and most notable was the journey of the young Linnaeus into Lapland, financed by the Royal Scientific Society of Uppsala. The Royal Botanic Garden at Kew seems to have been the first scientific institution to press botanical exploration abroad. A well known instance of the traffic in useful plants was the voyage of H.M.S. *Bounty* in 1787 to the South Pacific under the command of Captain William Bligh for the purpose of introducing the bread fruit tree from the South Sea Islands into the West Indies.

Efforts to conserve have sometimes resulted in the survival under artificial conditions of species that have disappeared in nature. For example, the Ginkgo tree (*Ginkgo biloba*) survived under cultivation in China and Japan, although it has never been found in historic times in a truly wild state. Once widely distributed throughout the Northern Hemisphere, the tree was reintroduced into Europe after specimens were discovered in Japan by Engelbrecht Kaempfer about 1690, and the first living Ginkgo in America in the modern era was imported from England and planted in Pennsylvania in 1785.

An interesting case in which a species survived because of international effort is that of Pere David's deer, the Milu.[6] This unusual deer, never found in a wild state, existed in modern times only within the confines of the Imperial Hunting Park of the Manchu Dynasty near Peking. Through negotiations with the Chinese imperial government, two specimens of the deer were sent in 1869 to the London Zoological Society and in 1883 two more exported. Subsequently, the Duke of Bedford undertook to form a herd on his estate at Woburn Abbey. His efforts undoubtedly saved the species. In 1895 a severe flood toppled part of the walls of the Imperial Hunting Park and many of the deer herd were eaten by starving peasants whose crops had been destroyed. The remaining deer were killed in 1900 by the international military forces that invaded Peking to suppress the Boxer Uprising.

The flowering tree, *Franklinia alatamaha*, is another case of a plant preserved from extinction through human efforts. The Franklinia was discovered by an American naturalist, John Bartram, on the banks of the Alatamaha River in Georgia in 1765.[7] Seed from the tree was propagated both in England and Pennsylvania. In 1778, his son, William B. Bartram, once again

57

found the Franklinia in Georgia, but the tree has never been seen in a wild state since; and the existence of all present specimens must be attributed to the efforts of the Bartrams and indirectly to the Lord Petre and other persons of wealth and title in England, who financed their exploration of the little known flora of North America.

Early Action Toward International Conservation

THREE GENERAL OBSERVATIONS may be made concerning international efforts on behalf of conservation.

First, they are comparatively recent. All major international agreements for the protection of the natural environment and notably of wildlife have been negotiated within the twentieth century. Serious international efforts to protect the natural world have thus occupied hardly more than one long generation of human history.

Second, with relatively minor exceptions, all conservation treaties negotiated before the London Convention on Oil Pollution in 1954 were concerned with the protection of migratory wildlife. Moreover, they were largely concerned with the direct killing of wildlife for sport or commerce and afforded little or no protection from indirect threats, such as environmental pollution or loss of habitat. The sovereign signatories were careful not to commit themselves to any specific action to establish sanctuaries, reserves, or national parks within their own territories, although sometimes the need for the protection of habitat was recognized. The language of the treaties did not go beyond such cautious phrases as "explore the possibility of," and "give consideration to," or even more guardedly, "consider the possibility of establishing."

Third, with the exception of the fur seal convention of 1911, the earlier treaties appear to have been indifferently effective. They were important as commitments of national governments to the idea of the conservation of nature. They marked the emergence of a new public attitude toward nature and the human environment. But whether they significantly retarded the attrition of environmental quality and of the Earth's wildlife is debatable. In almost every instance, protracted, complex, and desultory negotiations were required before even minimal agreements could be formalized. And even these frequently were qualified by reservations that reduced their already limited effectiveness.

The case in point is the convention concerning the Conservation of Birds Useful to Agriculture.[8] Signed by eleven nations at Paris on March 10, 1902, this treaty capped an effort of almost thirty-five years, beginning with a request by an assembly of German farmers and foresters in 1868 for the aid of the Foreign Office of Austria-Hungary in obtaining an international treaty for the protection of birds and animals useful to agriculture and forestry. During the following year, Italy, Switzerland, and France responded favorably to the idea, which at that stage was to establish a net of bilateral agreements. In 1872, the Swiss proposed an international regulatory commission, but the sovereign states of Europe were not interested in institutional arrangements. The issue was discussed at International Ornithological Congresses in 1873, 1891, and 1900, and an International Ornithological Committee, from which came the idea of a treaty was set up at Vienna in 1884. In 1887, a joint Austro-Italian declaration committed the respective governments to "strict and comprehensive legislation" for bird protection, but in fact the declaration was not implemented. It did, however, afford a basis for discussion at conferences in Paris in 1895 and 1902, at which the international convention was finally drafted.

Protection of migratory birds and animals in North America was less complicated than in Europe because of the simpler political boundaries and cultural differences. The Canadian–American Treaty of 1916 for the Protection of Migratory Birds[9] has been described as "simply a game law, imposing closed seasons and limitations on commerce."[10] A practical reason for the negotiation of this Treaty (technically with Great Britain, which at that time represented Canada in foreign affairs) was the apparent lack of constitutional authority of the federal government of the United States to protect wildlife through statutory legislation. Whatever the reason, however, it is a point of some importance that it was an international agreement that enabled the United States to enact implementing legislation and to provide subsequent administrative measures. The implementing legislation established a Migratory Bird Commission and began a system of permanent wildlife refuges that today totals thirty million acres.[11]

Efforts to extend protection southward to Latin American countries were begun persuant to a resolution of the United States Senate in 1920. However, not until 1936 was a Treaty for the Protection of Migratory Birds and Game Mammals [12] negotiated with Mexico. In 1940, under the sponsorship of the Pan American Union, a draft Convention on Nature Protection and Wildlife Preservation in the Western Hemisphere [13] undertook to commit the signatory nations to establish national parks, reserves, nature monuments, and wilderness areas; to safeguard wildlife habitats; and, under Article 7, to "adopt appropriate measures for the protection of migratory birds of economic or aesthetic value or to prevent the threatened extinction of any given species."

The treaty became effective in May 1942, following ratification by five of the twenty-one signatory nations. The language of the treaty represented a major step towards international policy for the quality of the environment. The purpose of the treaty, stated in its preamble, was "to protect and preserve in their natural habitat representatives of all species and genera of their [the signatory nations] native fauna and flora, including migratory birds, in sufficient numbers and over areas extensive enough to ensure them from becoming extinct through any agency within man's control" and to "protect and preserve scenery of extraordinary beauty, unusual and striking geological formations, regions, and natural objects of aesthetic, historic, or scientific value, and areas characterized by primitive conditions in those cases covered by this Convention." Like most treaties for wildlife protection, however, this convention is basically an exhortation, as Article 7 permits "insofar as the respective governments may see fit, the rational utilization of migratory birds for the purpose of sport as well as for food, commerce and industry, and for scientific study and investigation."

The African Convention Relative to the Preservation of Flora and Fauna in Their Natural State (London 1933) [14] marked a further advance in international efforts toward wild-life protection, particularly in its more specific prohibitions regarding the hunting and harassment of wildlife and in the protection and administration of habitat. Article 21 of the treaty provided that "each contracting government shall furnish to the government of the United Kingdom information as to the measures taken for the purpose of carrying out the provisions of the preceding articles." The United Kingdom agreed to communicate all the information so furnished to all the governments "which signed or acceded through the Convention."

The London Convention of 1933 was, of course, an agreement among the European governors of pre-World War II Africa. It logically followed that with political independence of the African continent a new treaty was needed. The African Convention for Conservation of Nature and Natural Resources [15] was approved and signed in Algiers in September 1968 by representatives of thirty-eight member states of the Organization of African Unity. The broader conceptual base of the new African agreement—to "ensure the conservation, utilization, and development of soil, water, flora, and the faunal resources in accordance with scientific principles and with due regard for the best interest of the people"—reflects the transition from the earlier conservationist view to the broader scope of environmental policy.

Conservation of the Fur Seals

INTERNATIONAL CONSERVATION EFFORTS have few success stories, but among them perhaps the least equivocal is the protection and management of the fur seal herd in the Bering Sea. The Convention between the United States and Other Powers Providing for the Preservation and Protection of Fur Seals,[16] signed July 7, 1911, demonstrates that it is possible for man rationally to exploit and manage a perishable resource. Although the administration of the treaty has not been without contention (notably Japanese agitation over alleged depredations of the fur seals on commercial fisheries) the signatory nations—the United States, Canada, Russia, and Japan—have obeyed its terms and based their management of the fur seal herd on a sound scientific research program.

Following World War II, a new treaty was necessary. An Interim Convention on Conservation of North Pacific Fur Seals was adopted in 1957 and has been extended at six year intervals.[17] A North Pacific Fur Seal Commission was created to formulate and coordinate research and to recommend management.

Eighty percent of all fur seals breed on the Pribilof Islands, which are under the jurisdiction of the United States, and the four nations party to the convention have a direct interest in the preservation and management of the herd—circumstances that have no doubt contributed significantly to its success. There has been a continuing exchange of scientific personnel and research material among the treaty powers. The United States and the Soviet Union and the United States and Japan have exchanged observers aboard research vessels, sharing information on pelagic research techniques and visiting rookeries to observe the behavior of seals, the taking of seals, and the preliminary processing of seal skins. Cooperative pelagic research has been carried out by the United States and Canada.

The administration of the treaty has been an outstanding example of sustained-yield management. In the sixty years since the treaty took effect, the first seal herd has grown from less than 150,000 to almost 1.5-million, the maximum number that feeding grounds can sustain. The periodic need to reduce the size of the herd by killing surplus animals (taking the skins) has aroused protest from persons who have failed to comprehend the ecological and political circumstances. Death is one of nature's universal and inexorable controls, and if man presumes to take over tasks once performed by nature, he must accept the disagreeable necessity of acting as a surrogate for nature.

In 1970, a new threat to the seal herd was discovered. In the course of searching for DDT residues, marine biologists in the United States found concentrations of mercury in the livers of Alaskan seals at levels considered toxic to humans.[18] The seals spend the greater part of their lives in the open ocean fifty to a hundred miles from polluted coastal areas, but mercury is concentrated in the aquatic food chain, being absorbed from the water by plankton and other small animals that are in turn eaten by fish and finally by the seals. Following further investigation, the United States Food and Drug Administration ordered withdrawn from the market 10,000 iron supplement pills made from the livers of fur seals, and the United States Public Health Service began preliminary examinations of the native Aleut population in the Pribilofs to whom the fur seal has been an important source of meat.

The threat from mercury illustrates how swiftly and unobtrusively man-made ecological change can overtake erstwhile effective legal and institutional arrangements. The Fur Seal Convention of 1911 was remarkably effective in protecting the seals from the direct impact of man. It was sufficient to control the taking of seals on the islands and in the surrounding seas. But the new threat could not be so localized, nor was it necessarily the result of industrial activity within the nations party to the treaty. The implications of contamination by DDT and mercury were becoming increasingly clear. International protection, either voluntary or coercive, that could not police the industrial practices of nations, would be unable to protect.

The Tragedy of the Great Whales

IF THE CONSERVATION of the fur seal is one of the brighter chapters in the history of international conservation efforts, failure to protect the whales is one of the most dismal. Following the rapid decline of whales in the North Atlantic Ocean, the first step toward international control of whaling was taken in 1920 with the establishment of an International Bureau for Whaling Statistics at Sandefjord in Norway. Cooperation with the Bureau was purely voluntary, all countries participating in whaling being urged to send it complete data on their operations.

Meanwhile, the League of Nations attempted to secure multipartite agreement to a program of conservation for whales. A Convention for the Regulation of Whaling [19] was finally signed at Geneva in September 1931. Twenty-four nations ratified or adhered to the treaty by December 1935, but Japan and the Soviet Union, which were to play a major role toward the extermination of the whales, were not even parties to the treaty. The treaty obligations were minimal. No limits were placed on the taking of any species. Restrictions were placed only on destructive and wasteful methods of operation. Whaling vessels were to be licensed by the participating governments and each vessel was required to give a full report of its operations and complete biological data to the International Bureau at Sandefjord. The convention prohibited the taking or killing of calves or suckling whales, immature whales, and female whales accompanied by calves or suckling whales. This treaty, which for all practical purposes was unenforceable, was supplemented by an agreement concluded in 1937 and by a protocol amending the agreement signed in 1938 intended to make the 1931 treaty something more than mere exhortation.

An agreement signed by nine governments in 1937 provided for at least one government inspector on each factory ship. Moreover, certain areas of the Atlantic, Pacific, and Indian Oceans were closed to the taking of certain species of whales, a whaling season was established and minimum lengths were pre-scribed for the taking of certain species. Parties to the 1937 agreement expressed concern about the unrestricted operations conducted under the flag of governments not party to the con-vention and the flight of whalers from the regulating to the unregulating states.

World War II brought the whales a temporary reprieve from the virtually unchecked rapacity of the whalers. Near the war's end in London in 1944, a majority of the parties to the 1937 agreement undertook to establish a new conservation prin-ciple. The so-called Blue Whale Unit (BWU) was established to regulate the maximum take of whales in any one season. The blue whale was taken as a measure of catch, being equivalent to two fin whales or two and one half humpback whales or six sei whales. Unfortunately, this unit of measurement, which it was hoped might prevent further over-expansion of whaling, was utterly unscientific and in effect legitimized indiscriminate reduc-tion of all species.

Following the war, at the initiative of the United States, a new international whaling conference was held in Washington in 1946 and an International Whaling Commission (IWC) was established.[20] A code for the whaling industry was formulated and the commission was empowered to amend it without the necessity of further formal conferences. The IWC conformed to the structure that had been established for international fisheries commissions, consisting of one member of each contracting government with one vote for each member. Ordinary decisions were to be taken by simple majority with changes in the code requiring a three-quarters majority. Although authorized to administer regulations for open and closed waters, periods, methods, and intensity of whaling, including the maximum catch in any one season, the commission had no power to restrict the number or nationality of factory ships or whaling stations ashore or to allocate specific quotas to any one nation.

In its subsequent history, the International Whaling Commission has been unable to overcome the studied and stubborn defense of the short-range interests of the whaling industry and its consistent disregard of the findings and recommendations of its scientific advisors.[21] Although the preamble of the 1946 treaty refers to "the interest of the nations of the world in safeguarding for future generations the great natural resources represented by whale stocks," the document is filled with qualifications which have been used to legitimize the short-range exploitations of the whaling industry. Among such phrases, for example, are "to achieve the optimum level of whale stocks as rapidly as possible without causing widespread economic and nutritional distress" or "make possible the orderly development of the whaling industry" or "shall take into consideration the interests of the consumers of the whale products and the whaling industry."

No one familiar with the history of whaling could possibly believe that the provisions established under the treaty of 1931, the agreement of 1937, and the code of regulations adopted in 1949 when the International Whaling Commission became effective, would be obeyed without enforcement. Violations of the treaties and the code of regulations have been widespread and endemic. The 1937 agreement, requiring each government party to the treaty to provide at least one inspector on each ship under its flag, has never been satisfactorily implemented and, even if implemented, would be a dubious form of protection. In

1959, the International Whaling Commission accepted a plan for placing neutral observers aboard ships, but efforts to implement this proposal have been ineffective.

Meanwhile, the great whales have been hunted toward early extermination. The anger, dismay, and protest of conservationists, scientists, and ordinary informed citizens of moral sensitivity had no effect whatever on the whaling industry or on most of their governments. In 1970, however, the United States government, over strong objections from commercial interests and the Navy, placed whales on the list of endangered species, thus prohibiting the importation of whale products.[22] Meanwhile, the rapid depletion of the whales was followed by the collapse of the whaling industry in country after country, and it now seems that the whaling fleets of the Soviet Union and Japan have the capability of exterminating all but the lesser species of this magnificent animal.

Managing Marine Fisheries

ONE OF THE EARLIEST and most widespread areas of international conservation has been the effort to conserve and manage marine fisheries. By the early twentieth century, the pressures of increasing human populations and advanced fishing technology were reflected in returns gradually diminishing in relation to the effort expended. The decline of fisheries, first in the North Sea and North Atlantic, was soon followed by decreases in other parts of the world, notably in the North Pacific. Because the high seas were beyond the jurisdiction of any nation, international cooperation was necessary to assist the fishing industries and to conserve the diminishing stocks of fish and other marine life. Two approaches were taken toward international conservation: first, cooperative research, and second, regulation. Being easier to organize and less susceptible to political controversy, cooperative research preceded regulation by several decades.[23]

First efforts were undertaken where diminishing returns were first felt. The International Council for the Exploration of the Seas (ICES) was established following organizing meetings in Stockholm in 1899 and in Christiania [Oslo] in 1901. Since its inaugural meeting in 1902, headquarters of the council have been in Copenhagen. Its membership was drawn initially from the northwest European states; Portugal, Spain, and Italy subsequently joined, and cooperative relations were established with the United States, Canada, and Japan. The council has collected and published data supplied by its members and has engaged in cooperative and planned research through committees, organized both by species of fish and by geographic areas. Within the limits of its activities, it has been generally considered a success and has afforded a model for similar efforts.

In 1919, the International Commission for the Scientific Exploration of the Mediterranean Sea was established, supplemented in 1949 by the General Fisheries Council for the Mediterranean sponsored by the Food and Agriculture Organization, for problems of marine science not directly connected with fisheries. From 1920 to 1938, the North American Council on Fisheries Investigation laid the groundwork for the International Convention for the Northwest Atlantic Fisheries. Following a general plan to encourage the formation of regional research councils for the scientific exploration of the sea in parts of the world not served by such bodies, the Food and Agriculture Organization in 1948 sponsored the establishment of the Indo-Pacific Fisheries Council (IPFC) for the "development and proper utilization of living aquatic resources."

Research may provide the information needed for conservation, but it does not of itself conserve. For that, regulation and management are necessary. The successful negotiation of a treaty between the United States and Canada in 1923 for the preservation of the halibut fishery of the North Pacific Ocean was the first of a number of international conventions leading to the establishment of continuing regulatory fisheries commissions. The International Pacific Halibut Commission consists of three members from the United States and Canada, respectively appointed by the governments of each country. The original convention (1923) was supplanted and modified by treaties concluded in 1930, 1937, and 1953. The commission was at first highly successful in rebuilding the halibut stock and maintaining a high annual sustained yield. From a low annual catch of 44-million pounds in 1931, an annual catch of 70-million pounds was reached in 1954, and it was hoped that this level might be indefinitely maintained. However, incursions into the halibut fisheries, and especially into the eastern Bering Sea, by Russian and Japanese trawlers raised doubts regarding this possibility. In 1971 a two-year agreement went into effect between the United States and Japan with regard to special halibut areas off United States territorial waters in the North Pacific and the eastern Bering Sea, and the United States and the Soviet Union have held scientific discussions on more general fisheries conservation problems in the area.

Much more restricted was the convention signed by the United States and Canada establishing an International Pacific Salmon Fisheries Commission to regulate the catch of salmon originating in the Fraser River system. Among other international arrangements for the conservation of fisheries are the Inter-American Tropical Tuna Commission and the International Commission for the Northwest Atlantic Fisheries, both established in 1949; the International North Pacific Fisheries Commission, established in 1954; and the Permanent Commission for Exploitation and Conservation of the Marine Resources of the South Pacific, also established in 1954.

It has been shown to be technically possible to employ research and management effectively to conserve fisheries resources and to provide a sustained yield for the fisheries industries. But whether it is politically possible and, in a narrow sense, economically profitable to take a long-range view of the conservation of marine fisheries is, as yet, far from certain. There has always been a tendency in international negotiations to divide the spoils rather than to conserve the resource.

All circumstances concerning the protection of marine life involve ancient arguments over the freedom of the seas and national rights, which, as we have seen, have often crippled efforts to implement protective policies. In 1943, at the request of the League of Nations, the International Council for the Exploration of the Seas created a committee of jurists with J. L. Suarez of the Argentine as rapporteur. His "Report on the Exploitation of the Products of the Sea," presented on January 29, 1926, urged a biological basis for policy, with primary attention to the preservation of economically valuable species rather than to the traditional concern of the parties with reciprocal commercial rights. The Suarez report proposed international regulation of the continental shelf to a depth of two hundred meters, provided for a rotation of zones of fishing to avoid over-exploitation, for closed seasons, for the protection of the young, for standardization of methods of capture, and for the fullest possible use of all animals taken. But the Suarez report was not implemented and had no direct consequences. Subsequent consideration under committees of the League of Nations and the International Council for the Exploration of the Seas led eventually to the Treaty on Whaling of 1931, which, as we have seen, proved tragically ineffective. Proposals to regulate fisheries and to establish international jurisdiction over any part of the seas were never seriously considered by the League.

In 1955, the United Nations tried where the League had failed. At the request of the General Assembly, an International Technical Conference on the Conservation of the Living Resources of the Sea was held in Rome at the headquarters of the Food and Agriculture Organization. The meeting was called to assist the International Law Commission in the preparation of draft articles on certain basic aspects of the international regulation of fisheries. The conference, as its name implied, was concerned almost entirely with technical problems involved in the conservation of fisheries. Legal or political matters were not discussed, although these have been the fundamental obstacles to the conservation of marine resources. Nearly two decades were to pass before the United Nations was prepared to confront the legal and political issues in a world conference on the law of the sea, which has been called for 1973.

With the exception of the Alaskan Fur Seal Convention, a case could be made that, if none of the international conservation agreements negotiated before 1970 had ever existed, the state of fisheries and world wildlife generally would not have been significantly different. Perhaps there is a better case for contending that, although the practical effect of the treaties was disappointing, they represented moral commitments which concerned people might work to realize effectively. Where public attitudes favored conserving behavior, as in the United States, Canada, and northwestern Europe, the treaties were generally observed;

conversely, where the commitments were not supported by the traditional culture or public opinion, the treaties were often rejected or given no more than token administration.

The Growth of International Concern

To PERSONS SENSITIVE to the rapidly declining quality of the human environment and aware of the increasing precariousness of man's ecological situation, the slow and reluctant movement of nations toward a more realistic assessment of man's predicament can only be described as painful. Worse yet, much of the international energy mobilized to improve the human condition, especially during the years before 1968, appears in retrospect to have been misguided, its ultimate effect often worsening rather than improving the human environment. Nevertheless, when one compares the assumptions, agenda, and emphasis of the 1949 United Nations Scientific Conference on the Conservation and Utilization of Resources at Lake Success, New York, with those of the 1972 United Nations Conference on the Human Environment in Stockholm, it is clear that major changes have occurred in public and national attitudes toward man's relationship to the Earth and the use of its resources.

If one judges accomplishments in relation to needs, the United Nations Scientific Conference on the Conservation and Utilization of Resources might as well never have occurred. Yet the effort was well-intentioned. Initiative for the conference came from the President of the United States, Harry S Truman, who in a letter dated September 4, 1946, to the United States representative on the Economic and Social Council (ECOSOC) of the United Nations, declared "that a congress composed of engineers, resource technicians, economists, and other experts in the fields of physical and social science would offer the most desirable method of presenting and considering the definite problems now involved in the resource field." [24] The idea was adopted by ECOSOC, which asked the Secretary-General of the United Nations to proceed with arrangements. Its limited potential is evident in the ECOSOC Resolution (109 VI) of February 11, 1948, in which the Secretary-General was reminded that "the task of the conference is to be limited to an exchange of experience in the techniques of the conservation and utilization of resources."

Among participants in the conference were persons who understood what its functions should have been. Prominent among them was Fairfield Osborn, President of the New York Zoological Society and of the Conservation Foundation, who declared in an opening address, "This world meeting on resources is a sign of the evolution of human society" and observed, "Despite the growing evidences of cooperation between nations, it is unlikely that this world meeting would be taking place, even now, were it not for conditions of obvious increasing seriousness." [25] Developing this theme, he continued:

> Within the last century startling developments of a worldwide nature have taken place. These changes have been so rapid, in some cases so violent, that adjustments to them, socially as well as materially, have barely kept pace. Unquestionably the greatest factor of change is the explosive upsurge in population in virtually all countries resulting in a doubling of the world population within the last century, or an increase of more than a thousand million people. . . .
>
> This doubling of the Earth's population in merely four generations has been accompanied, as we are well aware, by an almost fantastic series of inventions which have brought about what may be described as the second industrial revolution. The consequence has been that the drain upon the Earth's resources has increased not upon a mathematical scale related to population growth, but upon a geometrical scale related to greater numbers of people demanding a greater variety of products from an infinitely more complex industrial system.[26]

Unfortunately, a quarter of a century was to elapse before the United Nations arrived at the point of perception from which Osborn's assessment of needs began. He said in summary:

> This world meeting may make a great, perhaps even an epical contribution to the future of civilization [regrettably it did not]. It will inevitably serve as a correlator of existing knowledges, and that result in itself will prove of large value. The exchanges of opinion that will occur here will themselves reach new advances

in knowledge. However, the lessons of history demonstrate, with compelling force, that knowledge in itself is transitory, even impotent, unless widely applied and permanently integrated into the everyday viewpoint of people as a whole. What we are seeking is the acceptance of a clear concept regarding man's relationship to his environment.

In the light of experience, and in these terms, conservation becomes a political and administrative problem, an educational, even a social, cultural, and ethical problem. Therefore, it is not one with which the scientists or technologists can deal singlehanded. Further, conservation in the sense that it implies the wide use and equitable distribution of the Earth's resources, offers a point of synthesis for international cooperation for which the world is waiting.[27]

How unready were the nations to receive Fairfield Osborn's message was illustrated by the address immediately following. In it, Dr. Colin G. Clark, lecturer at Cambridge University and economic advisor to the government of Queensland, Australia, recognized that "man has proved himself capable of the most appalling misuse of natural resources under certain circumstances" and that the "world rate of population growth has accelerated since 1920," but he saw no problem in population increase, confining his analysis to an optimistic appraisal of the ability of nations to enlarge food supplies. He concluded that "the claim that in countries where fertility is high it should be artificially reduced is thus groundless economically." [28]

The agenda of the conference was divided by categories of resources, including minerals, fuel and energy, water, forests, land, and wildlife and fish. Although the guiding importance of ecological knowledge was mentioned in several papers and addresses, at no point was a truly holistic view taken of the relation between population, resources, and environment. However, an International Technical Conference on the Protection of Nature, sponsored jointly by the International Union for Conservation of Nature and Natural Resources and UNESCO, met at Lake Success (August 22–September 1) during the period of the Resources Conference and to some extent counterbalanced and supplemented the United Nations effort.

The United Nations Conference on the Application of Science and Technology for the Benefit of the Less-Developed Areas, held in Geneva in 1963, was in many ways a replay with elaborations and refinements of the Lake Success Conference. Fifteen years of experience had given almost no change in orientation. During the interim, several other scientific conferences on resources had been held under United Nations' auspices, notably one on New Sources of Energy at Rome in 1961, and two which were convened in 1955 and 1958 to discuss the Peaceful Uses of Atomic Energy. Without question, these conferences were important for exchange of views and the marshalling of information about man's use of the resources of the Earth. Their lack of results may be attributed in part to their failure to ask the questions that should have been suggested by the growing stress of human demands on the Earth and to bring under consideration the full range, not only of human needs and values, but of the biological and sociopsychological parameters of human welfare and survival, inadequate as our present knowledge of them is. The strongly economic and technological bias of the conferences and their generally uncritical optimistic tone precluded any realistic assessment of the trend toward a rapidly worsening human environment.

In contrast to the preceding international gatherings, the Intergovernmental Conference of Experts on a Scientific Basis for Rational Use and Conservation of the Resources of the Biosphere, the so-called Biosphere Conference that met in Paris in September 1968 represented a major advance toward recognition of ecological relationships. The conference did not consider inorganic resources except as they provided a medium for the support of plant and animal life and gave little attention to man-made environments like towns and cities, but within its context, the conference examined a broad spectrum of ecological issues. Unlike earlier conferences, this one was not conducted merely to exchange views and experience, but adopted twenty recommendations for future action by the participating governments, by the United Nations system, and especially by UNESCO. In the concluding paragraphs of its final report, the conference summed up its assessment of man–environment relationships and their political implications:

Until this point in history the nations of the world have lacked considered, comprehensive policies for managing the environment. It is now abundantly clear that national policies are mandatory if environmental quality is to be restored and preserved and land-use planning is to have a sound base. Although many of these changes have been taking place for a long time, they seem to have reached a threshold recently that has made the public aware of them. This awareness is leading to concern, to the recognition that to a large degree, man now has the capability and responsibility to determine and guide the future of his environment, and to the beginnings of national and international corrective action. . . . It has become clear, however, that earnest and bold departures from the past will have to be taken nationally and internationally if significant progress is to be made. No man, no people can travel this road alone. This recognition of the necessity of cooperative action has given the conference a spirit of optimism in the face of unprecedented challenges to man's wisdom and his good will.[29]

International concern with natural resources is, of course, not confined to international conferences and commissions. The conservation and management of natural resources and, more recently, of environmental values have been a major part of the activities of the Food and Agriculture Organization and have also been an important concern of UNESCO. Other United Nations specialized agencies and the International Atomic Energy Agency have limited concern with natural resources and the environment in relation to their principal missions. Chapter six of this book will take a close look at the structures of international organization for environmental affairs.

Some of the more significant conservation efforts have been carried on by nongovernmental international organizations. Some of these are essentially professional bodies, like the International Union of Forestry Research Organizations or the International Federation of Landscape Architects. Private organizations like the American Committee for International Wild Life Protection have been formed explicitly to promote various aspects of international conservation. The principal international conservation organization, however, is the International Union for Conservation of Nature and Natural Resources (IUCN). Because of its unique role in efforts to preserve the biosphere, the organization and activities of the IUCN will be mentioned often in this volume, and a brief description of its background, structure, and relationship to international conservation efforts may be useful at this point.

IUCN: The International Conservation Organization

SINCE ITS ESTABLISHMENT in 1948 following a conference at Fontainebleau sponsored by UNESCO and the government of France, the IUCN has been the primary organization concerned with protection of the natural world.[30] Its formation followed a series of previous efforts to obtain international cooperation in dealing with the natural environment, as distinguished from natural resources in a predominantly economic sense. Among the meetings were the first International Conference on the Protection of Natural Landscapes, and a meeting of a Consulting Commission on the International Protection of Nature in Berne, Switzerland in 1913; the first International Congress on the Protection of Flora, Fauna, and Natural Sites and Monuments meeting in Paris in 1923, and the establishment in 1928 in Brussels of the Office International pour la Protection de la Nature.[31] These efforts were advanced by the drafting in London in 1933 of the Convention Relative to the Preservation of Flora and Fauna in Their Natural State, pertaining to Africa, and the drafting in Washington in 1940 of the Convention on Nature Protection and Wild Life Preservation in the Western Hemisphere.

The membership of IUCN is complex. More than seventy national governments are represented, some directly, others through governmental agencies. Nongovernmental members consist principally of environmental protection and conservation organizations in a large number of countries throughout the world, some of which groups are international. Although not a member of the United Nations system or of the International Council of Scientific Unions, IUCN maintains cooperative relationships with both bodies and with several of the UN specialized agencies and regional economic commissions as well as with such regional organizations as the Council of Europe, the Organization of African Unity, and the Organization of American States. IUCN's mission is to promote the conservation of the biosphere—the interacting matrix of soil, water, air, plants, animals, and all physical elements upon which all living creatures of the Earth depend. The Union is especially attentive to threats to the quality of the natural environment, especially to wild lands and vulnerable species. It investigates and proposes methods by which man–environment problems may best be resolved, and it promotes educational measures to further general understanding of the values to be protected in the natural world. IUCN has given particular attention to the protection of rare species, particularly those threatened with extinction and to the perpetuation of natural habitats for wild plants and animals. It has encouraged the establishment of national parks, reserves, and sanctuaries for aesthetic, scientific, and recreational purposes and took a leading role in convening the First World Conference on National Parks held at Seattle, Washington, in July 1962.[32]

Because of its unique role and independent nongovernmental status, the Union is able to act directly and quickly in critical matters involving national action or international cooperation, where political considerations would restrain or complicate the efforts of governments or intergovernmental agencies. The Union has on many occasions drawn the attention of national governments to threats to the environment or to natural resources within their country.

The IUCN operates through an executive board, a secretariat, and six commissions. A general assembly is convened every third year to discuss international conservation problems and to act upon issues of current importance to the Union. Associated with the general assemblies are meetings of technical experts on more specialized problems of conservation. Regional meetings have been held to focus upon the conservation problems of more restricted areas as, for example, the Arusha Conference in Africa in 1961, the Bangkok Conference for Southeast Asia in 1965, the Bariloche Conference for Latin America in 1968, and the Conference on Productivity and Conservation in Northern Circum-Polar Lands in 1969 in Canada.

The work of IUCN is largely initiated through its commissions. The Survival Service Commission was formed in 1949 to prevent the extermination of threatened species of wildlife. Under its auspices, IUCN investigates the status and ecology of rare species of plants and animals, maintains the *Red Data Book*[33] of endangered species, an *Amber Data Book* of depleted species, and wherever possible begins appropriate protective action. The Commission on Education serves as a clearing house for the exchange of information and material about conservation education and has carried on much of its work through regional committees. The Commission on Ecology is the primary scientific advisory body for the Union and consists of smaller committees specialized, for example, in ecological aspects of soil and water conservation, ecological aspects of chemical controls, ecological problems of introduction (plant and animal species exotic to particular areas), and ecological aspects of marine, mountain, and arctic habitat. The International Commission on National Parks assists governments with information on the establishment and management of parks and different kinds of reserves and has sponsored international conferences in 1962 in Seattle and in 1972 in the Yellowstone Park. On request from the United Nations, it has now published both in French and in English the UN list of national parks and equivalent reserves.[34] The Commission on Landscape Planning is concerned with the protection of both natural and man-made landscapes and with land use and environmental planning.

The newest IUCN commission is on Environmental Policy, Law, and Administration. Its establishment reflects a growing realization that the problems of protecting the biosphere, although requiring scientific and technical knowledge for their solution, are ultimately social, political, and in the broad sense, moral. The commission is also intended to remedy the almost universal tendency in conservation and environmental protective efforts to ignore the processes of administration through which goals must ultimately be reached. The commission is concerned with comparative studies of environmental administration and with providing assistance and advice upon request to countries undertaking to strengthen and improve their management of environmental affairs.

Separate from but historically associated with IUCN is the World Wildlife Fund (WWF), perhaps best described as an international foundation, formed in 1961 to provide financial support for wildlife protection generally, to assist the IUCN, and to act to safeguard the wildlife of the world wherever it was threatened.[35] The annual worldwide fund appeals of the World Wildlife Fund is truly an international mobilization of resources for more effective protection of the wildlife of the biosphere. WWF has enjoyed the active support of an exceptional number of persons highly placed in government, science, international society, and public affairs. Also closely associated with IUCN is the International Commission on Bird Protection (ICBP), which, however, maintains a seperate identity.

International Effort in Retrospect

AT THE BEGINNING of the twentieth century, the environment as such was not an object of concern. International efforts were concerned with conserving economically valuable resources, and the means were mostly technical and legal. The first efforts were in the form of cooperative research and it was only in the light of experience and with considerable reluctance that nations agreed to minimum cooperative regulation of the exploitation of fish and other wild life. The second stage in the development of international action developed after World War II with the establishment of UNESCO and IUCN, and was reflected in the Biosphere Conference of 1968. The third stage, toward which there are now clear indications of movement, is one of concern with the social, political, and ethical aspects of man–environment relationships.

It may be premature to say that nations now generally recognize the need for protective management of human impact upon the biosphere, but it is in this direction that a strong current of informed thought is moving. The trend of thought has moved from diplomacy, economics, and engineering, through ecology, to ethics. But the ethics of the environment are not only individual, they are social and hence political.

In retrospect, the international conservation efforts of the first seventy years of the twentieth century may be seen as a phase through which it was necessary to pass to obtain a foundation upon which positive managerial methods could be built. If any lesson is to be learned from the conservation efforts of nations during the first two-thirds of the twentieth century, it is that unilateral national action alone cannot stem the threat to an increasingly endangered Earth. Unless effective transnational institutions can be devised to uphold at least minimum worldwide standards of ecological conduct, the defense of the Earth will be a lost cause.

4

Underestimating the Danger:

UNFORESEEN DIMENSIONS OF

HUMAN IMPACT ON NATURE

WHY WERE THOSE BEST EQUIPPED TO PERCEIVE THE threat to the integrity of the biosphere so slow to do so? Among those best qualified to assess the worsening environment on a global scale were scientists, engineers, statesmen, and world travelers. But few saw what was happening and few of those did more than deplore what they observed. As we have noted, there were warnings as early as 1864 implicit in the writings of George Perkins Marsh, and made more explicit toward the mid-twentieth century by Fairfield Osborn, Paul Sears, and William Vogt.[1] But not until the late 1960s did the concern of the informed minority become sufficiently pervasive and intense to arouse a wider public and, more importantly, to give power to an emotionally-committed political movement.[2]

Limitations of Foresight

IN RETROSPECT, there are several obvious reasons for failure to assess the danger. First, individual horizons and attention spans are inevitably limited. No individual can focus his attention on an unlimited number of activities, and his understanding and interpretation of what goes on around him is shaped by his personal experience and expectations. Second, many of the ecological changes were widely diffused and unobtrusive. Before the 1960s, the embryonic science of ecology had not opened people's eyes to the symptoms of environmental deterioration; to see something one must first become aware of it. Third, the sciences that could have made people aware are still under-developed. Even now, the techniques for measuring environmental change are not fully adequate, and means for conveying meaningful ecological information to the public are only now being developed. And fourth, men's view of the deterioration in progress was obscured because there was no prevailing valid coherent image of man and society in relation to nature.

These reasons are interrelated. The limited observations of individuals, if somehow systematically combined, might have provided a broader view of environmental trends. But, until recently, there were few journals, forums, or clearing houses providing a regular means for collating and disseminating information about individual efforts. Until recently, there were no large-scale systematic means of monitoring, measuring, and recording environmental data. There were neither instruments nor techniques able to measure minute but cumulative changes, for example, of carbon dioxide in the atmosphere or concentrations of artificial chemical compounds in living tissues. There is as yet no adequate system for monitoring global environmental changes in the atmosphere and the oceans, although such systems are now being planned.[3] In the absence of adequate environmental benchmarks, and continuing long-range statistical studies and projections, the scientific community could not develop the indices that would have alerted them to the growing dangers to the biosphere.

One of the reasons that the means for surveillance were not earlier developed is that the global environment was nobody's business. No governments exercised effective jurisdiction over the high seas or the atmosphere, and nowhere had the state of the environment, in a holistic sense, become a matter for public policy. Individuals and governments were concerned with specific environmental disorders within the nation as, for example, soil erosion, environmental pollution, and the depletion of specific resources, especially of the ones like forests or minerals which had industrial and military significance. But the

81

cumulative human threat to the biosphere itself could hardly be discovered before the nature of the biosphere itself was understood.

Lacking a concept of the biosphere, people have not seen it as a dynamic integrated phenomenon even though it surrounded them and they were a part of it. Those individuals who have become most alarmed about the human threat to the biosphere are almost invariably those who see most clearly the finite character of the Earth and the frequently fragile and, in all cases, evolved nature of its balances and interrelationships. The dynamic character of the living world implies a latent instability—a propensity for change which can be toward deterioration as easily as toward what our culture calls progress. Evolution does not preclude retrogression. The evidence of science would seem to indicate that life and growth are exceptional in a universe subject to the Second Law of Thermodynamics which describes the tendency of activity to reduce all order to static random distribution.[4]

There is thus no single answer to the question of why men have failed to perceive the full dimensions of the human threat to the biosphere. The danger was underestimated because of (1) limitations of individual perception, (2) the subtlety and initial unobtrusiveness of the environmental changes, (3) lack of an adequate system of gathering and communicating data, and (4) the lack of an adequate concept of the global environment or biosphere. Most people were conditioned to see man's activities as progress, not as irremedial depredations of the biosphere and, in consequence, they failed to see or else rejected the evidence of its deterioration.[5]

Impact of Population

AT THIS POINT, it seems hardly necessary to elaborate on the thesis that the world is confronted by a crisis of human numbers. The so-called population explosion has now become common knowledge among all literate people, although all do not assess its significance in the same way. For some, the issue is largely the technical one of feeding and clothing vastly increased numbers of people. For others, questions of individual freedom, of the quality of life, and of the survival of the living world itself are more critical. In consequence, even literate people have not reached the same conclusions regarding the urgency of efforts to develop policies to control and restrict population growth.

Among all the aspects of the human impact on the Earth, the threat to the biosphere from sheer increase in human numbers was perhaps least foreseen and certainly the one modern society was least prepared to cope with. Although the classical theory of the causes and consequences of overpopulation was expounded by the British economist and clergyman Thomas Robert Malthus in the early nineteenth century,[6] it was not until the mid-twentieth century that overpopulation began to be perceived as a worldwide problem and that the need to bring population growth under control began to receive attention from voluntary popular organizations and, reluctantly, from governments. For more than a century after Malthus, demographers (and there cannot have been many) who foresaw the course of population growth and understood the consequences of exponential increases had no influence and attracted little attention either in the scientific community or among the public at large. The world was not prepared, therefore, when in the 1960s the explosion of human populations was suddenly discovered to be a disaster of unprecedented proportions.

Awareness of a population problem and of its significance developed unevenly throughout the world and even within particular societies. Before World War II, there was almost no popular awareness of a problem anywhere, and indeed the general presumption favored increasing populations. Except for a Malthusian minority, these attitudes were generally pervasive through the years of World War II. The countries that had population policies mostly sought an increase in numbers through rewards for childbearing and support for large families.[7] Sweden had adopted a comprehensive program of family planning, but it was designed to deal with all aspects of family life and not necessarily to reduce population increase.[8]

Although there had been a continuing but little noticed literature on the problem of numbers, the publication of *Human*

Fertility: The Modern Dilemma by Robert C. Cook in 1950
marked the beginning of the growth of serious public concern
with the growth of population.[9] Among public leaders and
opinion shapers, attitudes developed through a series of stages.
The first reactions to the warnings of the demographers were
It can't be that bad. The *avant garde* of the population movement were seen as alarmists, but those who took the time to
examine the evidence and to check the arithmetic of demography
were forced to concede that the situation might be "that bad"
except for an important mitigating factor that the so-called
neo-Malthusians had overlooked. The escape hatch from the
Malthusian trap was marked "technology." Science and technology could be relied upon to find ways of meeting man's
basic needs without artificially limiting his numbers. What the
world needed was not fewer people but more efficient use of
resources and a more rational organization of the economy.

Groups that had almost no other point of agreement—
Marxists, liberals, industrialists, politically ambitious militarists,
and religious conservatives—found agreement in the proposition
that the real problem of society was economic productivity and
distribution. There was no agreement about how society should
be organized for increased production or efficient distribution,
but there was agreement that mere numbers were no cause for
alarm and that the Earth could absorb an indefinite number of
people provided that its productive facilities were properly
organized.[10]

Although some observers thought the ultimately catastrophic consequences of exponentially increasing populations
incontrovertible, they were nevertheless controverted, even by
scientists as distinguished as Harrison Brown, who declared:

> Our basic problem, really, is not that of supporting comfortably
> the distressingly large numbers of people who we know will in-
> evitably inhabit the earth in the decade ahead. I am convinced that
> technically this can be done.[11]

"We have the power," wrote Brown, "to create a civilization
as yet undreamed of in its beauty and its accomplishments. Yet
somehow we can't seem to organize ourselves to use that power
effectively to solve mankind's basic problem." Or as *U.S. News*

and World Report declared in 1958, "The big hope is that technical progress will answer all demands." [12]

Unfortunately technical solutions to the basic problems of subsistence in a world populated beyond any possibility of support through natural processes left other critical problems unresolved. Science and technology might, as Harrison Brown conjectured, feed, clothe, and support a population of ten billion persons (more than three times the number of people now living on the Earth). But even if by the year 2000 the population of the Earth grew to no more than seven and one-half billion persons, and if those persons were to be brought to the material standard of living now enjoyed in the United States, the basic needs of such numbers would "virtually deplete the earth of all high-grade mineral resources" and would, as Harrison Brown conceded, "necessitate our living off the leanest of earth substances: the waters of the sea and ordinary rock." It is difficult to imagine how life could be either free or abundant under such circumstances.

Optimistic scientists and technologists have found it easier to speculate on how the physical needs of enormous populations might be met than on the social and political arrangements and administrative controls over the lives and behaviors of people that such conditions would necessitate. By the beginning of the 1970s, there was an apparent and evidently growing popular skepticism that "our science and our technology have given us the power to create a world in which virtually all people can lead free and abundant lives." If science and technology have not given us the power to avoid the exponential increases in human population that now menace all human values, they have failed to give us the power that we need most. The most perfect contraceptives devised by science will not help if people will not use them. Yet, although Harrison Brown was optimistic about what science, if effectively mobilized, might do to close the gap between people and resources, he observed that "in 1950 many students of the population-resource situation concluded that major world catastrophe was in the making. Today, when we view the growth of world population in relation to what mankind is doing about the situation, that catastrophe appears a near certainty." [13]

85

The mounting tide of environmental pollution and the growing evidence of general environmental deterioration were beginning to impress themselves upon the public consciousness quite apart from the population question. Moreover, pioneering studies in the social and behavioral sciences began to raise disturbing questions about the extent of human adaptability to ever-increasing numbers and congestion. By the mid-1960s, it was widely accepted that the population explosion was indeed a reality and a menace, and that technology offered no more than a temporary palliative and not a cure. But many of those who accepted the reality of the population crisis found themselves unable to agree that whatever *must* be done *should* be done in order to cope with it.

David Lilienthal, writing in the *New York Times Magazine* in 1966, declared that "three hundred million Americans would be wrong," but he firmly opposed any compulsion or coercion to restrict population growth. Lilienthal, like many others of liberal persuasion, accepted the "right" of people to procreate, and felt that the only legitimate instruments of population control would be persuasive education and the human conscience.[14] By the end of the 1960s, however, the issue and its implications were becoming more fully evident, and a milestone in the road toward public policy for population control was marked by the publication in December 1968 of the essay "The Tragedy of the Commons," by Garrett Hardin.[15] Hardin declared that unrestricted freedom to breed was no longer tolerable and that public regulation to control and prevent the increase of population was the only means by which human society could realistically cope with the problem.

By 1970, the issue of birth control had become pervasive enough to threaten schism within the Roman Catholic Church which had long resisted acknowledging a worldwide population problem. Attitudes were changing even in communities in which opposition to population control had been deeply entrenched. For example, on January 17, 1970, the news and review section of the *Montreal Star* devoted more than half a page to the population issue under the headline "Universal Birth Control Plan a Necessity."

More refined and extended analysis of the consequences of the human impact made the threat appear ever larger and more imminent. It became increasingly apparent that much of the earlier optimism was based upon oversimplified and incomplete analyses of the actual impact of people upon environment. In particular, whether the environment could absorb the waste products of vastly increased numbers of human beings and domestic animals had been almost universally overlooked. Almost no attention had been given to obtaining sufficient energy to maintain the kind of technology that had developed in Western Europe and North America, much less to means of disposing of the waste products of the energy—the heat and toxic substances produced by burning fossil fuels or nuclear reactions.

The "Green Revolution"—the use of plant genetics and fertilizers and pesticides to increase agricultural production—only postponed an ultimate day of reckoning with respect to food supplies. Dependence on new high-yield plant strains of uncertain resistance to disease further increased the vulnerability of human populations, and careless application of agricultural chemicals added to the burden of pollution carried by soils and waters, in some cases to the extent of endangering human health.[16] Norman E. Borlaug, one of the Nobel Prize winning architects of the Green Revolution, frankly stated that the best that he had done was to buy time for humanity. Unless population growth could be stopped, there was no ground even for the earlier optimism that human populations could be fed, whatever sacrifices and austerities might be required in other respects.[17]

Most of the governments of the world and presumably their peoples were a long way from accepting this pessimistic conclusion. But the issue could not be avoided. It continued to trouble international conferences and led to lengthy arguments and debates over proposed revisions of the United Nations Declaration of Human Rights. The International Conference on Human Rights meeting in Teheran in 1968 posed the issue, but did not advocate any practicable course of action. Its Resolution 18 endorsed the ambiguous proposition "that couples have a basic human right to decide freely and responsibly on the number and spacing of their children. . . ."[18] But what were the criteria for responsible decisions? Did couples have a right to decide freely if they did not decide responsibly?

The single greatest obstacle preventing adequate recognition of the threat of overpopulation appeared to be psychological. Unwillingness to acknowledge that overpopulation is a threat to human welfare and survival was explained tersely by Joseph Wood Krutch: "Something deeper than rationality rejoices at birth and over the knowledge that we, as a species, are increasing. To admit a danger seems to put one's self on the side of death rather than life." [19] This reluctance was reinforced by "the vague assurance of many liberals that a properly organized society would somehow provide for every human being born into it," as unscientific an assurance as the belief that God always sends a loaf when he sends a child.

Impact of Technology

DOES THE ABILITY to invent and develop an advanced technology imply the ability to control it? The evidence suggests an answer in the negative, and for an obvious reason. Technological innovation depends on imagination, observation, intellectual and manual dexterity, and particularly on a certain aggressiveness or compulsion to dominate or control the elements of the environment. Control of the technology, on the other hand, is fundamentally self-control. It involves a special kind of imagination called foresight, and requires prudence and restraint.

Advanced modern technologies are almost wholly beyond the ability of the individual to maintain or manage. They cannot, therefore, be controlled by individual self-control; collective self-control is required. No human society, however, has been able to achieve collective self-control and at the same time to maintain a large measure of flexibility and individual freedom. Collective self-control may indeed be a contradiction in terms. It has historically been obtained through intensive socialization of communities, through taboos, folkways, religious beliefs, laws, hierarchical structuring, and other institutional arrangements which, in effect, remove the "self" from the control. Social conditioning would perhaps be a more descriptive designation for what actually occurs.

Although technological development has never been universally accepted in any society as an unmixed blessing, it has been overwhelmingly accepted in Western Europe and the United States as a largely unqualified good; but increasingly, the harmful potentialities of developing technology have become evident. Publication of the book *La Technique* in 1954 by the French sociologist Jacques Ellul may be taken as marking a point where the critical examination of the impact of technology upon society and the biosphere gained momentum.[20] Ellul saw technology as a force with its own innate dynamics and self-augmenting tendencies. Other critics including Raymond Aron, Lewis Mumford, Sigfried Gideon, and Friedrich Georg Jünger, saw technology as a dominating tendency evolving within society, thus implying that control of technology must be a political (judgmental) rather than an engineering or economic (technical) process.[21] The technological innovations stimulated by World War II induced a new concern with technological forecasting, and an effort to bring the benefits of science and technology to the less-developed areas of the Earth stimulated an interest in what was called technology transfer. These developments led in 1963 to the United Nations Conference on the Application of Science and Technology for the Benefit of the Less-Developed Areas.

This conference, which was a part of the United Nations Decade of Development,[22] was almost totally concerned with the exploitation of the natural environment for the satisfaction of human material needs. The president of the conference, M. S. Thacker, declared, "The story of how man is remaking his world by a more effective use of human and natural resources would open even reluctant eyes." [23] The story of this effort was told in more than two thousand technical papers submitted to the conference. The conference's underlying assumption was clearly stated when its president began it by declaring, "The air, the earth, the oceans and the sun contain riches which can support increases in population at higher and higher standards of living." Nevertheless, some warnings were issued. Professor Jean-Paul Harroy of Belgium drew attention to the worldwide menace of resource depletion and observed, "It is strange to find how little public opinion and national or international authorities seem to be aware of or even worried about this." [24]

The world as perceived by the conference was one of

unlimited possibilities only awaiting the applications of science and technology to make the possible actual. That it all had to happen within the parameters of a finite world did not seem to have been an assumption even implicit in the conference. In the relatively short retrospect of less than a decade it would appear that the assumptions of the conference were inconsistent with the conditions of the real world; and the optimistic and ambitious projections of the future advanced by its participants and by heads of government in messages to the conference, were fundamentally in error. It should not be surprising that at the end of the First United Nations Development Decade the general condition of humanity throughout the world was worse rather than better.

Following a reassessment of development efforts by the United Nations Economic and Social Council and a review and analysis of development efforts by Sir Robert Jackson, a Second United Nations Development Decade was launched for the 1970s, but the nations still were not prepared to acknowledge the ultimate need to conform to the inexorable parameters of a finite Earth.[25] Robert McNamara, Chairman of the International Bank for Reconstruction and Development, had spoken out on the necessity for bringing population growth under control;[26] and there was growing recognition that, whatever measures might be taken to raise standards of living in the less-developed areas of the Earth, attempts to universalize the type of industrial society that had developed in Western Europe, North America, and Japan, would be impossible. Indeed, anything like a serious attempt to do so would be disastrous.

Simplistic concepts of development were beginning to give way to a more sophisticated systems logic which took into account the multiple factors in the growth of population and technology. The impact of population on the environment grew not only with the geometric increase in numbers, but was exaggerated by the increase in human mobility in the demands of an industrial society upon natural resources, and by the quantities of waste products too great for the environment to absorb. As populations increase, technology must increasingly be used to sustain their minimum needs and (depending on national policies) to permit further increase. Natural systems become less and less able to supply society with food and water, clothing and shelter as populations mount. Artificial systems must be substituted, with new costs for society and exactions from the environment. Mass production becomes necessary in agriculture and manufacturing, and populations must be concentrated for efficiency both of production and distribution. Technological success in providing for minimum human needs permits social demands to expand. This renews pressure on the natural environment and makes necessary the transformation of more natural environments into managed ecosystems in which basic needs of human life-support take precedence over all other values and considerations. Advanced technologies permit industrial society to invade previously unoccupied or lightly occupied areas of the Earth—the Arctic, tropical regions, and deserts—in none of which industrial society developed and upon which industrial activity has had devastating effects.

By the last third of the twentieth century, it was becoming increasingly difficult to argue that the future welfare of the world could be guaranteed merely by indiscriminate applications of science and technology. It was equally evident that science and technology would have to be invoked in new areas if humanity was to escape from its worsening predicament. This realization has led to the movement of technological assessment, whose underlying assumption is that the threat of technology to the environment is more properly to be understood as damage wrought by the misuse of technology. Accordingly, it began to be proposed that technological innovations be tested before application and that studies of the second and third order consequences of technological innovations should be undertaken before technologies were applied.[27]

The movement for technological assessment marked a reappraisal of the uncritical view that benefits automatically followed applied science and technology. The possibilities for good were apparent, but what President Lyndon B. Johnson called "the darker side of technology" had also become evident.[28] To enjoy continuing benefits from the application of science and technology, society would have to pay a price that it had hitherto largely evaded. That price involved the careful and comprehensive analysis of the effects of technology, the testing of innovations before loosing them into society and onto the environment, and giving more attention to alternative ways of meeting social needs. In almost every aspect of life there was a growing practical need to control the uses of technology, not only to safeguard the present quality of life, but to prevent foreclosing options that might be needed to meet the exigencies of the future.

As the disastrous consequences of uncontrolled population growth aroused concern only when they became perceptible to ordinary people, it appeared that modern society had to experience adverse effects to be convinced of the need for the control of technology. But populations, having multiplied beyond any possibility of support from the unaided natural life-support base, were forced to improvise technological expedients which, although environmentally disastrous and ultimately self-defeating, did at least buy time for the governing classes and provide minimum subsistence for the population.

The practical necessity for governments to keep moving on the developmental treadmill led them to stage huge technological extravaganzas which had political publicity value, temporarily provided jobs, and promised relief from hunger and economic distress. Characteristic symbols of simplistic solutions to complex socioecological problems were high level dams constructed ostensibly for the purposes of irrigation, flood control, and generation of electricity. Probably the most notable of such developmental symbols was the Aswan High Dam on the Nile, which began to reveal serious damaging side effects even before its impounded waters had filled. The end of annual flooding in the valley of the Nile caused serious environmental changes: (1) A sharp reduction of fish in the eastern Mediterranean which had formerly lived on nutrients carried by the waters of the Nile,[29] (2) a scouring of the channel of the Nile, (3) erosion of the Nile Delta which was no longer replenished by the deposit of silt [30] and, (4) a loss of fertility in bordering farm lands which began to require artificial fertilizers. In common with virtually all impoundment and irrigation projects in tropical areas, the Aswan High Dam has resulted in the spread of schistosomiasis,[31] a fatal disease caused by a liver parasite concentrated in the impounded waters. Further, the weight of impounded water behind a high level dam can produce earthquakes in the area, such as the one that occurred following construction of the Koyna Dam in India that cost the lives of two hundred people in an area that had no previous record of earth tremors.[32]

The push to development in the technologically advanced countries is meeting increasing resistance from informed critics who question the wisdom of some of the more ambitious engineering spectaculars. For example, there seemed to be resistance in the USSR to untested implementation of plans of Russian engineers to control Arctic climate by transporting Atlantic ocean water to the Arctic basin and to increase productivity of the arid lands of central Asia by reversing the flow of great Siberian rivers from the Arctic.[33] Well-informed opposition also met American engineers when they proposed creation of a multi-billion dollar North American Water and Power Alliance to distribute water from the Canadian Northwest throughout large areas of the United States [34] and construction of the immense Rampart dam on the Yukon river,[35] which wildlife biologists testified would have a catastrophic effect upon the waterfowl populations of North America. In a move almost without precedent in the history of technology, the Ninety-second Congress of the United States refused to appropriate money to complete the final stages of the supersonic transport prototype. Fortunately, these projects encountered questioning within the countries for which they were proposed, but less-developed areas are more vulnerable to technological experiments untested for the socioecological consequences.

The Paradox of Progress

BY THE MID-TWENTIETH CENTURY, one could readily have drawn up a long list of trends and events that, properly interpreted, would presage impending disaster. These indications of massive environmental changes in the modern world, when noted by most people, were seen only as separate and discrete events. In fact, they were interrelated aspects of the impact of modern society on the world environment. The effect was two-fold: (1) to diminish the quality of life and (2) to impair the life-support system of the planet. As previously indicated, the interrelationships among these indicators were not perceived in part because the conventional configurations of knowledge, especially of the sciences, did not cause man to perceive it. The methods of modern science had hitherto been overwhelmingly reductionistic, concerned with reducing knowledge of physical phenomena to its lowest common denominator. Generalizers and synthesizers were viewed with skepticism by the scientific community and were distrusted by a public-at-large that put its faith in specialists. The concept of synergism—effects produced by interactions among separate elements—explained many environmental consequences of air and water pollution, but were understood primarily in relation to medicine and pharmacology. It was only with greatest difficulty that this concept was made acceptable in legal and administrative action when applied to atmospheric science, although it was fundamental to understanding the cause of photochemical smog, one of the modern man's most disagreeable self-made hazards.

One of the hopeful developments of the 1960s was a growth of public recognition of the need for comprehensive and reliable systems for identifying and monitoring environmental changes.[36] Many dangerous environmental trends, especially in their early stages, were not obvious and could be detected only by instruments. A dramatic example is poisoning by invisible, odorless, tasteless, and lethal carbon monoxide gas; at lower levels of concentration it produces symptoms of impaired vision, slower reaction times, and headaches—all too often attributed to purely individual causes. We are only beginning to realize how widespread it is among persons working in urban areas heavily congested with automotive traffic.[37] First efforts to use technology in monitoring environmental conditions have had the constructive effect of revealing a whole new range of unexpected threats and dangers. For example, following a 1966 conference in Sweden on mercury pollution, awareness of this problem has grown and samples and analyses have revealed a widespread incidence and induced a corresponding alarm.

In this and other cases of environmental monitoring, not only the scientific community, but the public at large has become more aware of what uninformed and unguided applications of science and technology had been doing to the environment and to man himself. This awakening offered hope that society might be moved by the knowledge of its predicament to revise its priorities and redirect its emphasis to halt the destructive exploitation of the biosphere and to inaugurate an era of ecological sanity and environmental self-renewal.

Diminishing the Quality of Life

A PLAINTIVE BALLAD of the 1960s asked "Where Have All the Flowers Gone?" Wildlife, generally from the wild flowers of mountain pastures to the great whales of the sea, were being crowded off the planet by the inexorable demands of human populations. Nor was their passing universally lamented. The vision of a totally homogenized, managed Earth was hailed by some prominent scientists, engineers, and business leaders. Academician E. K. Fedrov of the Soviet Union expressed a viewpoint widely held in his country, but found also among the industrial states of Western Europe and North America. Addressing the 1963 Geneva Conference, he declared,

> We are not interested in oil, coal, certain kinds of animals or other natural resources by themselves—their amount may be larger or smaller and the moment may come when there will be no resources at all.
> They don't count, but what is important is to what extent the vital needs of human society in power, food, materials, etc., are satisfied now and how they will be met in the future.[38]

Academician Fedrov, in common with many of his capitalist counterparts in the West, seemed concerned only with the material side of civilization and not with the quality of life itself. Throughout the 1960s, however, there was a growing awareness among people, perhaps more often sensed than articulated, that the quality of life and opportunities to enjoy an open and varied environment was rapidly diminishing.

Throughout historic time, the inhabitants of even very large cities had not been beyond walking distance of open country. In the early twentieth century, tram lines and later auto-mobiles could take city dwellers in an hour or so to the edge of even the largest cities. But the tremendous urban expansion fol-lowing World War II rapidly put city dwellers out of reach of rural areas or open space. The larger cities were surrounded by mile upon mile of urban sprawl with factories, subdivisions, and government installations scattered over the countryside, homog-enizing the environment and depriving it of any native distinc-tiveness. Weekend houses of the affluent and commercialized recreation areas and resorts began to expropriate coastal areas and the more accessible parts of mountains and desert land.

Destruction of the countryside proceeded in some degree in every industrialized nation in Europe and North America, and in Japan; and if it was retarded somewhat in the Soviet Union, the reason was less regard for environmental amenities than the policies of the Soviet government regarding public housing and transportation. The world as a whole was rapidly losing diversity and distinctiveness, and it was also sacrificing stability.

Here was truly a paradox of personal freedom. Science and technology were liberating man from ancient servitudes and enlarging many options beyond anything imaginable in an earlier age. Modern men in numbers larger than ever before were freed by affluence and air transportation to visit almost any part of the world, and yet almost every part of the world was tending to become "the same place." In the United States, as citizens endeavored to save the distinctive areas of Florida from destruction by agricultural and commercial interests, developers undertook to transplant the African veldt to the Florida prairies with imported lions and zebras so that multitudes could go on safari conveniently from Miami Beach.

Not all would agree that the vulgarization of the environ-ment diminished the quality of life for all people in any abso-lute sense. There is room to disagree over matters of taste. Nevertheless, widespread destruction of the natural environment indicated patterns of individual and institutional behavior that did not augur well for the long-range safety or stability of the environment in the more fundamental sense. The extinction of whales and wild flowers might well be precursors of the extinc-tion of man himself.

Impairing the Life-Support System

As SCIENTISTS BEGAN to turn their attention to the actual state of the environment, to apply analytic techniques to air, water, and soil, disturbing evidence of an impending crisis of vast proportions began to accumulate. Threats to the planetary life-support system did not merely issue from short-sighted or avaricious individuals, corporations, or governments. The very processes of modern society were revealed to be causes, and many of the so-called triumphs of science and technology, in agriculture, medicine, and aeronautics, were revealed as the agents of dangerous environmental deterioration.

Even the air is threatened. The ability of the atmosphere to support animal life is dependent on the green plants that generate atmospheric oxygen. Atmospheric scientists discovered that the activities of man, notably the burning of fossil fuels, the reduction of vegetation over wide areas, and the use of persistent and indiscriminate pesticides, might very well impair the ability of the biosphere to renew its oxygen. If increasing pollution of the oceans reduced the generative capacity of the oceanic phytoplankton, the oxygen content of the atmosphere might fall to levels inadequate to support the so-called higher forms of life.[39] Moreover, increasing amounts of carbon dioxide in the atmosphere, together with increasing atmospheric turbidity due to smoke, dust, and other particulate matter, might result in profound climatic changes. Such events did not seem likely to occur in the immediate future, but if present trends continued, they were more than a theoretical possibility.

Even that area of the Earth seemingly least vulnerable to human impact, the oceans, was now demonstrably threatened. David Epel of Stanford University's Hopkins Marine Station has warned, "The oceans are beginning to die from chemical pollution and nothing is being done about it."[40] He argued for immediate establishment of an international environmental organization to prevent the release of persisting chemicals into the environment. Similarly, Thor Heyerdahl, Norwegian ethnologist and oceanic navigator, reported after crossings of the Atlantic in 1969 and 1970 a shocking deterioration of the open sea—floating masses of oil and sludge, floating cans, plastic cellulose—environmental degradation far from human habitation.[41]

Increasing dependence of industrial society on transported fossil fuels, especially petroleum, resulted in inevitable oil spills from the sinking of oceangoing tankers and the exploitation of oil wells on the continental shelves. The wreck of the tanker *Torrey Canyon* on the coast of England and oil blowouts on the coasts of Louisiana and Southern California at Santa Barbara aroused public opinion in the United States and Europe to loud but not very effective protest. The technological society runs on fossil oil and the fuel must be delivered if paralysis is not to occur. The United States Department of Interior, after reviewing a proposed pipeline to move hot oil from Arctic oil fields to the Gulf of Alaska, justified the effort on the grounds of economic necessity, despite the ecological damage that would inevitably result. Technology has been developed to contain and clean up oil spills at sea, but it appears to be only partially effective. The only really adequate remedy would be some other type of fuel, an alternative not on the horizon in the early 1970s.

It seemed possible that public opinion might be more effective in stopping the long-standing practice of governments dumping poisonous gases and other lethal military substances into the handiest parts of the oceans. Following World War II, the Western Allies and the Russians dumped tons of captured German mustard gas and other lethal materials into the Baltic, the North Sea, and the straits between Denmark, Norway, and Sweden. As the poison containers deteriorated, hazardous substances were liberated, injuring fishermen and possibly endangering bathers and boaters. In the autumn of 1970, the Danish government published a warning pamphlet entitled *Gas Bombs in the Sea Around Us*.[42] In the United States, shipments of surplus gases in obsolete containers were sunk in the Atlantic near the Bahamas during 1970, but the public outcry and objections from the Congress made it unlikely that this practice could be continued. At the request of the President, studies of ocean dumping were undertaken by the National Academy of Sciences and by the Council on Environmental Quality, possibly beginning to lay a foundation for an ultimate international policy on the disposal of harmful substances in the seas.[43]

Industrial pollution and domestic sewage were continuing to destroy the fresh water lakes of the world, from Lake Baikal in Siberia to the Great Lakes in North America. The Caspian Sea and the Baltic Sea were in danger. Ports of the Baltic and the Great Lakes had already been contaminated enough to destroy their ability to support any but the lowest forms of aquatic life. All pollutants ultimately found their way into the oceans. Norwegian scientists were able to trace the spread of highly toxic residuals of plastics industries through the North Sea and along the coasts of Norway toward the Arctic and across the North Atlantic past Iceland to Greenland.[44] The persistent pesticide DDT had been found in the body tissues of Antarctic penguins and in deep-sea fishes thousands of miles away from any possible source of contamination. Tissues of pilot whales stranded on the coast of California were found to contain excessive quantities of mercury, presumably concentrated from ingestion of mercury-bearing fish.

Concern with the harmful effects of pesticides had grown since the publication of Rachel Carson's *Silent Spring* in 1963. Even the beneficial effects of pesticides had had a reverse aspect. The tropical anti-malaria campaign of the World Health Organization had been highly successful, but there was no assurance that the lives saved would not be foreshortened by malnutrition or by starvation as populations rapidly increased. Moreover, there remained the risk of mutations of malaria vectors, mosquitoes that were resistant to the effects of DDT and other biocides.[45] The destruction of wildlife attributable to DDT and evidence of its concentration in food chains that ultimately put it in the human diet led to efforts to ban the use of the so-called persistent pesticides during the late 1960s and early 1970s.[46] Nevertheless, certain defenders of the use of the pesticides in medicine and agriculture continued to discount their harmful effects and to insist on their continued use.[47]

Immediately after the harnessing of the atom in the 1940s, public and even scientific opinion tended to see nuclear reactions as an ideal source of energy, pollution free, and virtually inexhaustible. These optimistic illusions, however, were soon shattered by the realization that nuclear reactors threatened potentially severe environmental dangers.[48] There was a problem of disposing of the water heated by the reactor's cooling processes which, if discharged into streams and lakes, could have pronounced ecological effects. Moreover, a certain amount of nuclear radiation was present in stack emissions and in the water discharged from the reactors; perhaps most seriously, there was a problem of disposing of the spent fuel in the reactors which was still highly lethal and much of which would remain so for hundreds of years.

Reinforced by a campaign among scientists, public apprehension over the effects of atmospheric testing of nuclear devices led in 1963 to the Nuclear Test Ban Treaty.[49] Although this treaty was signed by the two principal nuclear powers, the United States and the Soviet Union, it was not signed by certain other nations with nuclear capabilities, particularly France and Communist China.

By the beginning of the 1970s, it appeared that the problem of energy in relation to industrial society must command very serious attention in any future effort to safeguard the planetary environment. Not only did energy sources, water power, fossil fuels, and radioactive substances, endanger the environment in their mining or generation, but their residual effects posed equally difficult and perhaps more dangerous problems. Among these were the disposal of radioactive wastes, which must be encased in shielding and buried deep in the Earth or in the depths of the oceans. But the possibility remained that the decay of containers or unforeseen accidents might liberate powerful radioactive substances into the environment. We have already seen how gases and particulate matter from the burning of fossil fuels contaminate air and water. How much of the residual heat created by every form of energy production could be tolerated by the biosphere had not been established by 1970, but there was growing doubt that its absorptive capacity was infinite. It could be conjectured that the ability of the biosphere to absorb man's outputs of energy could be the ultimate limiting factor on the expansion of industrial society.

Misread Evidence and Misdirected Efforts

PEOPLE ARE SELDOM willing to blame worsening conditions on their own activities. Devil explanations have always been popular as alibis for social distress with which political leaders find it difficult or disagreeable to cope. If the bad guys can be shown to be operating from outside the national boundaries, or can be identified as a vulnerable isolated group within a nation, it is plausible and politically manageable to meet the difficulties by attacking those malefactors. Only under exceptional conditions of stress have popular leaders been able to persuade their followers that they are collectively responsible in large measure for their difficulties. To convince society that it is its own worst enemy requires a kind of political skill which has rarely achieved widespread or continuing success. Religious reformers have succeeded occasionally in persuading numbers of people (temporarily) to abandon sinful ways, but such successes fall far short of what would be required to change the fundamental attitudes and behaviors of individuals and societies, and to restructure institutions for continuing ecologically sound management of man–environment relationships.

The cures or remedies for deteriorating societies and environments, therefore, tend to be selected for their political feasibility rather than for their existential validity. Scapegoats are sought in imperialists, capitalists, communists, and the long list of 'isms of which traditionalism, colonialism, feudalism, tribalism, and racism are examples. The fundamental problem, that too many people are demanding too much of a finite world, is thus evaded, and so, as Georg Borgstrom declares, "Man threatens to deprive himself of a future by refusing to recognize his predicament." [50]

The dominant explanations for modern social difficulties fall into two related but distinct categories. The first may conveniently be labeled "political," and it was dominant throughout the seventeenth and eighteenth centuries. The prevailing theories of the times attributed social evils to faulty political institutions. It found popular expression in the English, American, and French Revolutions, especially the latter. In the nineteenth and twentieth centuries, the causes of social and environmental deterioration were largely redefined as "economic." Marxism combined some of the old-style concern with political institutions with a primary emphasis upon the economic aspects of social behavior, but the primacy of economics as a social force was accepted by many theorists who rejected Marx. Economic explanations were especially popular in a pluralistic and free-enterprising democracy because they lent plausibility to the hope that necessary reforms might take care of themselves.

Perhaps the ultimate expression of the economic explanation was in the technical assistance programs administered by the United Nations and by technologically advanced countries, especially the United States. Economic development was seen as the catalytic process that would bring about all other aspects of social change, enveloped under the term "modernization." Closely related to economic explanations of social difficulties were the remedies offered by technologists. Those who saw society's salvation through technology—industrialization, the Green Revolution, and technoscientific inventions—seldom concerned themselves with how society got into its difficulties. The doctors were pragmatic, taking society as they found it and showing no great interest in how it arrived at its debilitated state.

By the last third of the twentieth century, however, popular confidence that unfettered technology would solve the world's problems was beginning to weaken, and there was a visible growth of skepticism about the adequacy of conventional explications of the causes and cures of social disorder.

An economics-centered international development effort, such as that of the United Nations First Development Decade, had fallen short even of its economic goals. In both technologically advanced and less-developed countries, economic development efforts often actually worsened living conditions. The much relied upon indicator of economic activity, the Gross National Product, was widely misconstrued as an index of economic well-being.[51] The conventional measurements of economic growth and standard of living were thoroughly misleading, at least as popularly understood. Abstract econometrics did not describe the actual living conditions of the mass of the people, and relying on them resulted in misdirections of effort that both failed to satisfy the real needs of people and too often narrowed options for the future.

Errors of innocence or perversity were reinforced in action. Institutions and programs established to deal with socio-ecological problems reinforced the errors implicit in their establishment. Institutional operations—blending concept, structure, and behavior—tend to generate positive feedback. That is, intervention in the environment tends to generate more intervention. For example, control of floods through public works has always created the need for more and more control measures and more and more works. Resort to agricultural pesticides has reduced natural controls of pests and made necessary stronger and more frequent applications of pesticides. Whether experience is an unreliable teacher or man an incorrigible student, the evidence thus far would indicate that repeated ecological errors have seldom been corrected either by those making them or by those suffering the results. Blame for difficulties has always been lodged elsewhere. When an artificial manipulation of the environment has given a new and higher level of productivity, the economy and the population have expanded to take full advantage of it. Even if the advantage is relatively short-term, it may not be possible to drop back to the earlier natural state without painful social and economic adjustments. The almost invariable consequence has been, therefore, to push on into further intervention and technological innovation to salvage the earlier advantage and perhaps, and hopefully, to enlarge upon it; but productive success again is absorbed by repeated expansion, so the final situation remains relatively unchanged, except that the margin of unexploited opportunity is progressively narrowed.[52]

Overly simplified views of man's needs and relationships thus caused otherwise capable men and agencies to misread the situation at hand. Commenting on the misdirection of development efforts, John Kenneth Galbraith observed,

> Action will indeed be sound if the diagnosis of the development problem is sound. If that diagnosis is unsound we will be having a good deal of waste motion in the world. It is my unhappy feeling that the diagnosis leaves a great deal to be desired.[53]

> We have probably wasted a good deal of time and effort doing things which were right in themselves but which make little or no contribution to progress because they were done in an environment which was inconsistent with advance. The environment has not been examined. It has somehow been assumed to be favorable to development.[54]

Galbraith was asking that the total environmental situation, physical and social, be examined in the analysis of development needs. The consequence of the failure to fully perceive the field of action was almost certain failure of the effort. The unhappy outcomes of misread evidence and misdirected efforts become part of the problem. "In this regard," as C.A.O. Van Nieuwenhuijze has observed, "we still have to unlearn a considerable amount of ethnocentrism and of simplistic evolutionism, but we need not fear that our lesson will not be brought home to us." [55]

Does Eco-Catastrophe Impend?

Introducing *Environmental Essays on the Planet as a Home*, Paul Shepard wrote, "I believe that the threat to the biosphere is real, and that life on the planet is endangered by our numbers and our technology, though I am not qualified to prophesy catastrophe or to mark Doomsday on the calendar." [56] Writing in *The New York Times* for January 1, 1967, the science writer, Walter Sullivan, declared, "Since the first nuclear explosions at the end of World War II, we have been altering the environment of this planet at a rate catastrophic by nature's standards," [57] and he went on to echo the predictions of disaster voiced during the meetings in the late 1960s and early 1970s of the American Association for the Advancement of Science. Predictions of socio-ecological catastrophe received increasing attention in the popular press as well as in the scientific journals. In *Playboy* Magazine, Sir Julian Huxley spoke of "the crisis in mankind's destiny." [58] In *Esquire*, an article by David Lyle was given the title, "The Human Race Has, Maybe, Thirty-Five Years Left." [59] In a paper presented at the 1967 annual Meeting of the American Association for the Advancement of Science and published later in *Bioscience*, LaMont C. Cole of Cornell University asked, "Can the World Be Saved?" [60] Cole concluded with qualified optimism that the knowledge existed to save the world, but offered no assurance that men would use it. More sensational were the warnings of Paul Ehrlich of Stanford University whose science fiction essay "Eco-Catastrophe" was widely published in the early months of 1970.[61] (The sensational newspaper, *National Enquirer*, was inspired to print in its March 22, 1970, issue, the large black headlines, "TEN YEARS TO

SAVE THE WORLD: A most disturbing look into the future—The poisoned planet—A scientist's amazing view of how the earth will meet a horrible end.")

Were these warnings and alarms valid or were they exaggerated and counter-productive as some critics declared? [62] Would they cause people to disbelieve in even more sober and well-documented assessments of danger if the predicted catastrophes did not occur? No certain answer could be given. The warnings of ecological disaster inevitably lacked a certain credibility because no responsible scientist could seriously predict the specific occasion or combination of events that would produce the catastrophe. Still, some informed estimates could be made about the timing and intensity of impending crises.[63] The possibilities of enormous disasters were latent in the prevailing situation around the world, particularly in the less-developed countries, and the probability of disaster increased with the passing of time. Where and how could not be pinpointed but the possibility that somewhere, somehow man-made ecological catastrophe of enormous proportions would be triggered could no longer be rejected, even by those who professed that they did not expect it to happen.

Even though few chiefs of state and national political leaders would admit belief in the predictions of eco-catastrophe, many acted as if they half-way believed them. It was hardly coincidence that after predictions of ecological disaster, national governments, international science and conservation organizations, and the United Nations system itself began to mobilize resources to attack the problems that man was creating for himself in relation to his environment.

Although the primary threat to man's survival is now the uninhibited or misdirected behavior of man himself, this behavior to a considerable extent rests upon the institutions of custom, law, and government. The behavior of national governments remains largely unchecked by any higher political authority and largely untutored by valid ecological assessments of environmental potential and limitations. The unrestricted "right" of national sovereignty regardless of international consequences has been harmful to human welfare in many respects and has been a major obstacle to world peace. Not all, but many ecological disasters could have been averted had not the willfulness of nations and the inadequacy of the present disjunctive system of international organization blocked ecologically sound analyses of development plans. As the development economist Jan Tinbergen declares, "Other disasters will follow unless we recognize the need for international order." [64] And I would add that this recognition must be manifest through action. It is not a mystery that confronts the human race; it is rather a challenge to justify its own pretensions to suzerainty over the Earth.

In the opinion of some observers, modern society may have awakened to its predicament too late to avoid a major disaster and widespread suffering in the years ahead. But there are some grounds for hope that effective action in the present and immediate future might enable human society to find its way through this difficult and painful period and to avoid irreversible damage of the biosphere. The processes of restoring the ecological balance of the Earth and of obtaining an optimum level of human populations, one probably greatly below those now existing, would present as great a challenge as any that humanity has faced. But this might be the ultimate test of the capacity of the human animal for survival. If political rivalries, ideological tensions, and implacable refusals to face reality prevent human society from meeting the challenge, the rapid decline of civilization or the early extinction of the human species would be plausible predictions.

5

Mobilizing International Resources:

TOWARD MORE EFFECTIVE

PROTECTION OF THE BIOSPHERE

In the preceeding chapter, we observed that the threat to the biosphere was only gradually perceived and then greatly underestimated, even by competent observers. A few far-sighted individuals who perceived the interconnections among deteriorating trends had begun to sound alarms in the late 1960s and early 1970s—only to be called "false prophets of doom" in some parts of the press, the government, and the economic establishment. There was a deep and pervasive resistance to the idea that somehow modern society was itself the cause of environmental crisis. In the words of Paul Bohannan,

> There was little to indicate to us, in our innocence, that civilization itself was threatened—that we were witness not merely to human moral weakness and error, but to an overwhelming revolutionary process. Yet today we know that civilization itself is threatened—threatened by itself.[1]

The resistance, as we have seen, was rooted in the view of reality held by the masses of people and their leaders. Nothing in the prevailing state of public opinion or conventional wisdom offered a basis for a coordinated public response to the real danger—the mounting demands of expanding populations on a finite and easily disrupted environment. Failure to identify the problem as a whole made efforts to cope with its symptoms and manifestations partial, fragmentary, and specialized. Corrective

107

efforts, not being directed to the real causes, were often ineffectual.

The National-State and the Environment

IF THE WORLDVIEW of society itself has brought on an environmental crisis, it would follow that the institutions through which society operates would either contribute to environmental deterioration or be poorly adapted to cope with it. Even when the need has been recognized and new structures created to deal with it, social action is often slow to follow. Only the pressure of the most threatening events, as in total war, has moved societies to respond appropriately to problems not previously encountered.

To cope with global problems of a threatened biosphere, even to devise new institutional arrangements we must begin where we are, with an international political order based on ecologically unsound premises. The surface of the Earth has been subdivided among nations largely by military force, rationalized under the doctrine of national sovereignty. This situation reflects an almost wholly anthropocentric view of man–environment relationships. Although this viewpoint seems natural to most modern men, it is not inevitable. At various times and places, most notably in more primitive societies, men have seen their relationship with the natural world in ways far more consistent with ecological realities.

The political doctrines by which the organization of the contemporary world is rationalized are the unfortunate products of a transitory and exceptional phase of human history.[2] They grew out of the process of nation making in the seventeenth and eighteenth centuries, coincident with the emergence of modern scientific and technological capabilities that began to liberate men from the enforced immobilities of a pre-scientific age. The optimism of Sir Francis Bacon's *New Atlantis* dominated the age, and its influence has continued to the present. The monarchical heads of the new national governments co-opted science and technology to advance the purposes of the state. (The science of statistics began as a way to estimate the military capabilities of neighboring states.)

Under the exaggerated sovereignty of Louis XIV and his finance minister, Colbert, France mobilized science to serve the state, establishing the Académie des Sciences in 1666. Regulations to protect forests and other elements of the natural environment were undertaken not for ecological reasons but for economic and military ones.[3] In Central Europe, the conservation and development of natural resources, particularly in agriculture and forestry, was embodied in a statist political–economic doctrine called cameralism.[4] In Russia, Czar Peter I founded the Academy of Science in 1724 to advance learning and technology. This institution has had an unbroken history; today it is the Academy of Sciences of the USSR.

This concern with the resource base of nations was to some extent internationalized through the political–economic doctrines subsumed under the name "mercantilism."[5] Although mercantilism in practice was strongly nation-bound, the theoreticians of mercantilism read, criticized, and were influenced by one another's writings. The concern of the sovereigns for the practical application of science to forestry and agriculture stimulated scientific investigation and practice in these fields throughout northwestern Europe and brought about the development of at least a latent international community in those fields.[6] Such efforts were forerunners of the so-called development programs of the twentieth century.

The point to be noted is that, lacking world community or global view of man–environment relationships the men of early modern times could work only in and through nations, national institutions, and nation-oriented concepts. International institutions for environmental protection could not be created until there were national institutions in the field. Regrettably, if national sovereignty afforded a basis for the earliest efforts to conserve resources, it also encouraged competition among nations to exploit resources on a global scale and to preempt territory around the world primarily to control and utilize the so-called available raw materials for economic and military purposes. The harm inflicted on the biosphere by Western-style industrial society is now apparent; and after five hundred years of expansion and exploitation, a new steady-state relationship with the natural world has become necessary.

The paradox that we have noted in European and Western

civilization has become a paradox for the Earth as a whole. Before humanity could organize to cope with the problems which its expansion and its technology have created for the natural environment, apparently there first had to be created nations, that not only worsened the effect of man on the environment, but also created barriers to cooperation across national boundaries for the protection of nature and the biosphere.

The national-state system, as it further evolved in the nineteenth century and was extended in the twentieth, had little occasion to devise structures or procedures for coping with other than routine transnational issues, as in the International Postal Union. It was not organized to cope with problems of an ecological character, which until the mid-twentieth century were seldom perceived to exist. Ecosystems had no relation to national boundaries and, partly for this reason, early efforts to conserve wildlife fell short of their objectives because governments were not ready to take action to protect the habitat necessary for the survival of particular species.

Treaties between sovereign states were most easily negotiated and enforced where signatory governments were not required to go beyond abstaining from or denouncing certain action. Treaties were more difficult to negotiate and enforce where positive action was required that would affect the property or behavior of its own citizens. As we have seen, nations might agree to adopt police measures to prevent slaughter of migratory wildfowl or fur seals. This was a normal and unexceptional action for nineteenth and early twentieth century governments. But signatories to treaties were not in a position to compel one another to adopt national land-use policies which would, for example, make provision for adequate breeding or wintering grounds for wildfowl, protect them from agricultural pesticides; or, in the case of fur seals, protect the waters of the seas from contamination by mercury, DDT, and other chemical compounds that might originate in nonsignatory countries far removed from the habitat of the ostensibly protected species.

National action to protect those aspects of the environment beyond national territorial control was either ineffectual or only moderately successful, not only because of the great inequality of interest and capability among nations with respect to envi-

ronmental protection, but because the immediate self-interest of
particular nations was not consistent with the long-term interests of all peoples. This is the "Tragedy of the Commons," the
sequential stages of which have been described with great effectiveness by Garrett Hardin.[7]

The treatment of air, water (notably the oceans), and
wildlife as commons, free goods or common property, has
invariably led to resource depletion, pollution, and environmental degradation generally. The awakening apprehension over
the state of the biosphere has not as yet resulted in effective
action not solely, or perhaps even primarily, because too few are
concerned, but because there is as yet no way for them to put
their concern into practice. Effective structures and an informed
consensus to support them remain to be created.

Meanwhile, efforts to mobilize international resources for
protection of the biosphere have often been counterbalanced by
the unintended ecological damage that has accompanied international development. International mobilization for development
has been more vigorous and extensive than environmental protective efforts are likely to be for some time to come. For this
reason, and because the two movements must be reconciled both
at national and international levels, it is necessary for us at this
point to examine the assumptions and objectives of international
development. "Development," especially in its economic aspects,
is firmly in the Baconian tradition. In its name, science and
technology have been marshalled on behalf of national strength
and identity. It has an understandable appeal to the leadership of
the less-developed countries, many of whom suspect the environmental movement of being a covert way to curb their national
development. Such resistance must somehow be overcome if
protection of the environment is to win acceptance and support
in the less-developed nations of the world.

Development and the Environment

WITH THE DISINTEGRATION of the greater part of the European colonial empires following World War II, and the establishment of many independent and developing nations, a new and

III

serious problem in human political ecology began to appear. The new nations were, in the conventional language of the times, "under-developed"—that is, they were less-developed economically, technologically, and administratively than were the industrialized states of Western Europe and North America. Moreover, these less-developed countries were nearly all faced with rapidly increasing populations, in part as a consequence of effective international public health measures organized through the World Health Organization. Aid to the less-developed countries became a major international activity, issuing from the United Nations and several of its specialized agencies; independently from major industrialized nations like the United States, the United Kingdom, the Soviet Union, France, and Sweden; and from regional groups such as the European Economic Community, and the Organization for Economic Cooperation and Development.

Unfortunately, the concepts of "development" that dominated these efforts were largely unecological. Like their antecedents in the seventeenth and eighteenth century statist regimes, they were heavily economic in bias, but they were narrowly economic in the sense that they were based upon a set of highly specialized and contemporaneous sociological assumptions, influenced by Keynesian economics, which were more appropriate for developed than for less-developed countries. The dominant view of development was economic development, narrowly defined; and it was the generally accepted view taken by British, American, and Soviet planners. A different approach was advocated by a group of French development economists, notably François Perroux, Louis-Joseph Lebret, René Dumont, and Jacques Austruy. Their view of development was broadly humanistic. It looked to the needs of the whole man and relied less on economic growth to bring about social and political reform. Happily, this broader outlook and increased ecological sophistication is now also observable among Dutch, Swedish, and Anglo-American economists.

Development may be inadequately described as a complex process of purposeful change in the attitudes, behaviors, and institutions of human societies. But however difficult a social definition might be, to define it in theory or practice in narrow economic terms is a perversion of the hierarchy of human values, a posture termed "economism" by the Russian theologian, Nicholas Berdyaev.[8] Economism, he said, was a set of mind that postulates economic values (narrowly defined) as fundamental to all others and employs economic criteria as the primary measure of the worth of all human activities. "Combined with an uncritical acceptance of innovating technology, it has facilitated the creation of a new artificial environment incompatible with the needs of the whole man even as it threatens the natural environment in which man evolved." "Man," wrote Berdyaev, "has ceased to live close to the earth, surrounded by animals and plants; he lives in a new metallic reality, breathes a new and poisoned air." [9]

The term "development," in actual practice, has been applied to a much narrower scope of human activity than the total evolution of society, and yet just this totality is involved. As French sociologist Raymond Aron has shown, development theory is inherently evolutionary and implies social and environmental change.[10] The failure of development or, to state the criticism differently, the naive misuse of the development concept, is the result of oversimplifying a process that is not only itself complex, but causes change in the even more complex ecological relationships of the living world. "Le développemènt est scandale car il est creation," declares Jacques Austruy, Professor Agrégé in the Faculty of Law and of Economic Sciences at the University of Lille.[11] It is a scandal because it is creation —a process of changing something *that is* into something *that has yet to be*. Development is a process of "becoming," and the ends and the effects of the process are therefore of greatest importance in evaluating its costs and determining its justification. The scandal is not primarily in ignorant or self-serving misdirection of development efforts, although these abuses have occurred. It is, more importantly, in the overconfident, simplistic treatment of complex social and ecological processes. The goal of true development, as postulated by Austruy, is an optimal condition for human society which implies the conservation of diversities and their interaction to enrich the quality of human life in its full range of needs and values.

It is the profound social and moral implications of development that make it dangerous and inappropriate to approach its planning and administration with untempered optimism. Yet some measure of optimism or, better perhaps, of informed faith, is necessary to any improvement in the human condition. An optimism tempered by an appreciation of the complexity of the task and the difficulty of realizing good intentions is the attitude most consistent with an ecological approach to development. And whatever its meanings, and they are several, the development process is in fact an ecological force to the extent that it alters relationships between man-and-man and man-and-his-environment.

The mechanisms of international development are transfers of concepts, money, and technique from the more "advanced" to less "advanced" nations.[12] Among the more common facilitating arrangements are bilateral agreements between an aid-giving and aid-receiving nation, for example, the United States Agency for International Development and aid-receiving governments; multilateral aid arrangements such as the Organization for Economic Cooperation and Development, the European Economic Community, and consortia, for example, for India and Pakistan; international organizations such as the United Nations and its associated agencies, including the International Bank for Reconstruction and Development, the United Nations Development Program (UNDP), the United Nations Institute for Training and Research (UNITAR), and the United Nations Industrial Development Organization (UNIDO); quasi-public or private international business enterprises, development banks and finance companies, organizations such as the Development and Resources Corporation; and foundations, institutes, consultants, and advisers employed by governments engaging in development projects, such as the Ford Foundation and the Overseas Development Institute.[13]

The inadequacy of the development process has been partly due to inadequate concepts and partly to narrowly programmed institutions. But, of course, the two are linked, because the institutions and their programs reflect the way people think about their missions. Obeisance to the traditional concepts of sovereignty and autonomy has not only obstructed realistic planning for long-range development; it has also made aid-extending agencies wary of treading on national sensibilities in carrying out projects. Especially the less-developed countries tend to regard science as a servant and to resist it as a teacher.[14] Development projects accordingly have often dispensed scientific advice and technology in a less than scientific manner. Bilateral or international aid missions regularly provide technical advisers for the administration of development programs and, of course, engage in feasibility and preinvestment studies before extending aids.[15] But a taboo against interfering in local affairs frequently leads scientists and technicians to avoid more than a minimum of political or administrative decisions.[16]

The failure to build ecological considerations into the planning and execution of development projects is an obvious consequence of a previous failure to deal adequately with all of the parameters of the situation in which development is sought. The behavioral as well as the ecological aspects of change, although now receiving increasing attention, have seldom been adequately investigated in relation to development objectives.[17] Yet many of the untoward consequences of development projects—for example, increases in schistosomiasis, in nutritional ailments, and in depletion of resources and species—may be in large part attributed to failure to inculcate new human behavior patterns to safeguard use of the new techniques and conditions created by development efforts. Development agencies have sponsored programs of education and training intended to inculcate new methods of behavior for specific goals, for example, in agriculture and in health.[18] Some of these efforts recognize the importance of ecological factors; many, however, have merely indoctrinated men in specified techniques and have not necessarily altered their general orientation to the changing environments.[19]

This failure to get at basic attitudes and concepts has been a major cause of the frequently disappointing results of international development efforts. The circumstances of development require a holistic approach; and because man is engaged in manipulating his environment increasingly by means of a science-based technology, his goals and efforts need to meet the test of science. Yet the less-developed countries are notoriously weak in scientific capabilities, and their leaders tend to seek from their international benefactors stop gap projects to meet the urgent needs of their ever-expanding populations, and technoscience spectaculars (reactors, high dams, national airlines) to bolster their political prestige. Seldom do these projects solve the continuing problems of the less-developed country, especially the ecological ones. The disasters of development have followed largely either from politically-inspired undertakings or from projects whose ultimate consequences were insufficiently analyzed. To look before leaping is as good a rule in international development as elsewhere. Investigation implies research, an activity which, as W. Arthur Lewis, development economist and one of the architects of the UN Special Fund has pointed out, "is generally neglected in under-developed countries."

> These countries do not spend enough on geological surveys, on water measurements, on soil surveys, on agricultural research, or any other kind of research. The departments responsible for such matters tend to be unpopular because they are expensive, because they rely mainly on foreign experts, people of those countries not being specialists in these sciences, and because they are somewhat of a gamble. They cannot guarantee to deliver immediate and profitable answers.[20]

Guilt for such inadequate preproject investigation, is spread evenly between aid-giving and aid-receiving agencies. At the United Nations Conference on the Application of Science and Technology for the Benefit of Less Developed Areas, meeting in Geneva in 1963, Jean-Paul Harroy of Belgium observed that "When planning programmes for the economic development of these areas are being organized (based in the vast majority of cases on renewable natural resources), the power and the decision are all too often left in the hands of the economists, engineers, financiers, political leaders, and members of government departments, whilst the specialists on these resources—the naturalists, ecologists, and geographical surveyors—are not included in the exercise." [21]

The outcome of the 1963 conference illustrates the problem. The initial chapter of the conference report strongly underlined the importance of ecological considerations. Having described numerous instances of man-induced environmental disasters, the report declared that:

Ecology, that branch of science which is concerned with living things—all living things, the insects as well as the humans—their habits, their relationship to each other in the global community, and to the surroundings which they share, has become, belatedly, an essential study in the evaluation and development of natural resources.[22]

Nevertheless, although the ecological aspects of development appeared in various contexts throughout the papers and proceedings of the conference, they never came into focus as an organizing force or as a means of synthesis.

The hazard of a fractionalized science for accurate perception of development problems is evidenced in the make-up of national or international development missions. As Louis-Joseph Lebret has said, the work of technical assistance specialists tends to be juxtaposed rather than fused. Major development missions have almost always had major ecological implications for the countries concerned and yet, as we have previously noted, the membership of the working group has normally included only economists, engineers, and technical specialists. Ecologists and social scientists (other than economists) have seldom been involved in the initial stages of the development task, though occasionally some have been brought in as afterthoughts to minimize the potential ecological damage of decisions already made. Where the heads of missions genuinely fail to see how an ecologist, a sociologist, or a systems development analyst could contribute to the work of a mission, the chances are meager for dealing with all relevant factors.

There is nothing inherent in human needs and values, or in the basic principles of economics or ecology that places the goals of development and environmental protection inevitably in opposition. If the goals seem incompatible in some cases, deficiencies and contradictions will often be found in the goals themselves. It would be a tragic mistake to assume that genuine development must necessarily be threatened or constrained by international efforts to protect the biosphere. One must, of course, distinguish between the broad goals and purposes of development and those of specific development projects. It is the unsound development project that has given the development process a bad name, just as it is a narrowly conceived, particularistic brand of economics that has offended the critics of the development process.[23] A more adequate theory of development is needed, but such a theory could also be a theory of environmental protection and enhancement. The objectives of the United Nations 1972 Conference on the Human Environment, to harmonize development and environmental objectives, is thus both politically and intellectually sound. It would be especially fitting if leadership so oriented were to come from the less-developed countries. Their people have not yet been thoroughly acculturated with those unecological attitudes and assumptions of Western industrial society that are now becoming obsolete in the countries of their origins. It will also be the people of these less-developed countries who will suffer the disastrous consequences of development plans that fail to meet the needs of the whole man consistent with the laws of a self-renewing life-supporting biosphere.

It in no way denigrates the role of theory to recognize that, in fact, the meaning of development has largely been defined in action. Theoretical or conceptual changes are often slow to evolve and, indeed, are often influenced by practical events. The most direct route to finding more adequate meanings for development may therefore be through changes in development practices. These changes could occur within the existing structure of development agencies, by redefining their missions to include ecological values, by better orientation and training of personnel, and by developing more adequate criteria for project assessment and review. As development economist A. O. Hirschman has observed, merely "spelling out the probabilities of . . . unwelcome side-effects could lead to a modification of the investment decision or at least to giving the product in question a lower priority rating." [24] But even these operational changes require appropriate concepts and guidelines to direct them. The concepts underlying the development task and the values directing the goals are powerful shapers of the institutional structure and procedures in development. If the world is to have an international effort consistent with the full scope of human needs, as defined in the words of François Perroux, "de tout l'homme et de tous les hommes," concepts *and* institutions must be consistent with each other and with this broad humane ideal.

The Structure of International Environmental Protection

DEVELOPMENT HAS BEEN the principal continuing effort of international cooperation, but environmental matters are rapidly emerging as another major area of common concern. A very large number of international organizations are involved in a great diversity of activities having something to do with problems of the environment. For the most part, however, these activities are incidental to other purposes, like geophysical research, food production, or disease prevention. Moreover, with the rapidly growing concern for man's environmental relationships, many of these programs are also rapidly changing; and any detailed description of them would be obsolescent before it could appear in print. What we may do here, therefore, is to outline the general course of international activity related to the environment, to identify the principal organizations, to suggest the significance of the interrelationships among them, and to indicate the principal problems toward which international cooperation has been directed. Descriptions of the environment-related functions of principal international organizations can be found in a report, *Environmental Activities of International Organizations* (1971), prepared at the request of Senator Warren G. Magnuson for the Committee on Commerce of the United States Senate by the Environmental Policy Division of the Congressional Research Service.

Before 1968, the concept of the environment had not inspired international action, except for the establishment of the International Union for the Conservation of Nature and Natural Resources (IUCN). No balance sheet of the results of international environmental action has been drawn, and one cannot say assuredly whether the net effect has been harmful or beneficial. One's judgment would be biased by values and preferences, particularly concerning international development projects where a displacement of natural environments and wildlife by expanding agriculture may be very differently assessed by differing groups of well-informed observers. But whatever their effects, international programs for the environment have largely been *ad hoc* or unrelated to one another. Neither concepts nor machinery for planning and coordination have been available. The development of such concepts, and that machinery, has now become a practical necessity. But to confront the necessity effectively, it is also necessary to take into account the structure of international action.

The United Nations System

THE PRINCIPAL STRUCTURE of action in behalf of the international environment is, of course, the United Nations system. This includes the United Nations General Assembly and Secretariat, and also the so-called specialized agencies, several of which are involved in various ways in international issues. Within the United Nations organization itself, certain areas of policy have been made the responsibility of three subsidiary councils whose functions are suggested by their names: Security Council, Trusteeship Council, and Economic and Social Council. The United Nations concern with environmental problems has largely fallen within the province of the Economic and Social Council (ECOSOC), which carries on its business through commissions and standing committees. Among the environment-related activities of ECOSOC have been international development programs, low-cost housing and urban planning, the peaceful uses of outer space and of the Antarctic, and jurisdiction over the high seas and the deep seabed.

Within the permanent administrative structure of the United Nations, the Department of Economic and Social Affairs (ESA) has undertaken studies and disseminated information on environmental consequences of industrialization and urbanization, and has undertaken to assist developing countries in reducing the adverse environmental effects of natural resources exploitation and the expansion of transportation facilities. The UN Centre for Housing, Building, and Planning is administered by ESA and is concerned with a range of environmental considerations relating to the man-made environment. Since January 1971, the Centre has published an environment-oriented journal entitled *Human Settlements*. ECOSOC has a Committee on Housing, Building, and Planning which is serviced by ESA and is con-

cerned with the same problems as the Centre. The Public Administration Division of the Department has undertaken studies and
has commissioned papers on the management of environmental
programs. Associated with the work of ECOSOC are the United
Nations regional Economic Commissions—for Europe (ECE),
Asia and the Far East (ECAFE), for Africa (ECA), and for
Latin America (ECLA). Of these Commissions, only ECE has
shown a major concern with environmental problems. Both ECE
and ECAFE have established Committees on Housing, Building,
and Planning. ECE has given special attention to the environmental problems of urbanized areas, including problems of air and
water pollution, the impact of urban transportation upon the environment, and the relationship of urban planning to the suburban
landscape and the countryside. ECE has been the first of the
regional Economic Commissions to concern itself directly and
comprehensively with the environment, sponsoring a symposium
on Problems Related to the Environment in Prague in May 1971.

Associated with the United Nations is the International
Court of Justice, the World Court, successor to the pre-1945
Permanent Court of International Justice. A body of international law regarding national responsibility towards the environment has begun to develop as a consequence of actions brought
before the court.[25] The first court, like the second, was
established as a part of a structure of international organization
(the League of Nations) following World War I. The earliest
formal machinery for the peaceful settlement of international
disputes was the Permanent Court of Arbitration, established by
the Hague Convention of July 29, 1899. The expressions
"permanent" and "court" were misnomers, however, because
the court has consisted of a panel of arbitrators appointed by the
signatory parties. Arbitration has not been mandatory and
recourse to the court has been infrequent. At the Second Hague
Conference (1907) on the pacific settlement of international
disputes, an unsuccessful attempt was made to establish a continuing international tribunal, a true arbitral Court of Justice.
Further attempts to establish a binding obligation to arbitrate or
to accept judicial settlement have not yet proved effective, but
precedents have been established indicating the ultimate possibility of an international rule of law. Should international

agreements establish a new body of rules and obligations concerning the environment, the number of international disputes susceptible to arbitration or adjudication may increase rapidly. The question therefore arises whether new machinery may be needed for this purpose.

The principal actors within the UN system, whose activities impinge most directly upon the environment, are the specialized agencies; and among these, the most extensively involved are the Food and Agriculture Organization (FAO), the United Nations Educational, Scientific, and Cultural Organization (UNESCO), the World Health Organization (WHO), and the World Meteorological Organization, (WMO). More specialized are certain environment-related activities of the International Bank for Reconstruction and Development (World Bank), the International Civil Aviation Organization (ICAO), the International Telecommunications Union (ITU), the International Maritime Consultative Organization (IMCO), and the International Labor Organization (ILO). Outside the United Nations structure, but obviously significant to the environment is the International Atomic Energy Agency which does maintain regular communications with the Economic and Social Council, the Secretariat, and several of the specialized agencies.

There is no easy way to describe the environment-related activities of the specialized agencies in a way that is at once comprehensive, coherent, concise, and accurate. Their activities are disparate and their fields of interest sometimes overlap. As one might expect, a large part of their activities relates to pollution of the atmosphere, of the oceans, and of fresh waters. In addition to being a factor in air and water pollution, pesticides have been singled out as a special kind of problem, particularly in relation to human health and wildlife. A second group of environmental activities are concerned with land use, conservation of wildlife, and environmental amenities. A third area embraces urban–environmental affairs and also extends to human settlements in rural areas; it has been heavily involved with problems of housing and urban planning.

Neither international organizations nor officially related to the United Nations system are the citizen-sponsored United Nations associations in principal countries. These associations hold meetings, adopt resolutions, and in a general way act to support the United Nations, its objectives, and its programs. In at least one notable instance, a group of these associations joined to take action for the protection of the biosphere.

During December 15–17, 1969, a conference representing the United Nations associations in four Nordic countries met in Stockholm to prepare a proposed declaration for submission to the United Nations in connection with the 1972 Conference on the Human Environment.[26] Drafted by Scandinavian experts in the fields of natural sciences, international law, and administration, the draft declaration was circulated to the Nordic governments and to the agencies of the United Nations particularly concerned. Arguing that air, water, land, and natural resources are the common heritage of man and must be protected for the benefit of humanity, the declaration asserted that each individual has a right to live in an environment in which he can develop to his fullest capacity, physically and intellectually. It includes "the right to an environment with reasonably clean air, soil, water, and access to unspoiled nature, as well as protection against the damages which can accompany the uncurbed exploitation of natural resources." The Nordic group listed five practical areas for environmental policy and control:

1. Enforcement of laws and agreements for limiting pollution.
2. Considering environmental consequences in all social planning.
3. Increasing research on the best use of natural resources.
4. Conducting effective information campaigns on environmental problems.
5. Giving environmental control efforts high priority in funds.

The conference identified the global population explosion as the basic cause in the growth of environmental problems, declaring that only drastic and early efforts can insure that the environment will remain viable for future generations.

Another example of initiative from United Nations associations came from the Soviet Union. In an unpublished paper prepared for joint discussions with a special panel of the United

Nations Association of the United States, the United Nations Association of the USSR supported increased international cooperation, although not by means of new international structures. Recognizing that "existing means for combatting pollution of sea waters do not, however, insure their full protection," the Soviet paper declared, "The problem of ocean and sea pollution is mainly a technical rather than a juridical or legal problem." The paper called for international standards to govern maximum acceptable concentrations of the most prevalent agents of atmospheric pollution, and declared, "International standard methods of controlling air cleanliness should also be worked out, that would make it possible to detect immediately not merely any specific forms of pollution, but all the admixtures present in the atmosphere at a given moment. . . ." The foregoing problems, however, the Soviet paper observed, were "entirely within the purview of the World Health Organization and they could be solved within the framework of this body." The Soviet paper continued, "As far as the need for setting international standards for air and water pollution is concerned, we do not believe that any international agency has to control the cleanliness of the air and water." The Soviet position appeared to be that although international legislation and standards were required, enforcement should be a domestic concern. Nevertheless, the Soviet paper did support certain institutional innovations at the international level. Among the specific innovations proposed in relation to the 1972 Stockholm Conference were:

1. A declaration on the protection and improvement of man's environment.
2. An international convention (treaty) for the protection of the environment.
3. Wide and concentrated research over an extensive range of complex environmental problems.
4. International exchange of information on scientific achievements and technical findings through international centers for the gathering and exchange of such information.
5. An international network of stations to observe phenomena and processes of a global and regional nature (environmental monitoring).

6. An international exposition on the study and protection of man's environment.

Intergovernmental Organizations Outside the UN System

Two MULTI-NATIONAL intergovernmental organizations outside of the UN structure have been significantly concerned with international environmental problems. The Organization for Economic Cooperation and Development (OECD) has established an Environmental Committee and a Directorate for Environmental Affairs. Previous environmental activities of OECD had been concerned with air pollution, with control of technologies and with research on environmental problems posed by advances in transportation technology, including noise pollution and changes in the physical environment.

The Committee on Challenges to Modern Society (CCMS) was created by the North Atlantic Treaty Organization in December 1969. Among its activities are studies of water pollution control standards, and of the potential national and regional impact of air pollution; comparative studies have been undertaken in Frankfurt am Main, Ankara, and St. Louis. CCMS has also been concerned with the environmental problems of urban communities, and a Conference on Urban Affairs was convened in Indianapolis in May 1971.[27]

Regional Organizations

THE DEVELOPMENT OF STRUCTURES for regional international cooperation must be considered in any effort to mobilize international resources for environment protection. A number of regional organizations are already involved in cooperative research, in administering concurrent standards and regulations, and in environment-altering action programs, especially those related to economic development. A second reason for considering regional structures is their possible utility in dealing with certain environmental problems that transcend national boundaries but are less than global. These problems are usually very specific—seemingly few sets of problems are uniquely associ-

125

ated with particular regions. The campaign to control the desert locust, for example, can be localized within ecologically defined areas in Africa and Western Asia.[28] Conversely, diseases characteristic of the humid tropics are seldom so localized that regional organization alone can be a promising approach toward control.[29]

Consideration of existing regional arrangements may be divided between those organizations that are already engaged in environmental protection and control and those that are not now significantly engaged but might become so. This distinction is not clear-cut, first, because some regional efforts are indirectly or marginally related to environmental problems and second, because organizations heretofore inactive in environmental issues may suddenly become involved in questions of policy. An example of the first circumstance is the Soviet-bloc Council for Mutual Economic Assistance (CMEA). Although this body is primarily political in origin like NATO, it has fostered technical and scientific cooperation and research among its member countries. Its activities impinge upon certain environmental problems, but environmental policies as such only recently have been found among CMEA's higher priorities. The Organization for African Unity (OAU) and the Organization of American States (OAS) have similarly been primarily concerned with matters other than environmental, but the OAU sponsored the new (1968) treaty for the protection of African wildlife, and a Latin American Committee on National Parks has held periodic meetings and exchanged information in this particular area of environmental conservation.

Three regional intergovernmental groupings in Europe have been in various ways concerned with environmental issues. They are the Council of Europe, which in 1970 sponsored the European Conservation Year; the European Economic Community; and one of the oldest regional bodies, the International Council for Exploration of the Sea (ICES), established in 1902 to coordinate the oceanographic activities of its member governments (most of which are in the North Atlantic area), to promote research in marine sciences, and to assist the development of international conventions for the improvement of marine fisheries.

On May 2, 1966, the Committee of Ministers of the Council of Europe adopted a "Programme of Work for the Intergovernmental Activities of the Council of Europe" which included a section on Physical Environment and Resources, the objectives of which were "investigation into and adoption of planned action to insure that man's physical environment shall be balanced, wholesome and enjoyable, and that Europe's natural resources shall not be wasted, misused or destroyed." [30]

The European Economic Community has pursued more limited environmental objectives, largely concerned with air pollution by motor vehicles and by the coal and steel industries, water pollution, and contamination by radioactive wastes.

Two Scandinavian regional organizations, one intergovernmental and one nongovernmental scientific, have become concerned with environmental issues. The former, the Nordic Council established in 1952, consists of members elected by the respective legislative assemblies and certain other representatives of the five Scandinavian countries—Denmark, Iceland, Norway, Sweden, and Finland.[31] An older organization, Nordforsk (Scientific Council for Applied Research), was founded in 1947 on the basis of an agreement between institutes for scientific and technical research in the five Nordic countries. The work of Nordforsk is carried out primarily through expert committees and working parties. Committees have been established on air pollution research and water pollution research. In 1968, Nordforsk was asked by the Nordic Council to carry out an inquiry on environmental protection in the Scandinavian countries. The resulting proposals were accepted in 1969 by the Nordic Council as the basis for a recommendation to member governments. As a consequence, a new coordinative body to harmonize laws and regulations concerning environmental protection in the Scandinavian countries and to deal with other environmental questions of common interest, was convened in Helsinki on February 25, 1971. A permanent Secretariat for Environmental Sciences had been previously established by Nordforsk in Helsinki, Finland, on January 1, 1970.[32]

Other types of regional intergovernmental organizations whose activities have incidentally involved them in environmental matters are commissions governing international lakes and rivers.[33] The oldest of these appears to be the Commission for the River Rhine established in 1815 at the Congress of Vienna following the Napoleonic Wars. The commission, however, did not become active until after the Treaty of Mannheim in 1868. The Danube Commission was established in 1878 and, in addition to its primary concern for navigation, also assists flood control for member states and is involved in integrated hydroelectric planning and international water pollution control. In North America, the Joint International Commission, established between the United States and Canada by treaty in 1909, has a variety of responsibilities, more recently including environmental matters in the Great Lakes and the Saint Lawrence River and Seaway. The International Boundary and Water Commission of the United States and Mexico is concerned primarily with the management of the waters of the Rio Grande, but with those of the Colorado and Tijuana Rivers as well.

River basin commissions have been primarily developmental in purpose, and environmental protection has been an incidental part of their functions. Two examples from less-developed countries are the permanent Indus Commission, established in 1960 by treaty between India and Pakistan, and the Committee for Coordination of Investigations on the Lower Mekong Basin, established in 1959 under United Nations auspices. Both have been looked upon as experimental models for similar efforts in other developing countries. Mekong Committee members consist of representatives from Laos, Cambodia, South Vietnam, and Thailand. During the first decade of its existence, only minimal attention was given to the ecological aspects of its activities. In 1969, however, a team of ecologists was assembled to undertake an ecological survey of the Lower Mekong Basin for future development planning.

Non-Governmental Organizations: The International Structure of Science

As we noted in Chapter 2, scientific concern with the Earth as an entity began with attempts to map and measure it, to study its geophysical evolution, and to discover the origins and ecological interrelationships of living species. Systematic international efforts toward the exchange of information and the correlation and extension of knowledge of the world began in the mid-nineteenth century with the international science congresses. Among these gatherings, for example, were the International Health Congress in Paris in 1851, the International Statistical Congress in Brussels in 1853, the International Congress of Chemistry in Karlsruhe in 1860, and the International Congress of Geodesy in Berlin in 1862. These congresses, composed of individual scientists and representatives of scientific societies in the more scientifically advanced nations led to the establishment of continuing committees and then to international associations and unions. For example, the International Meteorological Committee was established at a meeting in Leipzig in 1872. The International Association of Geodesy was established in 1898 and was the predecessor of the present International Union of Geodesy and Geophysics which has played an important role in describing the physical unity of the Earth.

In 1901, a step toward structural unity in international science was taken with the establishment of the International Association of Academies in Göttingen. National academies have played an important role in the history of modern science, beginning in the seventeenth and eighteenth centuries largely as voluntary associations of scientists, but also representing an official sponsorship of science by government, as in the establishment of the French Academie des Sciences in 1666 and the Russian Academy of Sciences in 1724. The First World War temporarily arrested the development of an international structure for science. Afterward, the growth of unions of scientific societies led to the formation of the International Research Council at conferences in Paris and Brussels in 1918 and 1919. Three unions concerned with astronomy, geophysics, and chemistry formed the council; but in the following decade, additional unions were admitted, notably in relation to our concern, in the biological sciences and geography. In 1931, this evolving structure was reorganized to form the International Council of Scientific Unions (ICSU) in which representation from the unions was joined with national representation, chiefly through the national academies.[34]

ICSU has a complex and diffuse structure, its constituent

unions being in effect umbrella organizations covering a large number of subsidiary associations. For example, there are sixty-eight national members in the International Union of Geodesy and Geophysics (IUGG), and seven international associations relating to geodesy, seismology, meteorology, geomagnetism, oceanography, hydrology, and volcanology. In order to focus the diverse and specialized resources of the unions on major global problems, coordinative mechanisms are needed. The principal mechanism has been interunion, interdisciplinary committees addressing themselves to particular scientific questions and problems. Of the several types of committees established by ICSU, the continuing scientific committees are the more important to an international structure for environmental protection and control. Among these committees are the Scientific Committee on Oceanic Research (SCOR), 1957; the Committee on Space Research (COSPAR), 1958; the Scientific Committee on Antarctic Research (SCAR), 1958; and, of special relevance to us, the Scientific Committee on Problems of the Environment (SCOPE), 1970. Special committees have been created for special international cooperative programs, several of which have contributed significantly to the conception and understanding of the biosphere. Perhaps the most important of these have been the Comité Spécial de l'Année Geophysique Internationale (CSAGI), which planned and coordinated the International Geophysical Year of 1956–57, and the Scientific Committee for the International Biological Programme (SCIBP), established in 1963 and continued until 1974 for the study of large-scale transnational ecosystems.

And so at the beginning of the last third of the twentieth century, there was an international scientific community with an elaborate federative structure, one able to focus its resources on specific scientific and environmental problems, and which had demonstrated, over more than half a century, an ability to coordinate and advance large-scale scientific enterprises. Many of these efforts, as early as the pre-ICSU International Polar Years of 1882–83 and, more recently, the International Geophysical Year,[35] the International Biological Programme,[36] and the UNESCO–WMO-sponsored International Hydrological Decade[37] have added significantly to the knowledge upon which the international environmental policy of the 1970s could be based.

The nongovernmental international organization most directly, consistently, and comprehensively involved with the world environment has been the International Union for Conservation of Nature and Natural Resources (IUCN), which belongs neither to the ICSU nor UN systems although it has cooperative relationships with both.[38] IUCN grew out of earlier efforts for the protection of nature, described in Chapter 3. To recapitulate briefly, it was established in 1948, following an international conference at Fontainebleau sponsored by UNESCO and the government of France under the name, the International Union for the Protection of Nature. In 1956 at its Triennial General Assembly in Edinburgh, the name was changed to the International Union for Conservation of Nature and Natural Resources, broadening the original concept of the protection of wildlife to include the protection of renewable natural resources. Membership in the IUCN is composed primarily of governments, and independent, scientific, professional, and conservation organizations. At the beginning of 1971, seventy governments and more than two hundred organizations from seventy countries throughout the world were members. IUCN operates through a number of commissions and committees which specialize in different aspects of the Union's work.

Although the social and behavioral sciences have been in various ways concerned with environmental matters, their interest in environmental protection has until recently been relatively slight. In March 1970, however, the International Social Science Council (ISSC) sponsored in Tokyo an International Symposium on Environmental Disruption in the Modern World.[39]

To examine fully the role of international organizations in protecting the global environment, it would be necessary to describe the international structure of business and technology and the many international professional associations affiliated neither with the international structure of science nor with the United Nations system, and more specialized in their concerns than either the IUCN or the ISSC.[40] There is, however, space to name only a few such bodies here. Prominent among them, in addition to the International Union of Forest Research

Organizations (IUFRO) and the International Federation of Landscape Architects (IFLA), already mentioned, are the International Federation of Housing and Planning, the International Commission of Agricultural Engineering, the International Association on Water Pollution Research, and the World Medical Association.[41]

Thus by 1968, or by the beginning of the last third of the twentieth century, steps had been taken through international action—political, scientific, and professional—to identify and to deal with specific problems of the human environment. As we have seen, this development had been largely *ad hoc* and incremental, representing no conscious effort to mobilize the energies and resources of nations for the protection of the biosphere. The result, however, has been to create a complex, ramifying, and largely uncoordinated structure of international action which, although not in itself adequate to provide protection for the biosphere, offers knowledge and experience from which an adequate structure might be built.

Convergent Efforts Toward International Responsibility

At the beginning of the 1970s, changes in the structure of international action seemed probable, first because of the growth of worldwide concern with the general state of the environment, and second because of the cumulative and converging international efforts on behalf of the environment which would require institutional innovation at the international level. Opinions differed over the rapidity, scope, and precise institutional character of new institutional arrangements, but there was widespread agreement about their ultimate necessity.[42]

It is instructive to compare the Resolutions of the Biosphere Conference and of the General Assembly of the United Nations on the Human Environment (presently to be discussed) with the Agenda and Proceedings of the United Nations Scientific Conference of 1949 on the Conservation and Utilization of Resources at Lake Success, New York. The twenty years between the Resources and the Biosphere conferences may, in historical retrospect, be seen to mark as fundamental a change in the perception of international responsibilities as any since the establishment of permanent international organizations. Certainly, the prospects for international action on behalf of the biosphere depend on the willingness of the greater national powers to cooperate; and so any cooperative actions by these nations may indicate new possibilities. A chronological list of events relating to international responsibility for the biosphere is included in the appendix.

It is now possible to see a process of conceptual and institutional growth in the quarter-century between the end of World War II and the preparations for the United Nations Stockholm Conference of 1972 that was not evident in 1963 when Pierre Auger wrote concerning "the problem of ecological balance and its disruption by human intervention . . . no clear doctrine has emerged as yet, such as a synthesis accompanied by an appropriative evaluation of the conditions in the near future." [43] But even though the concepts upon which international action could be based had not yet adequately developed, there was a rapidly developing recognition that the intellectual and institutional capabilities of nations needed to be mobilized to arrest the worsening condition of the biosphere.

In the United States, the White House Conference on International Cooperation (November 29–December 1, 1965) recognized the connection between international development programs and impending crisis in the biosphere. A report prepared for the meeting by a National Citizens Commission recommended the establishment of a number of new international agencies and programs for environmental and ecological protection. These included a specialized UN Agency for Marine Resources, a World Institute of Resource Analysis, a UN-sponsored International River Basin Commission, and a Trust for the World Heritage in Natural and Scenic Areas and Historic Sites.[44]

In an address at Glassboro (New Jersey) State College on June 4, 1968, President Lyndon B. Johnson called for Soviet-American cooperation in forming, with other nations, an International Council on the Human Environment.[45] On July 22, 1968, an essay entitled, "Thoughts on Progress, Peaceful Coexistence and Intellectual Freedom," by the Russian academician. A. D. Sakharov was published in the *New York Times* and was widely circulated throughout the world: it contained a strong plea for cooperation between the Soviet Union and the United States in coping with the global problems of environmental pollution and deterioration. The primary significance of these proposals was that they were made—that they could assume a comprehending and sympathetic audience of sufficient size and influence to justify the risk and effort involved.

The Resolution of the General Assembly of the United Nations on December 3, 1968, calling for a world conference on the human environment, stimulated a great variety of efforts —scientific, academic, civic, and political—on behalf of international action for protection of the biosphere. Typical was a series of events that we have previously noted: the identification of environmental problems as a major social concern of the NATO Committee on Challenges of Modern Society (CCMS), the Nordic Declaration of Environmental Rights, the European Conservation Year under the sponsorship of the Council of Europe, and the ECE Symposium on Problems of the Environment held in Prague in May 1971. In addition, publications and seminars were undertaken, including an International Conference on the Environmental Future sponsored by the government of Finland in late June and early July of 1971. These and many other initiatives gave evidence of a cumulative and widespread recognition of the need for cooperative international action on behalf of the environment. But the extent of the concern can be better illustrated by a more detailed examination of three major international efforts to mobilize international resources for environmental protection. These efforts have to do with (1) an Ocean Regime and (2) UNESCO initiatives, which will be considered in the remaining pages of this chapter, and (3) the United Nations Conference on the Human Environment, the background of which will be discussed in the following chapter.

Toward an Ocean Regime

THOSE PARTS OF THE EARTH in which national sovereignty has not been or could not easily be established are most amenable to international cooperative action. It is, therefore, not surprising that outer space, Antarctica, and the oceans have been objects of efforts to achieve some form of international control. In each, environmental protection has been an important consideration and some measure of success in obtaining international agreement has been achieved. In December 1959, the UN-sponsored Antarctic Treaty was signed, establishing the South Polar Region as an international scientific reserve. In 1966, the International Treaty on the Peaceful Use of Outer Space was ratified. But concerning the oceans, their accessibility, the importance of their resources, and the long established traditions of use have made international action more difficult. The marine environment comprises approximately 71 per cent of the Earth's surface and is absolutely essential to the welfare and even to the economic survival of many nations. Indeed, in a more fundamental ecological sense, it is, as noted in Chapter 4, essential to the survival of all living things. Legal and technical literature on national and international jurisdiction over the sea and its resources is very great, and the number of international treaties, agreements, and reports of major importance pertaining to the oceans would be numbered in the hundreds.[46]

Two efforts to mobilize international action for protection of the sea have, in effect, initiated continuing actions. The first was the International Conference on the Pollution of the Sea by Oil in London in 1954, which resulted in the London Convention (Treaty) of 1954 on Marine Pollution by Oil[47] and marked the beginning of a slow and often frustrating effort to deal with the mounting menace of marine pollution. In 1955, an International Technical Conference on the Conservation of the Living Resources of the Seas was convened in Rome by the Food and Agriculture Organization. Subsequently, in 1958, the Geneva Convention (Treaty) on Fishing and Conservation of the Living Resources of the High Seas was adopted.[48]

These and earlier cooperative efforts were primarily concerned with obtaining national cooperation and fixing national responsibility for specified uses of the oceans. In no other area of the human environment has international cooperation a longer history or more extensive development. Yet these efforts, as we observed in Chapter 3, were only partially effective and were sometimes failures. The International Council for the Exploration of the Sea was established as early as 1902 to coordinate the control of fisheries in the Baltic, the North Sea, the Bering Sea, and the waters of the North Atlantic. Limited in scope and membership, it was nevertheless a move in the right direction. The subsequent development of international fisheries commissions and a largely ineffectual International Whaling Commission gave little hope that cooperation among nations, alone, could adequately safeguard the ocean environment.

As early as 1959, at the concluding session of the First Oceanographic Congress in New York, Columbus O-D. Iselin of the Woods Hole Oceanographic Institution declared, "Some very wise agency needs to be developing the ground rules within which the vast marine resources can be developed in an efficient and safe manner for the benefit of all mankind." [49] With the establishment in 1959 of the United Nations–sponsored Intergovernmental Maritime Consultative Organization (IMCO), a step was taken toward international rules for the use of the seas. But responsibility for the oceans remained widely dispersed within the United Nations system.

The General Assembly, the Secretariat, the Economic and Social Council, and the International Law Commission, all have addressed themselves to international agreement on the principles, rights, and obligations of nations towards the oceans. The role of the specialized agencies has logically been specialized. The Intergovernmental Maritime Consultative Organization (IMCO) has been concerned with navigation, maritime safety, and marine pollution. It has established a procedure for reporting oil spills, proposed changes to strengthen the London Convention of 1954 on Prevention of Pollution of the Sea by Oil, and called for an international conference in 1972 concerning all forms of marine pollution. The Food and Agriculture Organization (FAO) is concerned with fisheries, but its emphasis is largely upon food supply. In December 1970, it convened a conference in Rome on the Effects of Marine Pollution on the Living Resources of the Sea. The World Meteorological Organization (WMO) has taken an increasing interest in ocean management and has entered the field of hydrography. The sea–air interface is of the greatest importance to weather and climate, and the development of the World Weather Watch [50] necessitates monitoring and reporting stations at sea.

At the beginning of the 1970s, one of the principal UN organizations for international scientific cooperation in relation to the seas was the Intergovernmental Oceanographic Commission (IOC), established in 1960 as a semi-autonomous subsidiary of UNESCO. UNESCO's Office of Oceanography and the IOC have played primarily a coordinating role, sponsoring several large-scale international expeditions. Principal among these was the International Indian Ocean Expedition of 1959–1966 in which twenty-three countries officially participated in addition to FAO and WHO.[51] Fifty-five governments belong to IOC, whose purpose is "to promote scientific investigation with a view to learning more about the nature and resources of the oceans through the concerted actions of its members." Among the other environment-related activities of UNESCO and IOC are the Indian Ocean Biological Center established by an agreement between India and UNESCO, the UNESCO–IOC-sponsored training programs relating to oceanography and fisheries, and publication jointly by UNESCO and FAO of the quarterly newsletter *International Marine Science.*

The establishment of an ocean regime has been under consideration in the United Nations at least since 1966, when the General Assembly by Resolution 2172 (21) requested the Secretary-General to survey the activities of national governments and the UN agencies relating to marine science and technology, and to formulate proposals for expanded international cooperation in the exploitation and development of resources of the sea. Also in 1966, the Economic and Social Council by Resolution 1112 (40) asked the Secretary-General, in cooperation with the Advisory Committee on the Application of Science and Technology to Development and the specialized agencies, to survey the state of knowledge of the resources of the sea beyond the continental shelves (excluding fish); and to identify those resources "considered to be capable of economic exploitation, especially for the benefit of developing countries." [52]

This movement was given impetus in 1967 by the proposal of Ambassador Pardo, Malta's permanent representative to the United Nations, that a treaty should be drafted for "the creation of an international agency to assume jurisdiction, as a trustee for all countries, over the seabed and the ocean floor, underlying the seas beyond the limits of present national jurisdiction." [53] The Maltese proposal was intended to prevent the national appropriation and militarization of the seabed and ocean floor beyond the then present limits of national jurisdiction, and to insure that the resources of the ocean floor would not be monopolized for the advantage of technologically advanced countries but would be used exclusively for peaceful purposes and to promote the welfare of the less-developed countries.

After extended discussion, the twenty-second session of the United Nations General Assembly referred the issue to an *Ad Hoc* Committee to study the peaceful uses of the seabed and the ocean floor beyond the limits of national jurisdiction and to survey all relevant international agreements and activities of intergovernmental organization. It was noted that the Secretary-General of the United Nations was already engaged in studies relating to these matters under resolutions that the General Assembly and the Economic and Social Council adopted during 1966, and that a working committee on legal arrangements relating to the scientific investigations of the seas had been established in connection with the Intergovernmental Oceanographic Commission. As a consequence of these and other activities within the United Nations, a large amount of data was assembled on the law of the sea, marine technology, and alternative possibilities for effective management and control of marine resources. In December 1968, the General Assembly, following a report of the *Ad Hoc* Committee, adopted a resolution creating a permanent Committee on the Peaceful Uses of the Deep Sea-Bed and the Ocean Floor and the Subsoil Thereof Beyond the Limits of National Jurisdiction.

While the nature of international responsibility for the oceans was being debated in the United Nations, proposals for an international regime for the oceans were being developed in other places. The Commission to Study the Organization of Peace urged in its Seventeenth Report (1966) that the United Nations take title to the sea beyond the twelve-mile limit, and to the ocean floor beyond the continental shelves.[54] It recommended the establishment of a United Nations marine resources agency to control the exploitation of ocean resources. The World Peace Through Law Conference, meeting in Geneva in

July 1967, resolved (Resolution 15) that the United Nations declare its jurisdiction and control outside the territorial waters of any state and over the ocean floor beyond the continental shelves, fishery resources being excepted.[55] During the early summer of 1970, an international convocation, *Pacem in Maribus*, to explore the peaceful uses of the oceans and the ocean floor, was held on Malta under the sponsorship of the Center for the Study of Democratic Institutions at Santa Barbara, California. Before that meeting, the Center had issued for discussion in October 1968 a "model statute," prepared by Elizabeth Mann Borgese suggesting the kind of international structure which might assume jurisdiction over the oceans.[56]

In the United States, interest in the development of marine technology and oceanography was well-organized and active. The issue of international control was debated in the Congress; and at the annual meeting of the American Association for the Advancement of Science in 1967, Senator Clairborne Pell of Rhode Island told a symposium that an international ocean space treaty that would cover both the sea floor and the sea itself was urgently needed to avoid the threat of anarchy. He advocated placing the sea and its resources under the jurisdiction of the United Nations.[57] In its report for 1966, the Committee on Oceanography of the National Academy of Sciences recommended the establishment of a world oceanographic organization within the United Nations structure of organizations.[58] And the American Assembly, meeting at Arden House in May 1968, gave extended consideration in its final report to the development of more adequate international law and procedures, urging that the United States "support the creation of international machinery within the family of the United Nations organizations with responsibilities in respect to the exploitation of non-living resources of the deep sea floor" and urged "stronger regional and other international regulatory machinery" for the living resources of the seas, including new international agreements on the legal boundaries of territorial waters and the continental shelf.[59]

Notable among a larger group of meetings relating to an ocean regime were two conferences on Law, Organization, and Security in the Use of the Oceans held at the Ohio State University in March and October 1967 under the sponsorship of the Mershon Center for Education and National Security and the Carnegie Endowment for International Peace; and, since 1966, annual summer conferences sponsored by the Law of the Sea Institute at the University of Rhode Island, bringing together lawyers, marine scientists, businessmen, and government officials for exchange of information and ideas on matters of law and policy relating to the sea and its resources. Publications resulting from these conferences are a valuable source of information regarding jurisdiction over the oceans.[60]

In a number of proposals for international jurisdiction over the oceans, fisheries were excluded from consideration in part because fishing on the high seas and coastal waters was already governed by a body of international law and custom, notably by the Geneva Convention on Fishing and Conservation of the Living Resources of the High Seas, Article I of which begins, "All states have the right to engage in fishing on the high seas." However, in their study on the common wealth in ocean fisheries, Francis T. Christy, Jr., and Anthony Scott warned that under present-day conditions traditional assumptions regarding freedom of the seas may no longer be valid because modern fishing technology could seriously deplete fishery resources and obstruct methods by which living resources of the sea might be made more productive.[61]

The foregoing developments, which by 1970 had become a kind of movement, pointed strongly toward the establishment of some kind of international regime for the oceans in the not-too-distant future. Although the state of the oceans was of basic interest to the 1972 Conference on the Human Environment in Stockholm, the twenty-fifth session of the General Assembly of the United Nations in December 1970 by Resolution (2750C) called for a conference on the Law of the Sea to be held in 1973. Despite the vast amount of generally ineffective action—legal, technical, and political—that had already occurred regarding the oceans, it seemed probable that some kind of institutional innovation could be expected to come out of these conferences. The types of structures that may emerge will be considered in the succeeding chapter.

UNESCO Initiatives

THE VERY BROAD RANGE of the activities of the United Nations Educational, Scientific, and Cultural Organization makes inevitable its involvement in various aspects of environmental policy.[62] We have already noted its involvement in oceanography and marine affairs. UNESCO has cooperated extensively with other specialized agencies on environmental projects, notably with WHO, WMO, FAO, and with IUCN. An early UNESCO effort that miscarried, the International Hylean (great forest) Amazon Institute to study environmental relationships in the humid tropics may indicate some of the political and administrative problems to be overcome if internationally directed research is to be undertaken on resources within territories falling under the jurisdiction of national-states. More success has been enjoyed by UNESCO's Arid Zone Program. The two phases of this initiative have been exchange of information among countries and stimulation of research on desert problems. The program has been under the direction of an Advisory Committee on Arid Zone Research. Since 1951, UNESCO has published an Arid Zone Research Series, including reviews of research on various aspects of arid environments and the proceedings of symposia, many of which were sponsored by the advisory committee.

UNESCO has from its establishment pursued an active interest in the protection of cultural monuments. Under its constitution [Article I, paragraph 2 (c)], UNESCO is called upon to assure "the conservation and protection of the world's inheritance of books, works of art and monuments of history and science." Program Resolution 3.3411 authorizes the Director-General "to study the possibility of arranging an appropriate system of international protection, at the request of the states concerned, for a few of the monuments that form an integral part of the cultural heritage of mankind." [63] Associated with UNESCO in this area is the International Council of Museums (ICOM) formed independently in 1946 and the International Committee on Monuments, Artistic and Historical Sites, and Archaeological Excavations formed under UNESCO's sponsorship.[64]

On December 11, 1962, the twelfth session of the General Conference of UNESCO adopted a Recommendation "Concerning the Safeguarding of the Beauty and Character of Landscapes and Sites." [65] Considering that men have sometimes impaired the beauty and character of landscapes and sites forming part of their natural environment and so impoverished the cultural heritage of whole regions in all parts of the world, the general conference recommended that member states give effect by law, or in other ways, to the provisions set forth in the recommendation. These included general provisions for safeguarding landscapes and sites, protective measures, urban and rural planning, natural reserves and national parks, zoning of protected sites, and education of the public.

UNESCO has often taken a lead in mobilizing international action on behalf of cultural monuments and values. In 1955, at the request of the Egyptian government, UNESCO helped to establish a special center for research on the ancient art and civilization of the Nile Valley. In 1964, the lake to be created by construction of the Aswan High Dam on the Upper Nile threatened to inundate a number of the most extraordinary monuments of the high period of ancient Egyptian civilization. Among these were four colossal figures of the Pharaoh Rameses II at Abu Simbel, the temples at Philae, and archaeological excavations in Sudanese Nubia. Salvage of the temples and the colossi were beyond the means and inconsistent with the priorities of the United Arab Republic. Through the International Campaign to Save the Monuments of Nubia, UNESCO assembled teams of scientists, engineers, and stone cutters, financed by donations from fifty-two countries, to accomplish what must have been the largest task of archaeological reconstruction ever undertaken.[66]

A very different international salvage effort assisted by UNESCO followed the disastrous 1966 floods in Florence and Venice which damaged many of the first art treasures of the Italian Middle Ages and Renaissance.[67] An International Campaign for Preservation and Restoration of Cultural Property in Italy was launched on December 2, 1966, to assist the Italian people and authorities and "to receive voluntary contributions from governments, public and private institutions, associations and private persons" for this purpose.

In September, 1968, UNESCO sponsored the Intergovernmental Conference of Experts on the Scientific Basis for Rational Use of the Biosphere, which, for obvious reasons, has been foreshortened in everyday reference to the Biosphere Conference.[68] This gathering, at which sixty-four nations and fourteen intergovernmental and thirteen governmental organizations were represented, adopted twenty recommendations, of which the fourteenth urged that

> . . . member States and governing bodies of all United Nations organizations develop comprehensive and integrated policies for the management of the environment, and that international efforts and problems be considered in the formulation of such policies.

Nine aspects of the application of science and technology to environmental management were specified, of which the eighth called for

> The establishment of an appropriate structure and mechanism to assure periodic and comprehensive review of policy and with authority, responsibility, and resources to readjust guidelines and goals and to make deletions, revisions, and realignments in action programmes, based upon empirical experience, scientific and technological advance, and changes in national or world conditions.[69]

The Biosphere Conference also suggested prophetically (Recommendation 17) that the United Nations General Assembly might consider the advisability of a Universal Declaration on the Protection and Betterment of the Human Environment.

Recommendation 20 proposed that "a plan for an international and inter-disciplinary program on the rational utilization and conservation of the resources of the biosphere be prepared for the good of mankind." This recommendation was accepted by UNESCO's General Conference at its fifteenth session, and a plan was developed by UNESCO's Secretariat in consultation with member states, UNESCO's Advisory Committee on Natural Resources Research, and five working groups of experts, for a program of investigation covering the following areas:

1. Inventory and assessment of resources of the biosphere.
2. Systematic observations and monitoring.

3. Research in the structure and functioning of terrestrial and aquatic ecosystems.
4. Research in interchanges in the biosphere brought about by man and the effects of these changes on man.
5. Education and other supporting activities.

The resulting proposal, Man and the Biosphere Program (Document 16/C78), was submitted and approved in October 1970, at the sixteenth session of UNESCO's General Conference.[70] Man and the Biosphere (MAB) consists of thirty-one projects, some of which have already been initiated within the framework of other international programs. The role of UNESCO was not necessarily to execute these projects, but to stimulate and assist their development; to this end, an international coordinating council was proposed. The other United Nations specialized agencies, ICSU and IUCN, would play major roles in the effort as would the individual contributions of national governments. Consistent with the role that UNESCO seems best constituted to play, MAB appears to be primarily an initiative in bringing to bear the resources of international organizations and national governments on the ecological problems growing out of man's relationship to the biosphere. Thus, regardless of its operational capabilities, whose shortcomings critics have sometimes compared with those of academic institutions, UNESCO has been a major catalyst in mobilizing international effort on behalf of protection of the biosphere.

6

Inventing Transnational Structures:

GUIDANCE SYSTEMS TO CONTROL

THE HUMAN IMPACT

A REVIEW OF EFFORTS TO MOBILIZE INTERNATIONAL resources for more effective protection of the biosphere leads to at least three conclusions. First, the structure of international cooperation thus far developed has been inadequate to arrest the deterioration of the environment. Second, the inadequacy of the structure is largely a consequence of indiscriminate deference to the "sovereign" rights of nations—as interpreted by national governments. Third, the concepts guiding national development have tended to be narrowly economic, failing to take account of the full range of human needs, and especially of the ecological requirements for a self-renewing biosphere.

A concomitant of deference to national sovereignty is the difficulty in developing a transnational or supranational basis for protection of the biosphere. National interest, as defined by the heads of governments, has by no means always been consistent with the interests of the governed. It is hardly to be expected that it would be consistent with the protection of the Earth as a whole. The sovereignty concept today tells more about the insecurity of nations than about political reality.[1] International cooperative action is necessary to overcome national parochialism. If nations saw their interests and welfare protected by international action to an extent unattainable by their own unaided efforts, they could more easily dispense with exaggerated interpretations of sovereignty.

Assuming that the present ecological circumstances of humanity are unprecedented, it follows that unprecedented institutional innovations may be required to deal with them. But this line of reasoning is not as yet conceded by most people or their political leaders. It is accepted by a small group of informed persons, chiefly in the scientific professions and in the international conservation movement, whose influence is proportionately much greater than its numbers, in part, a consequence of the power of knowledge. Knowledge does not always lead to action, but it can, especially when events make the circumstances seem urgent. It has been a conjunction of knowledge and disturbing events that have led to a worldwide movement for protection of the biosphere.

Political and institutional conservatism is strong and persistent. If transnational institutions for environmental protection are created, it will not be because they are favored or deemed practicable by national officials; it will be because no other alternatives are available to meet unavoidable needs. Even then, we cannot be sure that modern societies will, or can, adequately accept responsibility for the condition of the world environment. Partial or total failure of present protective efforts cannot be ruled out. Whether the world is ready for the institutional innovations that we will presently consider will only be discovered by trial. Uncertainty about their feasibility should be no bar to discussing them. If they are in some respects utopian, they may be less utopian than the belief that the biosphere can be saved by arrangements now in effect.

Refining the Environmental Problem

IN HISTORICAL RETROSPECT, the latter half of the 1960s may be seen as a period during which an awareness of a world environmental problem gained public recognition. We have noted that the 1963 United Nations Conference on the Application of Science and Technology for the Benefit of the Less-Developed Areas gave little attention to ecological relationships or to the protection and maintenance of the interacting ecosystems of the world as a whole. A now familiar benchmark on the way to an integrating view of the global environment is the often quoted final address of United States Ambassador Adlai E. Stevenson to the thirty-ninth session of the United Nations Economic and Social Council, which met in Geneva on July 9, 1965. Henceforth, declared Stevenson, our thinking must be in the context of human interdependence in the face of vast new dimensions of our science and our discovery. "We travel together passengers on a little spaceship, dependent on its valuable reserves of air and soil; all committed for our safety to its security and peace; preserved from annihilation only by the care, the work, and I will say the love we give our fragile craft." [2]

The spaceship as a model of man's planetary circumstances rapidly passed into popular usage, appearing in the titles of published works by Kenneth E. Boulding, Barbara Ward, R. Buckminster Fuller, and William G. Pollard.[3] This holistic view of the planet and its natural and man-made systems was obviously incongruent with the way in which the world was organized politically. As we have noted, neither the concept, nor the objectives of earlier international conservation efforts, nor the institutions to which they gave rise were directed toward the condition of the world environment as a whole. The Spaceship Earth paradigm was a convenient popular symbol for the more complex and abstract concept of the biosphere. A belief that the viability of the biosphere was threatened and that Spaceship Earth was in jeopardy led logically to a critical look at the adequacy of international machinery for environmental protection.

We have noted that in 1968 and 1969 several major international efforts were undertaken. Among these was the Biosphere Conference sponsored by UNESCO in 1968, and the subsequent announcement of a UNESCO initiative under the project heading of "Man and the Biosphere." In 1969, the International Council of Scientific Unions proposed a major new committee, the Scientific Committee on Problems of the Environment (SCOPE); and the International Union for Conservation of Nature and Natural Resources at its tenth general assembly, meeting in New Delhi, began an extensive internal reorganization to increase its effectiveness. But the principal step

147

was initiated by the Swedish ambassador to the United Nations who, on May 20, 1968, proposed that the United Nations call a world conference on the human environment.

UN Conference on the Human Environment

THE CONFERENCE PROPOSAL was referred for consideration to the Economic and Social Council, which endorsed the idea and recommended it to the General Assembly. On December 3, 1968, by its Resolution 2398 (23), the General Assembly adopted "without objection" the recommendation of ECOSOC, thereby setting in motion preparations for the conference in Stockholm in the summer of 1972.

The resolution of December 3, 1968, seems certain to be a milestone in the history of the relationship between man and his environment. The actual conference aside, the action of the General Assembly marked a worldwide recognition of the need for, in the words of the resolution, "intensified action at the national, regional, and international level in order to limit and, where possible, to eliminate the impairment of the human environment and . . . to protect and improve the natural surroundings in the interest of man." [4]

The objectives of the conference stated in the resolution were "to provide a framework for comprehensive consideration within the United Nations of the problems of the human environment in order to focus the attentoin of governments and public opinion on the importance and urgency of this question and also to identify those aspects of it that can only, or at best, be solved through international cooperation and agreement." After 1968, not only the United Nations and its specialized agencies, but also many other organizations—governmental, nongovernmental, scientific, professional, and civic, were deeply involved in preparations for the conference.

The General Assembly requested the Secretary-General, in consultation with the Advisory Committee on the Application of Science and Technology to Development, associated with the Economic and Social Council, to submit to the General Assembly at its twenty-fourth session a report concerning the nature, scope, and progress of work being done in the field of the human environment, of the principal environmental problems facing developed and developing countries, the time and methods necessary to prepare for the conference, a possible date and place for its convening, and finally, the range of financial implications for the United Nations in connection with the conference.

On May 26, 1969, the Secretary-General submitted his report to the Economic and Social Council, convened for its forty-seventh session.[5] This important document surveyed the main problems of man–environment relationships, reviewed the nature, scope, and progress of research and preventive measures, and reported on the considerations required in planning the Conference. The Secretary-General also reported the invitation of the government of Sweden for the Conference to meet in Stockholm in June 1972. Pursuant to the Secretary-General's report, a preparatory committee for the United Nations Conference on the Human Environment was established under General Assembly Resolution 2581 (24), and an *ad hoc* working group was established by the UN Administrative Committee on Coordination (ACC) representing the specialized agencies, to work with the Preparatory Committee.

The first session of the preparatory committee was held at United Nations headquarters in New York on March 10–20, 1970. It agreed that its main task would be to assist the Secretary-General in selecting topics and headings for the conference as well as in formulating ideas, suggestions, and proposals for its program. The discussion revealed substantial consensus on the character and seriousness of environmental problems, but the complex diversity of the problems' manifestation in various countries was seen as complicating the protective task.[6]

Although problems of environmental pollution were recognized as highly important, the preparatory committee did not make the mistake of defining the problem of man–environment relationships solely as a matter of pollution. Moreover, it was agreed that there should be an appropriate balance in the subjects considered by the conference, between the environmental problems of the more-developed and less-developed areas. A major objective of the conference would be to help developing nations avoid undesirable effects of industrialization. This aspect of the conference might well be one of the most delicate because the leadership in many less-developed countries seems determined that protection of the environment must not retard economic development or the maximum rational use of natural resources. The Preparatory Committee, therefore, placed particular emphasis on the link between environmental protection and national economic development programs.

The twenty-seven member preparatory committee, consisting of the representatives of twenty-one nations, their alternates and advisers, was much too large a body to actually organize the conference, and so a special staff was appointed under the direction of Maurice Strong, an official of the government of Canada, who was also designated as Secretary-General of the conference. Under Strong's sharp and energetic leadership, preparations for Stockholm proceeded with a thoroughness unknown to previous international conferences. A number of intergovernmental working groups were organized to develop proposals and bases for agreement on the major items of an agenda. Emphasis was on action. The time at Stockholm, June 5–17, 1972, would be sufficient for the representatives to consider and adopt agreed statements only if the issues involved had been thoroughly considered by national representatives beforehand. The symbolic value of the Stockholm conference could be great, but its constructive role would heavily depend upon the preparatory work. The important agreements among nations would have to be achieved before Stockholm.

To enlarge the forum for discussion, a series of regional meetings in Asia, Africa, and Latin America were organized in mid-1971, dealing especially with the interests and problems of the developing countries. To assist the preparatory committee and conference staff, basic information and policy papers were invited from a wide variety of national, intergovernmental and scientific organizations. The preparatory committee and the intergovernmental working groups were assisted toward an action-oriented synthesis with great skill by Secretary-General Strong and a small, effectively deployed staff.

At its second session meeting, in Geneva, February 8–19, 1971, the preparatory committee considered a proposed agenda for the conference culminating in the adoption and signature of a Declaration on the Human Environment. The proposed agenda consisted of six main subjects, consideration of which would be divided between three principal committees: [7]

1. The Planning and Management of Human Settlements for Environmental Quality.
2. The Environmental Aspects of Natural Resources Management.
3. Identification and Control of Pollutants and Nuisances of Broad International Significance.
4. Educational, Informational, Social and Cultural Aspects of Environmental Issues.
5. Development and Environment.
6. International Organizational Implications of Action Proposals.

The preparatory committee held a general discussion on the declaration, its principal objectives, and possible form and contents. On December 22, 1970, the Secretary-General had invited governments to comment on the possible form and contents of a draft declaration, and it was now proposed that one of the intergovernmental working groups should be organized to prepare a preliminary draft to be considered by the preparatory committee before its third session, scheduled in New York, September 13–24, 1971. There was substantial agreement among committee members that the declaration should be a document of universally recognized fundamental principles, recommended for action by individuals, national governments, and the international community.

The prospect of an international declaration, and the possibility that new international treaties and new international institutions would come out of the Stockholm conference further stimulated preparations especially in the more-developed countries where environmental policy had already become a major issue. In the preceeding chapter, we noted the activities of the United Nations Associations in a number of countries, and especially the Nordic Declaration of Environmental Rights.[8] Not all of the increased concern with international environmental problems was directly related to the 1972 conference preparations, but much of it was. After 1968, action in many countries took into account the probability of a major increase in international environmental policies and programs in the years ahead.

In the United States, there was action on behalf of international cooperation for environmental protection on many fronts. The National Environmental Policy Act of 1969 (PL 91–190) declared part of its purpose to be "to promote efforts which will prevent or eliminate damage to the environment and biosphere." And Paragraph E, Section 102, stated that all agencies of the federal government shall "recognize the worldwide and long-range character of environment problems and, where consistent with the policy of the United States, lend appropriate support to initiatives, resolutions, and programs designed to maximize international cooperation in anticipating and preventing a decline in the quality of mankind's world environment."

Christian A. Herter, Jr. was appointed Special Assistant to the Secretary of State for Environmental Affairs, and a Committee on International Environmental Affairs was established by the Department of State with a large part of its activities looking toward the Stockholm conference. Relating specifically to Stockholm, a broadly representative committee of citizens was appointed under the chairmanship of Senator Howard H. Baker, Jr., of Tennessee to advise the Secretary of State concerning the United States position on the conference agenda.

International environmental programs and international environmental law and institutions were taken up by many other committees, working groups, and seminars throughout 1970 and 1971. Typical of these efforts were the Committee on International Environmental Programs established by the National Academy of Sciences; a Panel on International Law and the Global Environment established by the American Society of International Law; an International Institute for Environmental Affairs established through private foundation assistance; a Study of Critical Environmental Problems—Man's Impact on the Global Environment, sponsored by the Massachusetts Institute of Technology (July 1970); conferences on international organization and the human environment under the auspices of the

Institute on Man and Science; and the Aspen Institute for Humanistic Studies in the late spring and summer of 1971. These are no more than a sampling of many and varied activities throughout the United States concerning international environmental problems and the United Nations Conference on the Human Environment.

Merely to catalog the events and activities in various nations pertaining to international environmental protection and the Stockholm conference in particular would unduly lengthen this chapter. Before concluding this selective summary, however, it should be pointed out that as early as 1964 a Conference on Law and Science met in Great Britain, sponsored by the David Davies Memorial Institute of International Studies and the British Institute of Comparative and International Law; it dealt extensively with the growing problems of the international environment and with legal and institutional measures for their correction and control. Subsequent to this conference, the David Davies Memorial Institute, through a series of conferences and publications, contributed materially to an understanding of the nature of the international environmental problems and of international action necessary for their solution. Also concerned with the international law of the environment was the organization, World Peace Through Law, which undertook in 1970 and 1971 to prepare a draft convention on environmental cooperation among nations. A preliminary outline was prepared by Carl August Fleischer, Professor of Laws at the University of Oslo, for review by a committee of experts and subsequent consideration at the World Peace Through Law Conference in Belgrade in the summer of 1971.

It may thus be seen that a great deal of activity and organization preceded the Stockholm conference of 1972, all necessary to lay a foundation for more effective cooperation in protection of the biosphere. Even this highly selected listing of interest, information, and involvement is impressive, but it must be remembered that it is primarily the better-educated citizens of the more highly-developed countries who are primarily concerned, and among them, especially those with high-level scientific and governmental responsibilities. Although widespread public concern for environmental quality has developed in the more-developed countries, it could not be said that in many countries environmental quality, particularly when it cuts across what are believed to be national economic interests, has been a compelling public issue. Nevertheless, the activity discussed above suggests more willingness to undertake international cooperation for the environment than for most other international public issues. But the experience of more than a century of international efforts toward the protection of certain aspects of the biosphere has almost without exception indicated that no effective protection can be obtained if governments of the day remain the sole judges of their interests and responsibilities in environmental policy matters, and if the only enforcement of international environmental agreements remains that administered by self-interested national governments. The widespread approval in principle of the United Nations Conference indicated recognition that the present structure of international cooperation, outlined in the preceding chapter, is not equal to the need. It is therefore hardly surprising that early in 1970 a number of public officials and scholars concerned with environmental problems and international organization called for the establishment of new institutions for international cooperation.

Toward Transnational Alternatives

CRITICS OF THE prevailing structure of international cooperation differed, sometimes widely, over the form that institutional innovations should take. Disagreement was primarily over the amount of authority that international organizations could realistically be expected to obtain and to apply. Nearly all agreed that international jurisdiction must be clarified, strengthened, and enlarged; and there was also substantial agreement concerning the functions that might be served by either new or reorganized institutional structures.

Writing in the April 1970 issue of *Foreign Affairs*, George S. Kennan declared, "If the present process of deterioration is to be halted, things are going to have to be done which will encounter formidable resistance from individual governments and powerful interests within individual countries. Only an entity that has great prestige, great authority, and active support from centers of influence within the world's most powerful industrial and maritime nations will be able to make headway against such recalcitrance." [9] He observed that while a single organization possessing such prestige and authority is conceivable, it is harder to conceive of the purpose being served by some fifty to one hundred organizations, each active in a different field, all of them together presenting a pattern too complicated to be grasped by the world public.

Describing the needs which such an agency could fulfill, Kennan wrote,

> All of this would seem to speak for the establishment of a single entity which, while not duplicating the work of existing organizations, could review this work from the standpoint of man's environmental needs as a whole, could make it its task to spot the inadequacies and identify the unfilled needs, could help to keep the governments and leaders of opinion informed as to what ought to be done to meet minimum needs, could endeavor to assure that proper rules and standards are established wherever they are needed, and could where desired, take a hand, vigorously and impartially, in the work of enforcement of rules and standards. It would not have to perform all these various functions itself—except perhaps where there was no one else to do so. Its responsibility should be rather to define their desirable dimensions and to exert itself, and use its influence with governments, to the end that all of them were performed by *someone*, and in an adequate way.[10]

In an address on "The Human Environment and World Order," at the University of Texas on May 14, 1970, U Thant, Secretary-General of the United Nations, declared, "We are faced with an unprecedented situation. This is the first time in its history that mankind faces not merely a threat, but an actual worldwide crisis involving all living creatures, all vegetable life, the entire system in which we live, and all nations large or small, advanced or developing." After reviewing the growing threats to the biosphere, Thant concluded, "If effective measures are to be taken in time, we need something new—and we need it speedily—a global authority with the support and agreement of governments and of other powerful interests, which can pull together all the piecemeal efforts now being made and which can fill the gaps where something needs to be done." [11]

Writing in *The Saturday Review* of July 4, 1970, Richard N. Gardner, Henry L. Moses Professor of Law and International Organizations at Columbia University, called for a global initiative and argued that the United Nations must do much more than is now being done to deal with the deteriorating world environment. Professor Gardner recommended a series of measures by which the United Nations could deal more effectively with environmental problems. He advocated a massive educational and research program to inform the world's peoples, and particularly its political leaders, on problems of the environment. He suggested the organization of a worldwide observation network for monitoring changes in the world's environment, the negotiation of new international agreements to control pollution and build ecological safeguards into international development programs, and, finally, the establishment of a program for protecting the world's threatened scenic, historic, and natural resources heritage. Calling for some restructuring within the United Nations, including a central overview committee of experts on environmental problems, he underscored the need to establish within the UN system an authority to direct and coordinate the work of the specialized agencies. [12]

Similar plans for new approaches to international organization for environmental protection were voiced by Professor Richard A. Falk of Princeton University, [13] by Senator Gaylord Nelson of Wisconsin, [14] and by Senator Warren G. Magnuson of Washington. [15] And a panel of the Study of Critical Environmental Problems sponsored by the Massachusetts Institute of Technology saw a need for more effective international action to control the causes of environmental pollution and for a greatly increased commitment to the task. They observed that:

> Since we believe a realistic appreciation of the difficulties to be a necessary condition to any prospect for success in coping with them, we should perhaps note our present view that to date the inventory of existing organizations is far longer in names than in demonstrated resources, will, or appreciation of the functions to be performed or even of the problems and possibilities. [16]

Inventing An Adequate Structure

SKEPTICS WHO QUESTION the value of new institutions for environmental protection have usually assumed that the future will largely recapitulate the past. Inadequacies of the present United Nations system are often cited as objections to its further development, especially by the addition of new specialized agencies or committees. Suspicion, jealousy, and intransigence among nations are also cited as evidence of the futility of saving the world through institutional reform. There are indeed strong grounds for pessimism about the ability of modern society to protect the biosphere, but they are not conclusive.

Mere institutional reform, unsupported by conviction or commitment, will be ineffective. But even a powerful purpose and intent will be frustrated if the means to action are inadequate. An intent, if sufficiently strong, persistent, and pervasive, will seek the means to its realization. Those who doubt the need for institutional innovation correspondingly doubt the unprecedented danger of an imminent global environmental crisis. There is, as yet, a shocking ignorance of the present ecological state of the world among many otherwise highly educated people. The recalcitrance of many national leaders is all too real. But the environmental crisis is even more real; unchecked, it will override the opinions, lives, and fortunes of the skeptical objectors. The toughness of the environmental problems must be matched by toughness of the remedies—if there are to be remedies.

The unprecedented situation of a man-made global environment crisis requires unprecedented political action. Modern society has created a global technoeconomy without guidance, safeguards, or restraints to foresee or control its ecological effects; and the result has been ecologically disastrous. A limited world polity has become necessary. This is far less than general world government, for which no political basis presently exists. But specialized government, within agreed areas of common concern and based on demonstrable evidence regarding the state of the physical world, must be possible if the survival of human society as it has evolved thus far is possible.

Building on society as it now exists, it should be possible to invent institutional arrangements that would enable man to cope globally with the consequences of his unecological behavior within the framework of existing political realities. Some national prerogatives must be superseded, but national sovereignty, in an operational sense, has already lost much of its meaning because it is unable to protect peoples and nations from global environmental deterioration. A legalistic principle, with some historical basis but diminishing benefits, is relinquished in certain particulars to gain otherwise unobtainable advantages. This is not unprecedented behavior among nations, for sovereignty in practice has never been absolute—and national-states are themselves relatively recent inventions in the social history of mankind.

At this time, the first priority in institutional innovation is to identify those requirements for protection of the biosphere that are not being met in the present configuration of international agencies. And because these functions will inevitably interact, institutions to perform them must be structured for efficient interrelationships. Thus, the first tasks of invention should be to (1) identify the critical points of needed action, (2) determine the relationships among them, and then (3) devise a corresponding structure that will effectively implement international and transnational efforts for global environmental protection. In devising this structure, it would be prudent and practical not to disturb existing institutional arrangements more than necessary. But because the tasks and techniques of environmental policy cannot be fully foreseen, the structure should, by design, be open-ended and incomplete so that it may grow and evolve as need requires.

Although there are alternative ways in which nations may cooperate to protect the biosphere, not all are equally suitable to the purpose. Arrangements less adequate for environmental purposes may be preferred for other reasons—economic, military, or ideological. But the unity of the biosphere and the ultimate indivisibility of the sea and air set parameters for an adequate system of global protection. The complex systems of nature must be matched by coordinate systems of man if man's preferred relationships to nature are to be managed in the interest of continuing human welfare.

The structure needed for the protection of the world environment thus must be a comprehensive and evolving system. The need cannot be answered by a unitary, self-contained organization because of the diverse, complex, and dynamic character of the task. But an effective system for environmental protection must be a coherent system in which reciprocal relationships exist among its components, in which the parts sustain the whole and the whole reinforces each of the parts. And although this coherence requires a primary center for functional coordination, provision should also be made for the coordinative function to evolve within the system. The movement of authority within the system, necessarily decentralized in the initial international stage, should be toward more comprehensive and general coordinated action. Thus, the system should be inherently capable of transformation from an international through a transnational to a supranational structure at some future time without losing its confederative character.

The system cannot be fully established at its inception. In a dynamic world, its structure may never be completed. It is therefore important that its initial structure be expandable. The components of the system should be seen as building blocks, able to be fitted together in changing combinations as circumstances may require. To achieve such a system, some forecast of its possible futures is needed. As all possibilities cannot be foreseen, and prospects can be expected to change over time, no forecast can be precise. But precision is not needed, as one purpose of a forecast is to build appropriate flexibility into the system from the outset. Psychological flexibility is especially important in institutions dealing with progressive change. Administrative structures and their personnel tend to resist changes in function and status. Devices are therefore needed at both national and international levels to overcome organizational inertia and resistance. The expectation of organizational change should be established at the outset among governments, agencies, and personnel involved.

Development of the system would be influenced as much by political acceptability as by technical capability. The system could grow no faster than peoples and governments permit. It would, therefore, be a mistake to attempt to construct the system solely upon the basis of technical processes, which are subject to modification and displacement by new methods. The basis of the system should be its political objectives, not its operational techniques. Techniques can be developed within a policy-directed system. They are already being developed through national governments, especially in the United States. For this reason, extended discussions of how and what to monitor, for example, are not necessarily germane to the establishment of an environmental protection system. Technical requirements are, of course, important in various detailed aspects of organizational development, but it is no derogation to describe them as micro-aspects in contrast to the macro-outline of the general system.

Institutional Innovations: Possibilities and Alternatives

IN A WORLD OF NATIONS, global action must proceed on two levels. The national level is obvious, because it is the focus of jurisdiction over persons and property and of control over human uses of the environment. The organization and administration of national efforts will be considered in Chapter 7. International efforts heretofore attempted have been described in the foregoing chapters, and the need for strengthening or reconstituting many of them has long been evident. In the future, the urgent need for a common jurisdiction over the oceans and certain other critical aspects of the biosphere can be met effectively only by transnational structures—agencies or groups of agencies that, although created by international agreement, operate thereafter *with national consent*, directly upon certain problems or in relation to persons and property (such as ships on the high seas) without need to refer to national governments. Such bodies would, of course, be responsible to a common agent of nations, such as the General Assembly of the United Nations or the policy-determining bodies of the other intergovernmental organizations described in Chapter 5.

The following possible elements of a world structure incorporate a wide range of suggestions from many students and other observers of international organizations. Six types of international or transnational arrangements would seem to be necessary to undertake effectively the tasks of controlling human impact upon the biosphere. In summary, they are:

1. A high level intergovernmental body to formulate international environmental policy and to help coordinate the work of United Nations specialized agencies and other organizations concerned with the global environment.

2. An institutional extension of the functions of an ombudsman, providing procedures short of judicial action for the investigation and resolution of disputes and controversies regarding the protection of the biosphere.

3. An independent body for scientific advice, investigation, testing, criticism, and the development of scientific competence in the environmental sciences, with a limited research capability corresponding generally to the center proposed by the *Ad Hoc* Committee on Problems of the Environment established by ICSU.

4. A global environmental monitoring network; a systematic allocation of responsibility among existing or yet to be established agencies for monitoring selected phenomena in the biosphere.

5. An international regime for the oceans; a coordinative multiple-agency structure to supervise and administer the use of the high seas and the deep sea bed as far as nations are willing to intrust this responsibility to international jurisdiction.

6. A fund to assist nations in preserving their cultural treasures, endangered wildlife, and distinctive natural areas and landscapes, especially in emergencies.

Obviously, there are many possible variations in the organization of these institutions and in their relationships among themselves and with existing international agencies. In the following discussion, we will attempt to identify the more likely variations and alternatives. But it is not feasible to describe all possible combinations; and what, in fact, develops could be in directions other than those which now appear most likely. The proposals that follow are, therefore, most useful in the functions

and functional interrelationships that they represent. Nomen-
clature and structural details are, in this context, of secondary
importance.

An Environmental Council

THE MOST CRITICAL FUNCTION in a global system for protecting the biosphere is that of formulating and proposing
worldwide policies. This function implies an agency at the
highest levels of international politics because, to be effective, it
must command the cooperation and respect of both national
governments and United Nations specialized agencies. Although
such an agency could conceivably be established outside of the
United Nations structure, it is doubtful that it could be fully
effective if it were unrelated to what has become the major
configuration of international organizations for public purposes.
A principal function of such an agency would be to better coordinate the environmental policies and efforts of the UN specialized agencies, and it is not clear that this could be done by an
authority lying wholly without the UN structure.

The International Council of Scientific Unions (ICSU)
or perhaps a new and more broadly based scientific organization
could constitute an environmental science advisory council to
assist the United Nations and the specialized agencies in environmental policy making. But the functions of policy formulation
and coordination are political, in the broadest sense, rather than
scientific. Scientific bodies may play an important and objectifying
role in environmental policy making, but the task of actually
formulating and proposing policies for national and international
action is a political and not a scientific function. Nevertheless,
the policy-making process has need of a sound and credible
scientific input, and this could be substantially supplied by ICSU,
or perhaps more appropriately by an organization also competent
in areas not included in the present structure of ICSU—social and
behavioral science and engineering.

Although the contrasting modes of investigation and management in science and politics need to be distinguished and
generally separated, they must be brought together at the high-

est levels of policy. Thus, to the three councils which have been established at the highest levels of the United Nations—Security, Economic and Social, and Trusteeship, a fourth, Environmental, might be added. This Council should be co-equal to the three present councils. The environmental concerns of the United Nations have heretofore been channeled largely through the Economic and Social Council, which perhaps should continue to deal with certain aspects of man's environmental relationships, possibly those relating to the social environment. But the magnitude and urgency of the task of environmental protection requires an independent advocate, and a position at the highest levels of the United Nations structure somewhat different from that appropriate to ECOSOC. The Security Council (without the unilateral veto) might be a better model for the Environmental Council, with the nations of high technology that contribute most heavily to world pollution and which could contribute most effectively to its remedy as permanent members, and the more numerous less heavily industrialized countries represented by rotating members.

The council would not merely react to issues and attempt to resolve them; its role would be that of advocate on behalf of a self-renewing biosphere. Its primary function, as we have indicated, would be to aid positively in formulating and proposing policies for the General Assembly, and it would assist the Secretary-General and the United Nations Administrative Committee on Coordination in allocating and coordinating environment-related functions among the UN specialized agencies. The Environmental Council would also have formal liaison with nongovernmental organizations such as the International Union for Conservation of Nature and Natural Resources and independent international bodies such as the International Atomic Energy Agency. This would be the body that, in cooperation with the specialized agencies and an independent science advisory body, would promote the development and adoption of criteria and standards to govern the uses of the biosphere. It would issue an annual report to the General Assembly on the state of the biosphere and would recommend specific action in critical environmental situations. The most effective coordinative function of the council might be to develop a comprehensive plan of action in whose making and execution national governments, regional groups, scientific organizations, and the UN affiliates and specialized agencies would participate. Council initiative could organize the planning and assist in allocating responsibilities for a World Environmental Program. A goal of stopping or reversing all man-caused deterioration of the biosphere within a decade would be a mighty challenge to the new council, and also provide a new and constructive focus for international cooperation.

Although the Environmental Council would require a permanent secretariat, it would not need large scientific and technical staffs of its own. The resources of the UN specialized agencies and designated nongovernmental bodies like ICSU, IUCN, and the proposed science advisory body would be available to it. Although the council might establish its own staff, a more efficient arrangement might be to create an environmental policy unit under the UN Secretariat. The executive officer of the council might be a UN Commissioner for the Protection of the Environment, an officer proposed by the United States President's Commission for the Twenty-Fifth Anniversary of the United Nations,[17] or an Undersecretary-General of the United Nations, as recommended by the Committee an International Environmental Programs of the US National Academy of Sciences. This officer would be the head of such UN staff unit or office as might be created and might be hoped to provide major leadership in the work of the council.

In establishing an Environmental Council, lessons learned from experience with the first three councils of the UN should be applied. For example, unlike ECOSOC, its membership should be small enough for effective deliberations. Because of the complex issues that it would need to consider, it is doubtful if it should number much more than twenty-five. Its members should be required to have qualifications to assure its competence to deal with the difficult problems encountered at the interfaces of science, technology, economics, and politics. Although the council members must be acceptable to their national governments, it would be unnecessarily risky to leave the nomination solely to national political authorities. One possible arrangement for securing at least a minimum of competence would be for the

President of the General Assembly, to make appointments to the council, or, alternatively, for the Secretary-General of the United Nations to appoint members from a roster prepared by an independent advisory body. Not all council members should be scientists; and those scientists certified as suitable members should have shown competence in policy-making or administration, or else have demonstrated a broad grasp of human needs and values. The council must have both political ability and scientific credibility.

If the membership of the council is to reinforce its mission, it would be desirable to deemphasize inherently divisive combinations. National identity cannot be avoided in a world governed by nations, but national representation should be secondary to considerations of competence to deal with environmental policy. Division between more- and less-developed countries could encourage conflict within the council. Insofar as national representation by stages of technoeconomic development is useful or politically expedient, a wide range or full spectrum of stages might be preferable to a grouping into camps.

Establishment of the council could be accomplished in any of at least three ways:

1. Amending the Charter of the United Nations.
2. An international agreement supplementary to the charter.
3. Resolution of the General Assembly.

The latter arrangement would be the most expeditious, as the negotiation of charter amendments under Article 108 has caused misgivings in many national governments and could take as long as three years. There would, however, be an advantage to the council in receiving charter status because, under Article 103, its provisions would then prevail over the constitutions of the specialized and other UN agencies, thus strengthening its ability to assist in policy formulating and coordination. A practical sequence of action might be for the 1972 Conference on the Human Environment to recommend creation of the council, for the General Assembly to respond to establishing the council by resolution and simultaneously initiating an amendment of the charter. Thus, by the time that the amendment was adopted, the task of organizing the council could have been completed, and the new agency could begin to function with full effectiveness.

The council could also be established by a separate treaty, associated with the United Nations but not incorporated within its charter. Informal relationships could then be developed to serve until the day when need will compel reluctant nations to support practical improvements in the charter.

To be fully effective, the council would need real powers in relation to the activities of the UN specialized agencies and other international organizations. But its coordinative role need not involve direct action with the specialized agencies. To avoid the conflict inherent in direct council interposition, its recommendations should go to the political authorities to whom the council and the agencies are both responsible—the national governments. As the UN system is presently constituted, such coordination as is possible depends upon agreement among the member governments.

An annual report of the council to the General Assembly could be a persuasive instrument of policy. Although the General Assembly is not strictly a legislative body, the need for global action to protect the biosphere would tend to force it to become increasingly governmental within the broad but definable area of environmental policy. There is more demonstrable valid knowledge in that field than in many into which the Assembly and the existing councils have ventured. In no other area of worldwide common concern is there greater opportunity for objective, factually-based, problem-focused policy making. Perhaps in this specific area of public policy, some form of limited world government may find its first cautious beginning.

Agency for Prevention and Settlement of Environmental Disputes

THE MOST CONSERVATIVE approach to global environmental protection would be through a regime of international treaties administered concurrently by the respective parties. However, without a readily available means for the interpretation of treaties and for fact-finding in controverted issues among nations, the protective value of treaties would be minimal. This adjudicative function has been provided generally by the International Court of Justice which, under its governing statute, might adapt its structure and procedures to deal more effectively with environment-related disputes among national states.[18] For example, the court may establish special chambers composed of three or more judges for particular categories of cases. Environmental cases could constitute such a category. And under Article 30 of its statute, the court may appoint special assessors, persons of special technical competence to sit with the judges but without the right to vote on decisions. In addition, under Article 50, the court has broad authority to entrust "any individual, body, bureau, commission or other organization with the task of carrying out an enquiry or giving an expert opinion." For those disputes in which national governments are the actual or only appropriate parties, the International Court of Justice affords ample means for the resolution of differences. But Article 34 of its statute denies the right of access to individuals and corporations. As multinational corporations play increasing roles in the world's economy, and as we move to prevent environmental damage in preference to pressing claims for damages, additional means for resolving international differences on environmental issues may be required.

A facility short of full-scale international judicial action may be needed to obtain the cooperation of nations in observing international agreements pertaining to the environment. A United Nations Agency for the Prevention and Settlement of Environmental Disputes might, therefore, be established as an independent fact-finding body whose function would be to obtain peaceful compliance with treaty obligations and United Nations environmental policy. Consideration should be given to associating the agency with the International Court of Justice. Unlike the so-called Permanent Court of Arbitration, however, the agency should, as circumstances warrant, develop a full-time staff with the competencies needed to analyze and resolve environmental controversies.

There are precedents for such an agency. The 1958 Convention on Fishing and Conservation of the Living Resources of the High Seas provides under Article 9 for a special five-member commission to resolve disputes under the treaty. Similarly, provision has been made for procedures short of formal adjudication under the International Coffee Agreement of 1968 and in the draft treaty on an international regime for the deep seabed prepared for the Department of State of the United States. Action by the Environmental Council might help prevent disputes, but issues bearing upon law and legal rights and obligations would more appropriately be handled by an agency closely related to the International Court.

This agency might function somewhat as an international ombudsman. Its services should not be restricted to national-states, and should probably be available to international organizations within the United Nations system, to such non-governmental international organizations as the IUCN, and ultimately, perhaps, to all international organizations including multinational business corporations. As with the Environmental Council, an Agency for Prevention and Settlement of Environmental Disputes might have recourse to the research facilities of an independent science advisory body to assist in determining the facts in particular cases. The agency should probably be empowered to seek advisory opinions from the International Court of Justice; and cases beyond the competence of the agency to resolve could be referred to the International Court or to the United Nations Environmental or Security Councils in accordance with the circumstances. Cases calling for arbitration could be referred to the Permanent Court of Arbitration. Indeed, if it were reorganized along the lines proposed at the Hague Conference of 1907, the Permanent Court could be made to meet the environmental need. But the inquiry or ombudsman functions exceed the arbitral function, and whatever facility is established should not be restricted to only one mode of resolving conflicts.

It would also be important that such an agency maintain continuing liaison with the Environmental Council. In particular cases, the council might be requested to restate or clarify the policies or standards that it had promulgated if differences of interpretation threatened to create controversy. For a variety of reasons, it would seem undesirable for the Environmental Council itself to review specific disputes except to apply basic principles. Its deliberation should be concerned broadly with policies and principles; and it should avoid becoming involved in detailed altercations, which would distract it from its more fundamental and long-range purpose and which might make more difficult its interaction with national governments and the UN specialized agencies.

A Center for Scientific Advice and Research

WITHOUT A SUPPORTING FACILITY for the gathering, analyzing, processing, and dissemination of information on environmental issues, the work of an Environmental Council would be severely constrained. Although much pertinent data is available through a variety of sources, the means to bring it together in meaningful relationships and in forms useful to decision makers does not now exist. The task of formulating policy proposals and analysing their implications would be appropriate to the previously mentioned UN unit, which could provide a secretariat for the Environmental Council. These are policy-related functions, which, in the interest of objectivity and public credibility should be separated from basic scientific fact-finding and analysis. Hence the need for a politically independent body for scientific advice and research on global environmental problems.

Several proposals have been advanced for establishing an global environmental science center, notably United States Senator Warren G. Magnuson's Resoluton for a World Environmental Institute,[19] and the Report of an *Ad Hoc* Committee of the International Council of Scientific Unions recommending the establishment of the Scientific Committee on Problems of the Environment (SCOPE) with an International Center for the Environment (ICE) under its sponsorship.[20] Because the Magnuson proposal closely resembles the ICE, and because SCOPE has been created and is proceeding to consider the possibility of an international environmental research center, the ICE model will be drawn upon in part, as an example of what might be undertaken. But there are alternative ways that the functions of scientific information and research might be organized, even within the general plan proposed for ICE. The following discussion does not, therefore, reflect in all particulars the emphasis and priorities specified by the *Ad Hoc* Committee of ICSU.

Whatever its sponsorship or structure, the science advisory and research facility should be a credible scientific institution, and, therefore, should not be charged with policy-making, operational, or administrative functions beyond those essential to its tasks of investigation and interpretation. Seven functions may be distinguished as necessary and appropriate to its role in an international structure for environmental protection:

1. To collect, analyze, and publish data on the state of the biosphere.
2. To study, devise, and advise in relation to monitoring environmental phenomena.
3. To develop criteria and propose standards (to the Environmental Council) for protection of the biosphere.
4. To estimate the probability and extent of environmental hazards, and provide "early warning" service.
5. To investigate environmental problems, to establish facts and identify alternative strategies or solutions.
6. To train and develop researchers and technicians.
7. To provide reliable and credible scientific advice to the Environmental Council and the World Court and to national governments generally.

As an independent scientific organization interrelating with other scientific bodies established at national and international levels, it could be a source of objective information and analysis on environmental issues for the United Nations and other international agencies, and especially for the proposed Environmental Council.

The ordinary functions of this body would be performed by a multidisciplinary council of high competence, nominated perhaps by the world's leading international scientific unions or associations. This body, through its executive officer or chairman, would direct a limited research facility, supplemented by environmental research institutions throughout the world. This capability is needed for two reasons: first, to strengthen the independence of the advisory council which otherwise would be totally dependent upon UN or national facilities; and second, to strengthen the acceptability of its findings as coming from a center in which qualified nationals of all countries could participate and which was unconstrained by the views of particular nations or regional groups. Thus it is not so much the global nature of environmental problems that calls for its establishment as it is the need for international cooperation in their solution. Research on global environmental problems does not necessarily require an international research facility, but practical efforts to protect the biosphere may be helped greatly by such an institutional arrangement.

The information gathering and analysis functions of the center would be basic to all of its other activities. The center would engage in original research but, more importantly, would provide central collecton and collation of information and research findings generated in other institutions throughout the world. This function corresponds generally to the intelligence service suggested by the *Ad Hoc* Committee, a point at which the data collected by a decentralized Global Environment Monitoring Network could be assembled, analyzed, and evaluated. Thus, a very major function of this intelligence service would be to relate its research and information gathering directly to environmental monitoring. This collating and evaluating function could lead to the publication of environmental information both in ways useful to scientists and in ways useful to political decision makers and the nonscientific public generally.

The second of our listed functions, first of the services to be provided by ICE and recommended by the *Ad Hoc* Committee, is the development of a system of environmental monitoring.[21] In the language of the *Ad Hoc* Committee, the monitoring service would "administer the activities of the Monitoring Commission" of SCOPE. The word "administer," covers many meanings. It is doubtful that an International Center for the Environment should actually engage in routine technical and instrumental details of actual monitoring. Although it would probably be unwise to exclude the actual functions of monitoring from the activities of an International Center for the Environment, its more appropriate function would be to study and advise upon monitoring procedures and to design the operations and coordinate the scientific information of the Global Environmental Monitoring

Network. As it is highly improbable that the diverse aspects of environmental monitoring could or should be brought under one roof, it is important that there be, somewhere, an organization with scientific credibility and objectivity capable of monitoring the monitors.

The third function, following directly from the first two, would be to develop scientific criteria to assist the Environmental Council, the General Assembly of the United Nations, the specialized agencies, and national governments in guiding the actions of peoples and governments on behalf of the biosphere. On the basis of these criteria, standards of conduct in relation to the environment might be recommended by the center through the Environmental Council, but the center would not itself promulgate standards for action.

A logical fourth function would be to estimate the hazards in man–environmental relationships, and to recommend to the Environmental Council, or to the General Assembly and national governments, priorities for action indicated by scientific evidence. Thus, the International Center would provide a warning system for both immediate and longer-range effects, a service which it could probably perform best if unencumbered by operational responsibilities.

The fifth function would be the investigation of specific environmental problems, either on its own initiative or in cooperation with other organizations who might request its services. Among these organizations, an Environmental Council would in principle be the most important, the center providing in effect independent staff resources for the council. Special studies, however, might be undertaken for a United Nations Agency for Prevention and Settlement of Environmental Disputes, for the UN specialized agencies and the International Atomic Energy Agency, for national governments, and for regional groups. This investigatory function would be more like problem-solving than basic theoretical environmental research, and it could be supported through contractual or retainer arrangements with the organizations that were the recipients of the research findings.

The sixth function, not specifically identified by the *Ad Hoc* Committee, would be the training of researchers and technicians in the environmental sciences, and this training might be provided in several ways. The *Ad Hoc* Committee had listed the organization of symposia as one of the functions of the center; training grants and internships would be another conventional means of developing scientific competence in the environmental field. The center might also provide formal courses for administrators, field investigators, and environmental technicians, and some of this work might be done in connection with the UN specialized agencies and other international or regional organizations concerned with environmental matters.

Last but most important of these seven functions would be to give scientific information and advice on environmental problems. This advice would come from the governing council of the center and could take several forms. One might be annual or periodic assessments of the physical condition of the biosphere, identifying trends and noting significant events and consequences. Other reports might be issued routinely for specific environmental phenomena. Advice or information would presumably be made available to UN agencies and to national governments upon their request.

A substantial part of the budget of the center might be provided through the UN Environmental Council, but the integrity and credibility of the center would be enhanced by multiple sources of support. Some funds might be contributed through national academies of science and channeled through international scientific associations. A World Environment Fund might provide partial support for basic research activities, assuring support of long-range investigations that are seldom attractive to political budget makers.

Global Environmental Monitoring Network

In a survey of international environmental monitoring programs using intergovernmental or international nongovernmental organizational machinery to coordinate their activities, Robert Citron of the Smithsonian Institution found ten that were in actual operation in mid-1970, seven that were in various stages of planning, and five that were proposed.[22] None of the operational programs had been established exclusively or even primarily to monitor environmental pollution on a global scale, although the World Health Organization through its programs of global environmental health monitoring was concerned with the surveillance of air and water pollution and of radiation hazards. Among the planned and proposed programs, several were interrelated or overlapping so that the programs actually established may be fewer than those under consideration at the present time. Marine pollution problems in particular have been under study by an interagency group of experts formed at the request of the UN General Assembly (GESAMP).[23]

Effective action to protect the biosphere depends upon a reliable system for identifying, measuring, and analyzing destructive processes. Several movements have developed within the scientific community for monitoring environmental change, particularly in relation to toxic pollutants and changes in the atmosphere. Earlier monitoring efforts, such as the World Meteorological Organization's World Weather Watch, have been concerned chiefly with predicting the behavior of natural systems. By the late 1960s, however, concern with man-induced effects outweighed the more traditional aspects of scientific investigation.

Concern with the impoverishment, degradation, and pollution of the global environment found international expression in the Special Committee for the International Biological Program (SCIBP) established by the International Council of Scientific Unions. In 1968, SCIBP appointed an *Ad Hoc* Committee on Global Monitoring, which in September 1970 submitted a report recommending a global system for monitoring the world's environment and assessing short-term and long-term changes.[24] Accompanying the report of this SCIBP committee were three technical reports prepared, respectively, by the USSR Committee of Biologists, the Task Force on Global Networks for Environmental Monitoring of the United States Committee for the International Biological Program, and the Ecological Research Committee of the Swedish Natural Science Research Council.[25]

The SCIBP committee chaired by Bengt Lundholm of Sweden, with W. F. Blair of the United States, and M. M. Smirnow of the Soviet Union as the other members, were agreed that the technology is available to monitor both the physical-chemical environment and the biota. The committee observed that the various operating and developing networks for environmental monitoring generally neglected biological as contrasted with physical parameters and urged that global monitoring should have as a major aim the "acquisition of data pertinent to the global movement of biologically significant materials (such as pesticides, heavy metals, chemical compounds in general, and pathogenic organisms) in the world's air, waters, and lands, and the acquisition of data pertinent to their effects on the world's ecosystems and their components." The committee recommended further that after a United Nations survey of existing and planned systems for environmental monitoring, there be organized a global monitoring system taking cognizance of presently existing capabilities and expanding these where necessary. To implement this recommendation, it was urged that the United Nations draft and adopt a charter covering the necessary national and international agreements, and that the newly established Scientific Committee on Problems of the Environment (SCOPE) serve as scientific adviser to the global monitoring system.

SCOPE, officially established by the International Council of Scientific Unions in August 1970, moved to create a Commission on Monitoring. Close relationships existed between SCIBP and SCOPE, and the *Ad Hoc* Committee on Global Monitoring of SCIBP was adopted as a nucleus for the new Commission on Monitoring set up by SCOPE. There was obvious need for rapid and considered action if the scientific community was to make a significant contribution to the preparations for the United Nations Conference on the Human Environment in 1972. It was generally agreed, therefore, that the SCOPE Commission for Monitoring be asked to undertake detailed planning for the location and coordination of the global monitoring system, including the problems of central data storage and retrieval; and that, at an early stage, the planning include feasibility and methodological studies at national and transnational levels.

An important contribution to the discussions on environmental monitoring and to international action on behalf of the environment generally was made by the previously noted Study of Critical Environmental Problems (SCEP), sponsored by the Massachusetts Institute of Technology. Among its recommendations, the final report urged "an immediate study of global monitoring to examine the scientific and political feasibility of integration of existing and planned monitoring programs, and to set out steps necessary to establish an optimal system." [26]

Illustrative of the diversity and complexity of the movement for environmental monitoring have been the efforts of the UNESCO-connected International Oceanographic Commission (IOC) which in May 1969 sponsored a meeting of scientists and administrators on the Mediterranean island of Ponza. Among the agencies represented were the Advisory Committee on Marine Resources Research of FAO, the Scientific Committee on Oceanic Research (SCOR) of the International Council of Scientific Unions, and the World Meteorological Organization. The meeting issued a report entitled "Global Ocean Research" which recommended a global monitoring system for marine pollution and a biological program oriented to fisheries development. [27] The report also recommended studies in ocean circulation and ocean–atmosphere interaction and a massive research effort in marine geology. (In discussing the relationship between the earth sciences and oceanography, Gifford C. Ewing, Senior Scientist at the Woods Hole Oceanographic Institution, has said, "The relationship between the ocean and the overlying atmosphere is so intimate that neither can be adequately described without including the other." [28])

One of the more extensive operational environmental monitoring systems is the previously noted World Weather Watch, sponsored by the World Meteorological Organization to develop global facilities for meteorological observations, communications, data analysis and processing. One outcome of the WWW should be improved weather predictions, and especially long-range weather forecasts. [29] Full implementation of the World Weather Watch calls for the development of more comprehensive global data collection and data processing systems. Designed in part to meet this need is the projected Integrated Global Ocean Station System (IGOSS), sponsored by the International Oceanographic Commission with cooperation of WMO.

But questions of what, how, who, and why promise to

complicate any attempt to establish a global monitoring effort. And beyond these questions remains the problem of coordinating a global network and applying its findings to policy decisions and action. Commenting on the establishment of global monitoring systems using instruments deployed routinely over the oceans, Henry Stommel, Professor of Oceanography at the Massachusetts Institute of Technology, observes, "there is a deep division between those who want to establish a large-scale operational system in the ocean and those who want to understand the phenomena occurring in the ocean." There will have to be a major engineering effort to develop this understanding, but the organizers propose a fairly rigid and permanent observing network and the scientists want a varied series of experiments.[30] Professor Stommel argues for a "carefully steered evolution of large-scale experiments before setting up a routine global monitoring system." IGOSS, he declares, "is not a scientific program, it is a future system for reporting data internationally, which is meant to serve needs of immediate protection." [31]

Many concerns and anxieties underlie these proposals. But growing awareness of the threats to the biosphere, the international origins of the proposals, the prestige of their sponsors, and practical experience already gained give hope for the establishment of a comprehensive global environmental monitoring network before the mid-1970s. And, although presently established monitoring may continue under present management, the expansion of monitoring efforts now recommended will probably require the establishment of new agencies or the reorganization of old ones, so that at the very least there will be a coordinative mechanism through which the information relevant to international policy and action for protection of the biosphere may be brought together.

It has been suggested that the center for environment advice and research should help to design a worldwide network of monitoring but not undertake to operate any substantial part of it. The operational functions would be performed according to a comprehensive and systematic plan in which a large number of national and international agencies would be involved. The task of devising a workable system would be partly one of coordination. The various monitoring programs could be coordinated by appropriate agencies; for example, atmospheric phenomena by the World Meteorological Organization, soil conditions by the Food and Agriculture Organization, and wildlife populations by the International Union for Conservation of Nature and Natural Resources. To a large extent, however, actual monitoring operations will be undertaken by agencies of national governments. In some of the developing countries, special education and training may be required so that nationals from those countries may participate in the global effort; if wisely planned, such training could improve the general level of understanding and technical ability to deal with environmental and scientific issues.

The tasks of monitoring the primarily physical aspects of the environment, for all their complexities, are the simpler and might be the more easily coordinated; because the greater number of them involve interactions of the oceans and the atmosphere, there would be logic in bringing them together in one agency. There are, however, objections both within the United Nations system and among certain of the leading national governments to the creation of new UN specialized agencies. One possible way of resolving this problem would be to reorganize the World Meteorological Organization into an Oceanic and Atmospheric Organization or, if seismic and other related phenomena were included, into a World Geophysical Organization. The WMO is already engaged in developing a system of monitoring atmospheric change through the World Weather Watch and has also been involved in hydrological studies. It would do no violence to scientific or administrative structure to reorganize this agency as the primary operational and coordinative body for the global monitoring of geophysical changes. A World Geophysical Organization would logically provide forecasting and warning services in all geophysical areas, including earthquakes, volcanic activity and electromagnetic phenomena not caused by man. Going beyond the present responsibilities of WMO, the new agency might be authorized to inspect the uses of the air and sea in relation to the criteria and standards of conduct adopted by the Environmental Council, although this function might more appropriately be performed by whatever authority was established to administer the uses of the oceans. At the outset, it would probably be unwise to burden the organization with policing functions, but arrangements could be made to report its findings to the proposed body for scientific advice and research, to the Environmental Council, and, logically, to the organization responsible for controlling uses of the oceans, as well.

The biological aspects of environmental monitoring would be less easily allocated, since they need not be confined to the United Nations agencies. Organizations such as the IUCN may play an important role in the systematic surveillance of wildlife populations and ecosystems. Monitoring the status of wildlife has been a major function of IUCN, which publishes the *Amber Book* of depleted species and *Red Book* of endangered species. Changes in the biota may, like the canary in the coal mine, provide significant indications of pervasive trends in the biosphere and of emerging environmental hazards.

The monitoring of social and economic phenomena raises some obvious methodological and jurisdictional questions. There are highly important social and economic parameters to the total human environment, but there is also the Economic and Social Council of the United Nations charged with concern for social and economic affairs. Some, but not all, social and economic data is environmentally significant, just as there is frequently social and economic significance in physical science and biological data. It would seem desirable, however, that such social and economic information with important environmental implications should be made available to whatever agency was created for scientific advice and research and which should have facilities for research in social and behavioral science at least sufficient to enable it to obtain assistance from those sciences, professions, and disciplines not otherwise represented in the agency staff. In the social and economic area, data gathering, analysis, and reporting might be coordinated or, so far as feasible, undertaken jointly between the proposed science agency and research center and those UN and other international agencies primarily concerned with human affairs, including public health. In this effort, the International Social Science Council (ISSC) might play an advisory role.

In summary, a Global Environmental Monitoring Network

is more likely to emerge as a coordinated structure of autonomous components than a single organization. Design and review of the network might appropriately be undertaken by the ICSU Scientific Committee on Problems of the Environment or perhaps by a completely new institution for scientific advice and research. A large and important sector of the physical environment, however, might be monitored by an expanded WMO, possibly redesignated as the World Geophysical Organization. The network could serve the advancement of basic scientific knowledge as well as the routine surveillance of environmental change, but its main *raison d'être* would be the protection of the biosphere.

An International Regime for the Oceans

IN THE PRECEDING CHAPTER we noted evidence of a growing movement for international action to protect the oceans from resource depletion and pollution. Need for more effective methods of control were voiced in the preparatory committee for the 1972 Stockholm Conference; and the General Assembly of the United Nations in Resolution 2750 (25), December 17, 1970, called for a world conference on the law of the sea in 1973. Marine pollution, uses of the seabed, and the protection of the living resources of the sea have been and continue to be the subject of innumerable seminars, working groups, and conferences. The International Maritime Consultative Organization has sponsored a major conference on oil pollution also for 1973.[32] Documentation on oceanography and marine affairs is as extensive as in any field of environment-related studies.

As man began his discovery of the biosphere through navigation of the seas, it may be that through the necessity to create a regime for the seas man will discover how to organize a truly global governing body with jurisdiction over the Earth's surface covered by the seas. This would not be world government; but it would be worldwide limited government, with ramifications extending far into the continents and into a wide range of non-maritime matters. As Maurice Strong, Secretary-General of the United Nations Conference on the Human Environment, observed to the second meeting of the preparatory committee:

Major sources of serious marine pollution are frequently removed from the marine environment itself. I suggest that we may
be assisted in the task of dealing with this problem by the existence
in international law of an obligation on States to cooperate in the
prevention of pollution of the oceans resulting from harmful
agents regardless of their source. There is, I believe, great promise
in the language of Article 25 of the 1958 Convention on the High
Seas that "all States shall cooperate with the competent international organizations in taking measures for the prevention of
pollution of the seas or the air space above, resulting from any
activities with radio-active materials or other harmful agents." [33]

With so vast and portentous a subject, the alternatives for
international or transnational organization are many. The
absence of national territorial jurisdiction over the high seas
and the unequivocal evidence that concurrent national action
will not afford effective protection points strongly toward the
ultimate emergence of a transnational regime with authority to
act directly on persons and property in relation to the uses of
the seas. The most comprehensive and carefully worked out plan
for an ocean regime is that developed by Mrs. Elizabeth Mann
Borgese and cited in the preceding chapter.[34] The Borgese
Ocean Regime, although associated with the United Nations,
would itself almost constitute a special United Nations for the
seas, with a maritime assembly, commission, planning agency,
secretariat, regional arrangements, and a maritime court. It
would encompass the commercial uses, mining, and food
resources of the seas as well as the scientific and technological
aspects of oceanography, marine biology, meteorology, and
engineering. Thus, the maritime assembly under the Borgese
proposal would not only determine the rules for issuing licenses
to explore and exploit the seabed, but it would also issue rules
and regulations for the conservation, development, and exploitation of the living resources of the sea.

There are arguments both for and against joining commercial exploitation and development and scientific research in
the same agency. The World Geophysical Organization, which
we have suggested might be developed around the present
structure of the World Meteorological Organization, would not

necessarily overlap the intent of the Borgese proposal, provided that those functions of the maritime assembly and commission primarily relating to scientific study and engineering development be performed by the WGO or in close cooperation with it. Nevertheless, there are functions specified in the Borgese proposal that could be performed by the more general environmental agencies previously described. More strictly maritime functions, however, such as issuing regulations concerning the pollution of the oceans, could be performed as at present by the International Maritime Consultative Organization. Although it may seem impolitic for two separate international organizations to be given major responsibilities relating to the oceans, this arrangement might not be illogical or uneconomical if the respective functions of the agencies were to be clearly and practically distinguished.

To establish a comprehensive Ocean Regime of the type envisaged by the Borgese plan would represent a far more drastic change in international relations and international institutional structure than the proposed modifications of existing structures just discussed. The Borgese plan includes many maritime functions not primarily connected with protection of the biosphere, although nearly all the functions of the proposed regime relate, in one way or another, to man–environment relationships. If one's concern is with the biosphere and with the oceans as a major aspect of it, then an international oceanic agency or agencies should be organized to facilitate the coordination of their policies and activities with broad biospheric and environmental considerations. If an international regime for the biosphere were, in effect, to be created, guided by an Environmental Council, then the judicial and many of the scientific functions incorporated in the Borgese Ocean Regime should perhaps be vested in more general environmental agencies. If there is to be effective international control of the mineral and living resources of the sea, some type of international maritime organization is needed. But its functions would be primarily regulatory and administrative; and its policies and procedures would be subject to the overriding priority of environmental and ecological considerations promulgated through the Environmental Council—with, of course, adequate regard for the full range of human needs, including the nutritional and economic.

The Ocean Regime would be a more difficult political innovation than the conjectured new agencies and reorganizations previously described, because it would not only impinge upon present assumptions in international law but would also invade territory now partly occupied by other agencies, especially the International Maritime Consultative Organization, UNESCO's Intergovernmental Oceanographic Commission, FAO's marine fisheries program, and WMO's hydrological interests. Moreover, there has been persistent opposition among leading nations to the establishment of additional United Nations specialized agencies. The most practicable approach to the institutional problem, although perhaps not the most ideal, may be some reorganizing of existing agencies and programs.

We have suggested, for example, that the scientific aspects of oceanography be embodied in an enlarged and reconstituted WMO which should be redesignated as the World Geophysical Organization. It would be logical, although perhaps not essential, that the Intergovernmental Oceanographic Commission and special projects such as the International Hydrological Decade and other geophysical programs of UNESCO become associated with the WGO. UNESCO's loss in this area could be more than compensated by enlarged activities in other aspects of science and in cultural affairs such as the World Heritage Foundation, presently to be considered.

The natural resources management of the oceans, including control over exploitation of the deep seabed and the effective regulation of pollution, might be vested in an expanded and reorganized IMCO, with FAO retaining its concern with marine food production, and the IUCN its activities in the protection of wildlife. A special coordinative committee on oceanic and maritime affairs might be established by the Environmental Council for assisting the development of mutually consistent or reinforcing programs affecting the seas. Under this arrangement, IMCO would gain greatly in the scope of its activities and responsibilities. Becoming far more than a consultative organization, it would necessarily have to be reconstituted, perhaps as the International Maritime Organization. The new IMO would administer whatever responsibilities the community of nations saw fit to confer upon a common agent to protect the more than 70 per cent of the surface of the Earth covered by the seas. Most of this area is beyond the general jurisdiction of nations, and international authority over the deep seabed or surface of the high seas would abrogate no existing sovereignty.

Thus by restructuring and improving the present UN system and without creating additional specialized agencies, the nations of the world could create an Ocean Regime. It is clear, by the criterion of human welfare, that the nations cannot treat the oceans as a commons much longer. The burden of proof should rest upon those who would contend that nothing need be done.

World Environment Fund

THE NEED FOR A FOUNDATION or fund to assist the protection of man's heritage in cultural and natural history follows from the difficulty experienced by many countries in the preservation and management of their unique noncommercial assets. If indeed these assets are of value and concern to the world community, it would then seem reasonable that it should bear some part of the cost of protecting and maintaining these areas, species, and monuments. Whether a protective structure should be created under the United Nations' auspices, related perhaps to the activities of UNESCO, or whether an international trust or other appropriate organization should be established on an entirely voluntary and nongovernmental basis, or whether some combination of both arrangements should be developed, are among the alternatives to be considered.

The problem of preserving and protecting natural areas, species, sites, and monuments is complicated by the location of the greater number of these natural and cultural resources within the territorial confines of national-states, which thus have political jurisdiction. Moreover, the movement to preserve and protect such assets has been concentrated in North America and Europe, whereas the sites and monuments are distributed throughout the world. Not a few national political leaders in less-developed countries have on occasion expressed resentment that their governments were burdened with the responsibility of preserving historical monuments and wildlife of greater interest to scientists and conservationists from technologically more advanced countries than to the people of the country in question. Nevertheless, other national leaders have seen that their wildlife, landscapes, and cultural monuments were important not only to their nation's identity, but also to its economic future.

International cooperation to preserve distinctive areas has evolved with notable but still insufficient success in the movement to establish national parks and monuments. This effort has been the particular concern of UNESCO (to a lesser extent of FAO), and of professional nongovernmental organizations such as the International Federation of Landscape Architects, and the International Union for Conservation of Nature and Natural Resources. In 1933, an International Convention on Parks in London adopted a set of basic guidelines for the preservation of natural areas. Proposal for a world conference on national parks was made in 1958 at the sixth general assembly of the IUCN in Athens by the Japanese landscape designer and conservationist, Tsuyoshi Tamura; and in 1962, as noted in Chapter 3, the first World Conference on National Parks was held in the United States at Seattle under the joint sponsorship of IUCN, UNESCO, and FAO, in association with the United States National Park Service and the Natural Resources Council of America.[35] Under similar sponsorship, the Second World Conference in 1972 is coincident with the one-hundredth anniversary of the establishment of Yellowstone National Park.

In 1965, a preparatory committee for a White House Conference on International Cooperation recommended "that there be established a trust for the world heritage that would be responsible to the world community for the stimulation of international cooperative efforts to identify, establish, develop, and maintain the world's superb natural and scenic areas and historical sites for the present and future benefit of the entire world citizenry."[36] For example, the committee cited unique and irreplaceable resources like the Grand Canyon of Colorado, the Serengeti Plain of East Africa, Angel Falls in Venezuela, and Mount Everest on the Nepalese–Tibetan frontier. Among cultural and archaeological sites, it cited Angkor, Petra, the ruins of Inca, Mayan, and Aztec cities, and historical structures such as the Egyptian pyramids, the Athenian Acropolis, and Stonehenge. The committee also recommended that attempts be made to provide for animals and plants threatened with extinction an appropriate area of natural habitat in national parks, wildlife refuges, wilderness areas, or their equivalent. Special protection was urged for those natural areas "whose main value lies in the spectacular animal species they support, the Indian rhinoceros, mountain gorilla, and the orangutan, for example."

Meanwhile, the world heritage idea has been adopted as a project of the IUCN, which has prepared a draft proposal for the Stockholm conference. Richard N. Gardner has written about the need, and a book dealing with the subject has been undertaken by John P. Milton and Noel Simon in association with the Conservation Foundation. The idea has been effectively advocated by Russell E. Train, former President of the Conservation Foundation and Chairman of the U.S. Council on Environmental Quality. Clearly, information regarding the world heritage proposal has been spreading.

The specific functions of the World Heritage (WH) would be:

1. To identify unique or natural areas that should be preserved.
2. To establish priorities for their protection.
3. To develop standards for their continuing maintenance.
4. To provide funds to aid their acquisition or protective custody by national government, other organizations, or the WH itself.

Among the more possible institutional arrangements for the World Heritage are the following. All involve some official or governmental status, because a purely private organization would probably find it much harder to obtain the necessary public financial support and to negotiate with national governments. The arrangements:

1. An autonomous international organization sponsored by UNESCO and/or FAO in association with IUCN and WWF.
2. A special trust established within UNESCO to receive voluntary contributions to be expended in a manner

similar to the Egyptian and Italian efforts (See Chapter 7).

3. A line item in the regular UNESCO budget for funds to be approved by UNESCO for WH projects.
4. A special United Nations facility for the conduct of the WH program, possibly administered as an activity of the Environmental Council.

These arrangements are not mutually exclusive alternatives. The historical initiative of UNESCO, FAO, and IUCN, would seem to make their continued involvement desirable. There would be logic in the association of the World Heritage Fund with a high level Environmental Council of general competence which could supplement its resources through allotment of funds to UNESCO, FAO, IUCN, or to other appropriate recipients. Assistance to recipient nations could perhaps be administered on a basis of matching funds, including definite national commitments to protective standards and performance. In an address to the International Congress on Nature and Man in the Netherlands on April 26, 1967, Russell E. Train, then President of the Conservation Foundation and an early advocate of the World Heritage, declared,

> The Trust should be established in close working association with such organizations as the International Union for Conservation of Nature and Natural Resources (IUCN) and the International Council of Monuments and Sites (ICOMOS). Under contract with the World Heritage, and in cooperation with the governments concerned, the IUCN could perform the task of survey, inventory, and of establishing priorities for action in the case of natural areas. An important outcome of such a task would be the production of a blueprint for a world program for the protection of natural environments—including specific targets for action programs and time tables for their accomplishment.[37]

In a message to the Congress of the United States on February 8, 1971, President Richard Nixon endorsed the World Heritage concept and stated that he was "directing the Secretary of the Interior, in coordination with the Council on Environmental Quality and under the foreign policy guidance of the

Secretary of State, to develop initiatives for presentation in appropriate international forums to further the objectives of a World Heritage Trust." [38]

How Much Innovation Is Feasible?

IT IS OBVIOUSLY FUTILE to speculate that the institutional arrangements just described or others resembling them will come into existence as the result of the United Nations Conference in Stockholm in 1972. But there is, nevertheless, reason to believe that a structure of some sort will come into existence well before the seventies have run their course. This expectation is based upon the belief that nations will find an international structure for environmental protection to be in their national interests. It is based upon the belief that there is enough rationality in the world, enough regard for validated scientific evidence, enough clear-mindedness about the price of survival, to obtain reluctant consent from otherwise self-seeking and politically-biased governments and popular leaders. The implications of the movement for protection of the biosphere extend beyond conventional international agreement to a new level of transnational effort. Particularly with the oceans, the arbitrary exercise of national sovereignty must be relinquished to an authority empowered to protect and administer a heritage common to all people and upon which all living creatures ultimately depend.

Beyond the pressure for action engendered by the evidence of deterioration and distress that has been recounted, action on behalf of the common responsibility for the protection of the biosphere may conceivably be forced by a dramatic and disastrous ecological collapse in some part of the world which would necessitate aid and intervention from the community of nations. It is all too probable that within the coming decades, especially in tropical areas, a number of smaller national-states may be confronted by a convergence of overpopulation, depleted resources, environmental pollution, fiscal insolvency, and social instability that exceeds their political capabilities. Faced with the socioecological collapse of one or more of its members, the United Nations system would face a severe test of its ability to respond rationally and humanely to a situation for which there was little precedent. Conceivably, under such a test, the United Nations system might develop new responses which would surely require a collaborative effort between the Economic and Social Council and a possible Environmental Council, with perhaps a new custodial role for the Trusteeship Council.

In December 1968, at an International Conference on Ecological Aspects of International Development, I suggested that the United Nations might consider how it would meet the need to establish receiverships for ecologically bankrupt nations.[39] The structure needed to operate a socioecological receivership does not now exist. Parts of the task would fall logically within the functions of the World Bank, the United Nations Development Program, and several specialized agencies. A central planning and coordinative facility would, in any case, be needed to make the most effective use of the available resources of international assistance and to supplement those resources where necessary.

Lest it be thought that the innovations which have just been discussed are new in concept as well as in proposed form, it should be recalled that many of them have been under consideration for a decade or more. The structures which ought to be invented and adopted by the community of nations would in some instances, as in the settlement of international disputes, serve purposes recognized before the beginning of the present century. The needs are not new; it is the will to action that eludes the nations.

In an address on September 20, 1963, before the eighteenth General Assembly of the United Nations, President John F. Kennedy spoke of the effort to improve the conditions of man. "It is the task of all nations," he declared, ". . . acting alone, acting in groups, acting in the United Nations, for plague and pestilence, plunder and pollution, the hazards of nature, and the hunger of children are the foes of every nation. The earth, the sea, and the air are the concern of every nation." He proposed a far-reaching program of international action:

A world center for health communications under the World Health Organization could warn of epidemics and the adverse effects of certain drugs as well as transmit the results of new experiments and new discoveries.

189

Regional research centers could advance our common medical knowledge and train new scientists and doctors for new nations.

A global system of satellites could provide communication and weather information for all corners of the earth.

A worldwide program of conservation could protect the forest and wild game preserves now in danger of extinction for all time, improve the marine harvest of food from our oceans, and prevent the contamination of air, and water by industrial as well as nuclear pollution.

And finally, a worldwide program of farm productivity and food distribution, similar to our country's "Food for Peace" program, could now give every child the food he needs.[40]

It is futile to speculate how much better the state of the world might be if resources devoted to military and other costly and destructive purposes could have been used to implement such a program as President Kennedy proposed. The Stockholm conference is perhaps the best chance in our time to take the collective action necessary to arrest the destruction of the living Earth. If effective action follows, it will not necessarily be because men have become more altruistic; it may be because they have become more realistic. There is evidence that peoples and their governments are beginning to understand the danger that more perceptive individuals have been trying to bring to their attention. But do they recognize the danger with conviction and intensity sufficient to press their representatives and leaders for appropriate and adequate action? We will perhaps learn the answer from the results of the Stockholm conference, but certainly before the end of the 1970s.

7

Strengthening National Capabilities:

ORGANIZATION

AND ADMINISTRATION OF

ENVIRONMENTAL PROTECTION

IN LESS THAN A DECADE, THE DECLINING QUALITY OF the human environment has become a public issue of worldwide concern. Direct personal effects drew attention to the nature of the impending environmental crises—to the exponential growth and maldistribution of human populations, to environmental pollution, to resource depletion, and to the deterioration of human settlements, especially in crowded urban centers and impoverished rural areas. Science and technology have been enlisted to arrest these trends and to ameliorate the damage already produced. And in order to implement scientific and technical remedies, law and economic planning have been taken up as instruments of environmental policy. Nevertheless, not enough attention has been given to the point at which action occurs—the point at which policies, programs, or projects are implemented through the organized efforts of people. Whatever their substance or intent, at whatever level of government they are formulated, environmental policies will be only as effective as their administration. But the key to effectiveness throughout the system is the national level; as the world is now politically organized, only national governments can ensure effectiveness at the other levels. And national governments can also hamper efforts, both local and international.

Growth of National Concern

EVIDENCE OF WORLDWIDE CONCERN for the quality of the environment has been growing steadily. Awareness of environmental deterioration and demands that governments do something about it are evident in public opinion studies undertaken in a number of countries, and expressions of public concern have been reported from almost every part of the world.[1]

Although public attitudes may be less evident in the developing countries, some of their better-informed citizens have joined the chorus of apprehension. Professor Francesco di Castri of Chile solicited the opinions of more than one hundred scientists concerned with environmental matters in the developing countries of Asia, Africa, and Latin America.[2] His results indicated that awareness of deteriorating environmental trends and dissatisfaction with degraded environmental conditions may everywhere be greater than casual observation might suggest.

That there was concern in the developing nations over deteriorating environments was confirmed by a number of conferences held in the summer of 1971 in preparation for the UN Conference on the Human Environment the following year. Among these were a Working Party on Environmental Problems in Developing Countries, held in Canberra, Australia, sponsored by SCOPE; an International Environmental Workshop held in Aspen, Colorado, sponsored by the International Institute for Environmental Affairs, and regional seminars on development and environment, sponsored by the United Nations Regional Economic Commissions.

The wide-spread belief that environmental problems are largely those of affluent industrialized nations is not confirmed by fact. Some of the most serious and worsening environmental problems of the present time are found in the burgeoning urban centers of developing countries.[3] In the backlands of these countries there is growing evidence of abuse and depletion of natural resources. Alleged differences in national values between developed and developing countries may be more semantic than substantive. The expressions "ecology" and "environmental quality" may not be the rallying cries in developing countries that they have recently become in many parts of the developed world. But if the environmental issues are broken down into the specifics of contaminated water supply, unsafe and unsanitary housing, polluted air, eroded or laterized soils, degraded forests and depleted wildlife, attitudes in developing countries may not differ greatly from those found in countries in which environmental quality has become a popular issue. Decision makers in developing countries may trade a degree of environmental degradation for needed economic development. But that does not mean that environmental pollution is welcome or that the degree of environmental impairment accepted as an initial necessity will continue to be tolerated as development continues and economic and ecological sophistication grows.[4]

In their concern to improve the economic well-being of their peoples, public administrators and planners should not make the mistake of equating a lack of protest against bad environmental conditions with popular indifference. Concern for economic well-being is not incompatible with regard for environmental amenities and ecological considerations. To the extent that countries demonstrate that economic well-being and environmental quality, far from being incompatible, are mutually necessary and reinforcing, no people anywhere upon seeing such proof will be content to suffer unnecessary environmental degradation. Success in environmental management anywhere will make people everywhere less willing to sacrifice environmental amenities; they will realize that the cause is failure to organize and administer well-balanced programs of national development in which ecological and environmental factors are an integral part.

Interrelationships of Development and the Environment

DEVELOPMENT INEVITABLY affects the human environment in many ways, and environmental protection implies requirements and restraints in reaching development goals. The ultimate goal of both processes is the same—improvement of the human condition, of the quality of human life. To the extent that development and environmental quality efforts contradict one another, they diminish the chances of achieving the common goal. It is therefore the particular task of policy planning and public administration to bring about a harmonious, mutually reinforcing fusion of developmental and environmental policy and action.

It is the nature of the problems of development and the environment that make organization and administration especially critical to their solution. They are characteristically complex and dynamic and do not conform to the boundaries of political jurisdictions; they also pervade all levels and sectors of human organization. Problems of development and the environment even when localized at a given organizational level—local, national, or international—can seldom be attacked successfully without cooperation from other levels. Markets, credit, labor supply, information, political ideologies, and energy cycles are in constant flux; and no nation, even the greatest, can unilaterally isolate itself from world-wide economic or environmental trends.

The environmental consequences of development may be diffused far beyond the boundaries of the developing or developed country. For example, in economically developing country A, unconsumed residuals are discharged into the air and water and carried across political boundaries to become costly, unwanted pollutants in countries B, C, and D. In many countries, food supplies from the sea are important sources of nutrition and export, but the living resources of the sea are now jeopardized by contamination from oil, toxic heavy metals, and pesticides—all consequences of technoeconomic development, and carried by oceanic currents from their points of origin to all parts of the world. The resources of the sea are further threatened by over-exploitation of advanced fisheries technologies; future food supplies could be destroyed by pursuit of present economic advantage. Thus, a technological innovation in country A, applied by operators from country B, may ultimately jeopardize the nutrition and health of people in countries C to T.

This ramifying quality of problems that are both environmental and economic in character explains why intergovernmental multilevel action is needed to resolve them. National-states, although juridically sovereign, are unable to protect fully either the environmental or economic welfare of their people solely by their own efforts. The international problem of reconciling economic development and environmental protection does not necessarily exist only between nations at different stages of development. Some of the more acute international problems are between countries with similar technological capabilities. For example, member states of the European Economic Community and the Economic Commission for Europe have sought ways to ensure that nations adopting and enforcing strict environmental controls on industrial production are not put at a disadvantage in the marketplace by countries that maintain lower production costs by failing to insist that their industries meet the full costs of production, including preventable damage to the environment.[5]

Now, to summarize the implications of development and environmental protection programs for organization and administration. Both development and environmental protection have international dimensions and require international cooperation. In the development process, the developing countries need assistance and continuing economic encouragement from the developed countries. But the environmental consequences of development, especially where development is mismanaged, are likely to be projected into the global environment. Failure of developed countries to control harmful side-effects of their industrial activity would also harm developing countries, especially those dependent upon food from the sea. Failure of the less-developed countries to bring their societies into ecological balance would strain international relations, diminish chances for world peace, and frustrate popular hopes for better life. Thus complex relationships are being created that demand new and improved organizational and administrative arrangements among and within nations if human welfare is to be well served.

The Key Role of National Governments

NATIONAL GOVERNMENTS, and especially their administrative services, play definitive roles in managing problems of the human environment. At present all other units of government and all international organizations are dependent upon their acquiescence and support. However universal an environmental problem may be and however urgent the need for concerted international action, the response will be forthcoming only to the extent made possible by national governments. But even though national governments may be willing to cooperate, international action will be effective only to the extent that nations are able to fulfill their commitments to international action. And among the many limitations on ability of a nation to fulfill its commitments, internationally or domestically, administrative inadequacy is one of the most common.

The ramifying nature of environmental problems, especially those of air and water pollution, makes local action on them especially dependent upon national cooperation and support. National policies, standards, and financial assistance are generally required before local or regional units of government can act effectively on most environmental issues. Even under federal governments where most state, provincial, or local authorities may tax independently, basic policies for the country as a whole —fiscal, economic, and environmental—are national. Policies for agriculture, natural resources management, and development planning are almost everywhere initiated and administered nationally. Localized problems such as those pertaining to urban and rural settlements and regional planning have nowhere been successfully attacked without the support of national policies conducive to sound population distribution and land use.

International efforts, regional or global, occur only with national participation or consent. The effectiveness of the United Nations, and of its specialized agencies and affiliated organizations, depends heavily upon the support, cooperation, organizational competence, and administrative ability of national governments. Even nongovernmental international organizations are to some extent dependent upon national action. Organizations such as the International Council of Scientific Unions and the International Union for Conservation of Nature and Natural Resources not only receive direct financial assistance from national governments, also indirect support in the form of aid given to scientists and other persons in attending international conferences and otherwise participating in their activities.

Only national governments, through representation on the

governing bodies of international organizations, can ensure the coordination of their activities. In a formal sense, the United Nations Administrative Committee on Coordination and the Fifth Committee of the General Assembly (for administration and budget) perform coordinative functions in relation to United Nations programs generally. But the ultimate power of decision rests with the national governments, and their ability to bring about coordination in the UN and the specialized agencies depends considerably upon the coordination of policy and administration in their own governmental structures. If nations have not learned how to organize their domestic programs for development and the environment, they are not well prepared to promote coordination at the international level.

There exists perhaps no nation in the world today in which the public services are as well organized and administered as the needs of the nation require, or as the people and their leaders desire. There is, however, a wide range in the abilities of national governments to deal with the complex issues of the modern world. Administration of environmental affairs is one of the most difficult areas, demanding inputs of scientific and technical knowledge and skill in the planning, organization, and administration of complex programs that are nowhere common attributes of public administration. The commitment of national governments to development efforts and, more recently, to the protection and improvement of the human environment has raised the necessity for upgrading public administration standards everywhere. The need may be greatest in the developing countries; but very few countries in the world today can achieve new and complex objectives for economic development and environmental quality without a substantial corresponding improvement in the organization and administration of the public services.

The state of knowledge regarding the actual goals and functions of national government in dealing with environmental problems, and with the administration inevitably involved, is fragmentary. Adequate assessments of the administrative performance of government agencies are almost nowhere available; and administrative actions in relation to the environment are among the more poorly defined public functions. There are large gaps in our knowledge of how specific problems of environmental management and protection are approached in various countries. This is partly because many environmental programs are relatively new and have run ahead of adequate description and analysis.

Descriptive papers submitted by participating countries to the Biosphere Conference in Paris in 1968, to the Economic Commission for Europe's Environmental Symposium in Prague in 1971, and to the United Nations Conference in Stockholm in 1972, might help to close this information gap. But the "country papers" submitted for international conferences frequently remain unpublished or largely undistributed. For this reason, the need for more comparative studies and analyses of organizational and administrative practices in government will surely be increased as nations respond to the stimulus of the Stockholm conference.

Common Problems of Environmental Protection

THE BASIC DIFFICULTY of governmental organization in relation to environmental issues is gaining an adequate conception of the problem. Comprehensive environmental protection and management have not been traditional public functions, despite a long history of governmental administration of certain aspects of the environment. Elements of the environment have been managed through public works and have been major agents of environmental change through programs of agriculture, forestry, transportation, industrialization, and nearly all of the activities covered by the term "development." The need to reexamine the impact of human activity upon the environment has arisen without a suitable theory of public responsibility to redirect the activities of governments. To formulate a declaration of national and international responsibility leading to programs of action may be one of the most useful acts of the 1972 United Nations Conference on the Human Environment.

Because of its relative novelty, the issue of environmental policy has not readily been understood by the public or by its representatives in government. As governments, especially through development programs, have increasingly intervened in environment, inadequacies in administrative organization and procedure have become evident. Government agencies, sometimes with international assistance, have found themselves in competition with one another for incompatible uses of the same natural resources. Action in one department of government has too often clashed with action in another.

For example, governments have sought to improve public health through environmental anti-malaria measures while simultaneously, although unintentionally, they have worsened health conditions by extending irrigation projects that spread the disease schistosomiasis. Nations have also tried to earn more foreign exchange by promoting spectacular scenery and wildlife to tourists, but have simultaneously pursued less lucrative programs in agriculture, forestry, and mining that destroy the scenery and the habitats of wildlife. Examples of cross-purpose action can be found in developed and developing countries alike.[6] In the United States, a costly controversy over construction of an international airport in the Florida Everglades [7] resulted from a failure of government to establish priorities for development and environment and to pursue coordinative planning or even adequate exchange of information among the principal federal and state agencies directly concerned.

Solutions to the problem of organizing for environmental protection while meeting other public responsibilities have not been easily discovered. There are differences in environmental needs and priorities among nations that must create differences in organization and administration. But there are also environmental problems universal to human society to which the organization and administration of governments must make coordinated response. The difficulty of containing environmental problems or their chain-reaction effects within political boundaries is a challenge to present governmental arrangements. With due regard to their particular needs and conditions, all national governments (and international organizations with major environmental responsibilities) face a common problem of organizing to cope with the complex, ramifying, and evolving character of man–environment interactions.

This organizational problem exists at all levels but, as ever, is most critical at the national. To cope with major environmental problems there is need for administrative organization that (1) is sufficiently comprehensive to encompass the problems under attack, (2) facilitates coordination of all related efforts, (3) is adaptable to the dynamics of environmental change and to progressive stages in the solution of environmental problems, and (4) is capable of obtaining, evaluating, and applying the appropriate science and technologies to the problems. In order to assist national governments to develop administrative organizations possessing these capabilities it may be useful to identify the principal deterrents that would have to be overcome. We will review these factors briefly, first at the national and second at the international level.

Comprehensiveness. A major obstacle to a comprehensive or holistic approach to problems of the environment (or of development) is the traditional functional and hierarchal structure of public administration. This structure has not been unsuitable for the things that it was designed to do under the conditions prevailing during the course of its development. But it was not intended for comprehensive tasks like environmental protection and management, and it seldom is flexible enough to make optimal reallocation of public resources to meet rapidly evolving problems. The classic description of this functional hierarchal structure has been provided by a German sociologist, Max Weber. And it is the developed countries that have most thoroughly adopted it, although of course modified by practical circumstances.

This structure has been legitimized by law and tradition and reinforced by career patterns in its public service and by the interests of civil service unions and client groups. It may, therefore, be more difficult to modify than more loosely organized and less professionalized public services in many developing countries. New coordinating structures to regroup functional units for problem-solving have been established in several developed countries. A well-known case of combining diverse skills and functions into a unified problem-solving structure has been the Apollo program in the United States for exploration of the Moon.[8] This program would justify careful study for its possible relevance to the problems of organization and management in the terrestrial environment. Among new comprehensive structures for environmental administration are the Department of the Environment in the United Kingdom[9] and the Ministry for the Protection of Nature and the Environment in France.[10] A super-department of natural resources has been proposed for the United States.[11]

Coordinating Ability. Reorganizing to provide for a comprehensive approach to environmental problems may facilitate coordination but it does not necessarily accomplish it. Bringing environment-shaping agencies together within a common organizational structure is only a logical first step toward coherent administration of environmental policies. The minister or cabinet-level official responsible for the coordination of environmental policy and action cannot be effective unless he has adequate information and techniques for the analysis of programs subject to his administration.

But no matter how well organized and equipped to coordinate environmental policy, the administrative performance of government will inevitably be influenced by political forces. In countries where political power is concentrated in a single political party, responsibility bears more heavily upon that party and its official representatives in government than in countries in which political responsibility is more widely distributed among competing parties and institutions. This same concentration of responsibility occurs where the development of the nation, particularly in its economic sector, is governed by centralized planning. Where the emphasis in central planning is heavily economic, environmental considerations are in danger of being thrust aside as adding to the cost and complicating the administration of development plans; but there is nothing inherent in single party political systems or in centralized economic planning to make them less responsive than other regimes to environmental considerations. Indeed, should these countries give high priority to ecological and environmental values, they may, perhaps, more easily implement them than those countries in which there must be widespread consultation and search for consensus before major actions can be undertaken. And, although centralized planning may have a tendency to augment a plan's built-in errors, environmental deterioration has more often resulted from the absence of planning or from inadequate coordination among planners. Planning is an essential element of environmental administration, but it must be adequate to the challenges that the environment presents.

In utilizing planning as an instrument of environmental protection, the developing countries may enjoy certain advantages. Their developmental needs have made both sectoral and comprehensive planning indispensable to the achievement of their development goals. Thus, planning machinery exists in many developing countries and could be adapted without great difficulty to serve the needs of environmental protection as well. Unlike many developed countries, these developing nations are seldom confronted by powerful domestic interests either in the bureaucracy or the private economic sector whose immediate values and objectives conflict with environmental protection and enhancement.

Operational Flexibility. A major problem for administrative organization and procedure, at all levels, has been the accelerating tempo of change in the modern world. All societies are developing, but the rates and degrees of change differ greatly within and among nations. New problems and new technologies strain the adaptive capacity of governmental organizations designed for a less turbulent age. Many problems of the human environment are relatively new because the technoeconomic developments that caused them are new. In less than half-a-century, a host of unprecedented environmental problems have been created by (1) a worldwide explosion of human populations and urban growth, (2) mass use of automobiles and aeroplanes, (3) nuclear energy, (4) a plastic and pesticide revolution in industrial chemistry, and (5) technologies for the exploration of hostile environments in the polar regions, beneath the seas, and in space. This enumeration could be extended but each of these developments has produced a wide range of environmental problems and opportunities.

For example, the jet plane that creates problems of air and noise pollution for urban centers also permits development of tourism as a major economic asset for countries rich in scenery, wildlife, or cultural monuments. Nuclear energy may eventually free nations from dependence on unevenly distributed and exhaustible fossil fuels, but its hazards have already brought nations together in treaties to prevent radioactive contamination of the planet. Pesticides have prevented disease and protected food supplies in fruits, grains, and vegetables, but have also produced destructive and even dangerous effects in the food-chain and reproduction of many animals. And it is characteristic of these, or of many other examples that might be cited, that (1) their cause–effect relationships are not confinable within national boundaries, and (2) are subject to rapid and not easily foreseeable change. Operational flexibility, which is the capacity of an administrative system to reassign priorities, regroup personnel, and reallocate funds, is therefore a desirable quality in present-day government.[12] To use a term proposed by Alvin Toffler, ad hocracy, as contrasted with traditional bureaucracy, has become a necessary condition.

Ability to Enlist and Evaluate Science and Technology. Most, if not all, man-made environmental problems are the direct or indirect results of applied science and technology. Given the present state of knowledge, not all of these problems are avoidable. Energy production and utilization in particular entail certain environmental costs that cannot wholly be avoided. All modern societies are dependent for their continuing existence upon a science-based technological infrastructure. Although the differences between the environmental problems of the developed and developing countries are frequently exaggerated, one significant contrast is the degree of dependence of the developed countries on the continuous operation of artificial interdependent systems, for example, in agriculture, food processing, materials handling, water supply, waste disposal, communication, transportation, and the generation and distribution of energy.

The developed society is vulnerable to the disruption of its interlocking systems; the developing society, employing subsistence agriculture and a large measure of self-renewing human and animal labor, is less easily disrupted. But population growth, pollution, and depletion of resources now pose serious environmental problems to the developing countries in addition to older problems of poverty, illiteracy, and disease. Yet, regardless of their origin, the problems of development and the environment cannot be solved without recourse to science and technology. In ability to enlist and evaluate scientific and technical knowledge and skill the less developed countries are generally disadvantaged.[13]

In the greater number of developing countries scientific, technical, and managerial leaders have received their formal education and training and much of their social and economic orientation in the developed countries. In the great majority of cases, however, their education occurred before environmental issues became matters of serious public concern. Most of them returned home before economic and development thinking had been modified to take cognizance of the need to harmonize production and conservation and to take account of the environmental costs of improperly directed economic and technological growth. There is thus a possibility that technicians and administrators in less developed countries today may be less sensitive to the dangers of environmental degradation than their former classmates in the more-developed countries where the adverse effects of misdirected development have appeared earlier.

It would thus appear to be a responsibility of the more-developed countries, and especially of international programs of assistance in education and technical training, to help the less-developed countries avoid the mistakes that, through lack of experience and information, the developed nations made in the past. It is especially important in this connection that the scientific, technical, and administrative leaderships in the less-developed countries learn at first hand in the more-developed countries the destructive potential of misguided applications of science and technology.

The force of scientific knowledge, inadequate everywhere, is generally greater in the more-developed than in the less-developed countries. Lack of commitment to science is, of course, not confined to developing countries; many technologically-advanced countries have been very selective in their support and use of science. But the developing countries are almost everywhere handicapped by deficiencies in scientific analytic capabilities. In very few is the influence of their young and growing scientific institutions and of their competent and dedicated individual scientists decisive at the higher and strategic centers of policy-making and administration.[14] Political leaders unversed in science and unaccustomed to the use of analytic techniques in decision-making find it easy to dismiss or to ignore scientific evidence inconsistent with their own perceptions of the conditions of the nation or of their dreams or ambitions for national development.

Most nations today are likely to find it easier to acquire the capital and technology to modify their environments than to acquire the knowledge and wisdom to modify that environment wisely or, indeed under some circumstances, to protect it from further modification at the hand of man. Technology assessment, or the analysis of science-based innovations to discover the full range of their effects before they are applied, is an urgent need in all countries today. Proposals for such review of technologies potentially hazardous to the environment have been made in a number of countries and by the International Council of Scientific Unions. The organizational problems of obtaining the information needed for this task and the dissemination of its findings among all nations deserve serious attention in the light of the Stockholm conference and the implementation of plans now under discussion at national and international levels.[15]

Problems of Multilevel Cooperation

BECAUSE NATIONS ARE confronted with environmental problems that cannot be solved unilaterally or within their own frontiers, international cooperation has been sought in a growing list of environmental issues. In preceding chapters, we have noted that cooperation was first sought through bilateral and multilateral treaties administered by the ratifying powers. Intergovernmental agencies with their own policies, personnel, and procedures were gradually established for a variety of purposes, including management of international rivers, protection of fisheries, and allocation of telecommunication wave lengths. The growth of large multipurpose international agencies followed establishment of the United Nations in 1945. The UN specialized agencies, some of which antedate the UN, have tended to broaden the scope of their activities, particularly in relation to environmental issues. UNESCO, from its inception, covered a broad spectrum of concerns, and WHO, WMO, and FAO have added new programs in the environmental field.

But two organizational problems have arisen from this largely *ad hoc* process of institutional growth. First, United Nations action and assistance to national governments is concentrated in those areas in which the specialized agencies have responsibility and competence. It does not encompass all environmental needs and issues, since large areas of policy are beyond the jurisdiction of any existing international agency. Among these gaps, at least within the UN system, are general responsibility for the high seas and the deep seabed, for manipulation of the weather, for protection of unique and threatened wildlife, landscapes, and cultural treasures, and for the conservation of nonrenewable resources upon which all nations are dependent. To some extent, these gaps have been filled by nongovernmental international organizations, such as the International Union for Conservation of Nature and Natural Resources (IUCN) for wildlife, the International Federation of Landscape Architects (IFLA) for landscapes and scenery of international significance, and the International Council of Scientific Unions (ICSU), through its Scientific Committee for Problems of the Environment (SCOPE), for a broad range of inquiry in environmental science. These and many other nongovernmental organizations become directly involved with planning and administration at national levels. Some, especially IUCN and ICSU, maintain close working relations with the United Nations and the specialized agencies. Without exception, however, they are handicapped by lack of funds and, to some extent, by ambiguity of status when dealing with governmental authorities.

The second organizational problem follows from the first. Although as we have noted, coordinative mechanisms for organization and administration have been established in the UN system (ACC and the G.A. Fifth Committee), there is widespread belief that existing arrangements are not fully adequate to ensure a harmonious and mutually supportive administration of international programs at the national level. Moreover, no means exists for acting on unmet needs short of major international negotiations; and the mechanisms for avoiding wasteful duplication and for making optimum use of available resources through coordination appear to be inadequate at all levels. In summary, (1) present international efforts do not fully or evenly cover those areas of environmental concern in which national governments need international assistance, and (2) there are no easily available means for extending international efforts where they are most needed, for coordinating those now in effect at the international–national interface.

There has been extensive opposition to the creation of additional specialized agencies, and it is therefore more likely that new areas of international cooperation will be served by the enlargement and reorganization of existing agencies. The preferred objective would appear to be a coherent linkage among existing agencies, with an environmental policy council and a research facility the most likely innovations. And in designing, or redesigning, national or international structures for environmental protection or management, it is important to consider how the various levels of organization will interrelate.

The world appears to be moving toward the development of multilevel intergovernmental systems for coordinated action in relation to the environment. The interlocking of environmental problems with many other public issues means that their solution requires the authority and action of general governments—which means primarily national government. But some aspects of environmental actions are most efficiently administered at local levels, and there are certain environmental problems that extend beyond national boundaries but do not directly affect all nations. For these problems, regional solutions may be the most practicable.

Regional intergovernmental arrangements are already taking form, for example, through the UN Regional Economic Commissions, and most notably perhaps for environmental problems, through the Economic Commission for Europe. Regional cooperation on behalf of the environment has already been noted in other groupings, such as the Organization for African Unity (OAU), the Council for Mutual Economic Cooperation (CMEA) and the NATO Committee on Challenges to Modern Society (CCMS), the European Economic Community, and the Nordic Council. Further regional cooperation may be stimulated by the series of pre-Stockholm regional meetings in Asia, Africa, and Latin America. Regional arrangements for specific environment-related purposes are among the oldest (and newest) instances of intergovernmental cooperation. The international fisheries commission[16] and the campaign against the desert locust are contrasting cases in point.[17]

In developing multilevel intergovernmental systems for cooperation, effective operations require that two conditions be met. Cooperative relationships must be organized and developed for the entire multilevel system *and* at each level so that related activities at each are *articulated* (fit together with minimal friction) and are *synchronized* (actions are timed to occur simultaneously or in planned sequence).

Although it is not reasonable to expect uniformity in national organization, it should, nevertheless, be possible to establish operational compatibility among local, national, and international agencies that must interact in the administration of environmental programs. This articulation among units of government must be procedural as well as structural. For example, if the principal water quality control agency in country A is in the Ministry of Agriculture, in country B in the Ministry of Health, and country D in a department of the environment, the ability of these agencies to work together or with international agencies will be heavily dependent upon the degree of autonomy that they enjoy, and the extent to which the orientations and priorities of the parent ministry or department are sympathetic. If an agency in country A can act expeditiously and responsibly on environmental issues, but realization of its objectives depends upon collaboration with its counterpart in country B, which is buried under layers of bureaucratic authority and subject to elaborate and protracted clearance procedures, the administrative effectiveness of country A is correspondingly diminished. Intergovernmental control over air and water pollution, and the application of pesticides, for example, can obviously be frustrated by such incompatibilities.

Synchronization of action between nations and among levels is also a concomitant of operational effectiveness. To the extent that nations operate on differing legislative and fiscal calendars, their ability to cooperate may be reduced. Innovation in budgetary procedures may be required to enable nations and international organizations to respond rapidly and in concert to unforeseen emergencies, and to reassign priorities in the face of unpredicted environmental changes. The establishment of development banks may help to increase national fiscal flexibility.

Synchronization is also important in relation to the timing of the contemplated action. In cooperative programs, organizational and administrative arrangements should, as far as possible, ensure that the activities of participating nations be synchronized in essential operations. The "critical path" method of program planning and analysis might usefully be applied to international programs for environment. A sequence of critical events is plotted on a time scale extending from the beginning to the end of a project. Through this chart, it is possible to show graphically the relationship between the consecutive phases of a task and to determine who must do what, when.[18]

Timing is also important in obtaining an adequate review of environment-affecting proposals, especially where the only remedy for damage may be in prevention. If the United Nations were to create an environmental council or world environment research center, an informational clearinghouse could be provided in either or both facilities with which nations could routinely file descriptions of proposed action affecting the environmental concerns of other nations. Nations would not be required to wait until environmental damage had happened to take up the issue with the offending nation through regular diplomatic channels or through the appropriate international organization. An international registry of chemical compounds, proposed by the International Council of Scientific Unions, would be a significant step in this direction. A practical example of this procedure is afforded by the environmental impact statements required of all agencies of the United States government under the National Environmental Policy Act of 1969, which requires a sharing of information with state governments as well as other federal agencies and with the public.

Although a nation might be free to initiate damaging action in the face of objections by its neighbors, the issue would have been opened to possible peaceful negotiation and reconsideration of the project before damage was done. For example, the West

Ford and Starfish experiments of the United States Air Force, involving a nuclear explosion and the scattering of copper dipoles in the upper atmosphere, did not result in permanent global environmental change, although such possibilities were feared by well-informed scientists and international protest resulted.[19] An international system of information exchange and review could reduce conflict and induce more careful ecologically-oriented planning at all levels.

Proposals for Action

HAVING REVIEWED some of the more common and significant problems encountered in the organization and administration of environmental programs, we may now consider what steps should be taken toward their solution.

Organization and administration are purposeful processes and never take place in a policy vacuum. Thus the organizational and administrative action proposed in this chapter implies policies and public decisions that cannot be fully spelled out here. The propositions that follow describe what needs to be done to facilitate the broad tasks of environmental protection regardless of the specific programs and projects through which the task is performed. As we have previously emphasized, the problems of organization and administration connected with environmental issues grow out of the nature of those issues themselves. The challenge of the environment to public administration, especially at the national level, is to adopt concepts, institutions, and technologies to cope with the complex, interrelating, ramifying, and dynamic properties of the biosphere. It is a severe test of the human capacity for management.

The following ten points apply at all organizational levels, local, national, and international, but all points are not equally relevant to all levels. They are primarily applicable to national and international levels although, in principle and by national action, they are also relevant to the administration of environmental policies at the local level.

A Ten Point Program

IN ORDER THAT IT MAY more effectively play its role in meeting the challenge of safeguarding the human environment, each nation or international organization, insofar as applicable to its circumstances, should consider action to:

1. declare a policy for the environment, with action-forcing provisions, to serve as a guide to legislative and administrative implementation;
2. survey and evaluate the overall state of the environment within the area of its responsibility as a basis for the establishment of priorities and plans of action in relation to human needs, available resources, and social goals;
3. appraise its organizational suitability in relation to the multidisciplinary, multilevel, and evolving character of environmental problems and where necessary restructure for more effective performance;
4. review its administrative processes and procedures for adaptability to environmental problem solving and, where necessary, seek new methods and techniques for the administration of environmental programs;
5. ascertain the personnel needs of environmental programs and devise procedures for recruiting, selecting, training, and optimum utilization of organizational personnel;
6. develop information systems to provide public decision makers and all affected parties with accurate, timely, and meaningful data on environmental problems and the estimated impact of human activities upon the environment (needed for implementing Point 7);
7. develop systematic means for coordinating and reviewing all environment-related activities under a common policy (Point 1) and especially with respect to planning, applied science, technology, and development;
8. establish a policy guiding and reporting council or commission at the highest policy levels to make visible

the environmental issue, to represent the environmental conscience of its constituents, and to assist in the practical tasks of program coordination (Point 7);

9. establish facilities for research on environmental problems, including their social and economic implications, and the organization and administration of environmental programs;
and

10. establish continuing programs for public understanding of man's relationships with both natural and cultural environments and his role in the administration of environmental protection efforts.

The elements of this program will now be considered in greater detail.

1. Declaration of Policy

MERE POSSESSION OF THE organizational and administrative capabilities for carrying out environmental policy is insufficient to insure effective action. If results are to be obtained, administrative machinery and action must be directed toward specified outcomes—administration never occurs in the abstract.

The first, and most obvious, prerequisite for administrative effectiveness is the establishment of general goals and guidelines for environmental policy. To be useful, these goals and guidelines should be stated as general rules or principles, and in operational language, that is, capable of being administered. Insofar as feasible and appropriate, they should be action-forcing; that is, they should not only state principles, but should also indicate or require administrative action to put the principles into effect. Agencies should be required to review all plans and programs to ascertain their probable environmental effects according to specified criteria. The declaration should therefore provide criteria by which existing and proposed programs can be evaluated. It should afford a basis for cooperation among all levels of public action and with the nongovernmental sector; it should not only enunciate a clear policy for the protection of environmental values, but should also indicate the desired relationship between them and other legitimate social needs, for example, population control, urban planning, natural resources conservation, nutrition, health, education, and recreation. For example, the declaration might state the relationship between the level of population, the availability of natural resources, and the quality of human life.

Because of the fundamental character of the declaration, and the differences between an international declaration which has largely moral force and a national declaration which could have the force of law, declarations are needed at both international and national levels. A statutory declaration has been adopted for the United States in the preamble and initial section of the National Environmental Policy Act of 1969. And as we have seen in Chapter 5, declarations of policy and objectives have been published by the United Nations Association of the Nordic Countries, and by the Council of Europe. An international declaration on the human environment is to come out of the United Nations Conference on the Human Environment.

2. *Environmental Survey*

A SECOND AREA OF ACTION needed to provide a basis for planning and administration is the assessment of environmental conditions within the geographical area of responsibility. Whenever a nation establishes a comprehensive policy for the environment, and administrative agencies to execute that policy, it is obvious that the comprehensive survey of environmental conditions is needed. A survey is necessary to identify the major problems, to indicate priorities, and to establish benchmarks against which subsequent trends can be measured; and also against which the success of preventive, corrective, and restorative efforts can be evaluated. As a part of its examination of environmental trends, such a survey should review the nature and probable effects of development plans, proposed or in operation. It is likely that many of these plans were initiated before the environmental side effects of development were as well understood as they now are.

Projects resulting in ecologically-damaging consequences should be reconsidered or redesigned. The survey of environmental conditions is not a one-time task, but should be a continuing function of whatever agency is charged with responsibility for assembling and interpreting environmental data. But the initial inquiry into the condition of the natural environment is of such great importance that it should be included as a major part in any comprehensive program of action.

There is, of course, a wide difference among countries in the comprehensiveness and detail necessary or possible for such a report. No national government has as yet undertaken anything approaching a thorough assessment of its environmental condition. However, the first annual report of the Council on Environmental Quality of the United States provides one of the more complete reviews of environmental conditions thus far undertaken.[20] Need for such an assessment, even a very general one, has been recognized by the United Nations Preparatory Committee for the Stockholm conference, which requested a general overview of the condition of the biosphere to be available before the conference.

3. Appraisal of Organizational Suitability

A THIRD AREA OF THE ACTION is appraisal of the suitability of existing organization for effective implementation of environmental policy. In order to estimate this suitability, it is necessary to analyze the relationships between legislative provisions and administrative structures as they affect policies and procedures connected with environmental goals. There are several ways by which this examination may be undertaken. Statutory provisions and administrative arrangements may be reviewed by some central authority competent to undertake this function. Conversely, each governmental department or agency may be required to review its own statutory authority and administrative policies and practices, and to submit reports on their conformity with the declared national policy. This latter approach was used in Section 103 of the National Environmental Policy Act of the United States as the more practical alternative to a costly and time-consuming centralized analysis of statutory and administrative law.

There is yet another approach to the analysis of organizational suitability, which is to examine selectively existing legislative and administrative provisions to ascertain their aptness to successful implementation of environmental policy. This approach is not concerned so much with finding inconsistencies between declared environmental policies and existing statutes and administrative practices as it is with finding positive ways for bringing existing practices into line with declared policy with minimal reorganization of the administrative structure. For this approach to be useful, obviously there must be authoritative means for reconciling through executive action, so far as possible, conflicting or inconsistent goals or objectives.

Special attention should be given to organizational structures at intergovernmental interfaces; that is, at the points of contact between national agencies and international organizations, and between national agencies and local authorities. To the extent that intergovernmental or multilevel cooperation is required, organizational structure should facilitate and not impede interaction. A United Nations initiative might usefully assist a comparative study of these organizational linkages to discover the nature and magnitude of such difficulties as may exist, and to propose needed remedial measures at all levels. A considerable amount of information regarding these linkages has been gathered for development programs.[21]

At national levels, offices of management analysis, often associated with budget administration, regularly undertake studies of organizational and administrative performance. It is, therefore, important that the criteria for organizational effectiveness in environmental programs be specified, especially in relation to the ability of government agencies to cooperate across political boundaries, as in international commitments. The logical place to specify these criteria is in basic national laws or declarations concerning the environment; although for particular purposes, it might also be done in international treaties.

4. *Review of Administrative Processes and Procedures*

THE PROCESSES OF ADMINISTRATION are not, in practice, fully separable from the organizational structures through which they operate. Nevertheless, they may be separately considered in analyzing their effects upon public policy and action. Deficiencies in a poorly-designed organization can partly be overcome by skillful administration; and conversely a well-designed structure may be poorly administered. It is unnecessary to the purposes of this book to detail all of the aspects of administration that might be considered in a review of its relationship to environmental goals and programs. Two aspects of administration—information handling and program coordination—are of such importance to environmental protection and management that they merited special listing as Points 6 and 7 in this enumeration.

The purpose of the review suggested under this point is to ascertain the actual effect of administrative operations upon environmental issues.[22] For example, answers should be sought to such questions as:

1. What is the effect of the administration of tax and fiscal measures upon environmental quality?
2. What requirements for care of the environment does government exact from licensees, concessionaires, and franchise holders?
3. How effectively does "the administration" communicate with its public and employees on environmental issues?
4. What use is made of the better developed tools of operations research, systems analysis, and program budgeting?
5. To what extent has "the administration" of any agency or program defined its sub-goals pursuant to the larger public purpose of environmental protection and enhancement?
6. To what extent is administrative action discretionary, and on what points is it bound by public laws on environmental issues?

5. Ascertain Human Resource Needs

THE RELATIVE NEWNESS of many aspects of environmental protection suggest that all levels may find shortages of personnel who have the knowledge and skills needed in environmental programs. A governmental or international agency that maintains continuing information on the capabilities of its employees is, to that extent, well-prepared to make the best use of available human resources. In an age of rapid technological and environmental change, a "skill file," a continually updated record of the various abilities of organization personnel, is a managerial tool that should be widely adopted.[23] Its usefulness could be great, depending upon the ability of administrators to use it in reassignments of work and transfers of personnel. Here is an illustration of the previously noted need for flexible administrative arrangements. But long-range planning for use of personnel is also implied. Programs scheduled to be reduced or terminated in either the public or nongovernmental sector should be examined to ascertain whether their personnel possess skills usable in other, especially new, efforts.

Education and training are important tools of human resources development. Reconversion training makes best use of public investment in public personnel by retaining their experience in the public service and adding new abilities to their basic skills. For example, programs are now being developed in the United States to reorient and retrain space scientists and engineers, whose field is phasing down, for work in environmental programs that are building up. Environmental protection may afford new employment opportunities, especially in developing countries where changes in agriculture have displaced people from the land, where industrial development is unable to fully absorb the surplus working force, and where environmental problems are growing. Many environmental protection measures involve labor-intensive tasks which highly mechanized societies find difficult and expensive to perform. Many of these tasks, for example, correcting soil erosion, replanting deforested areas, patrolling national parks and wildlife areas, digging wells, and laying sewers and water lines, are equally necessary to development and to environmental quality. Minimal training may be required for manual labor, but for planning and supervising the work, special capabilities are needed and more training may be required.

Secondary schools, technical institutes, and universities can assist the development of personnel resources if they understand the needs. Unfortunately, formal education has, almost everywhere, lagged behind the environmental needs of the times, both in teaching and in research. The universities, in particular, are organized around the disciplines and professions, and are much better at producing specialists than competent well-informed generalists. Although there are exceptions, university education has not developed that capacity for synthesis which is needed in the planning and administration of environmental (and developmental) policies. Governments might take more initiative in stimulating and assisting the growth of problem-focused education in the universities, with special attention to the art and science of synthesis in policy formulation and administration.

6. Information Systems for Decision Makers

POSSIBLY, THE SINGLE GREATEST contribution that organization and administrative analysis could make to environmental protection would be to develop systems for the flow of needed information into, through, and out of governments and international organizations. The changing conditions of the human environment are increasingly being observed and recorded through systems of monitoring and surveillance. The ultimate usefulness of this data depends upon its application to practical environmental problems. But to use this information, the administrator must receive it in a form appropriate to his decision-making responsibilities. And although public officials generally need to enlarge their personal capacity to understand and act upon environmental problems, their ability to perform effectively will still depend in large measure on the quality of the available information-handling apparatus.

We are as yet in the early stages of learning what information is needed for environmental protection and how to digest and present it for use by public officials and citizens generally. Not all of this task must necessarily be performed within the public service. As noted in the preceding chapter, the International Council of Scientific Unions has proposed the establishment of an International Center for the Environment that could handle the global aspects of environmental information. Its services would be available to national governments and international organizations. The International Union for Conservation of Nature and Natural Resources, in consultation with several UN specialized agencies, is preparing a handbook on ecological factors in development which could be a very useful aid to development planning and to the training of administrative personnel in developmental and environmental programs.

These organizational facilities must be supplemented by systems and procedures within governments and the international structure to make sure that environmental information is available in the right place, at the right time, in the right form and amount. Although no single organization could be expected to handle the flow of information at the international level, there might nevertheless be great value in a central information exchange, which could be linked with regional data centers and national research and information facilities through a worldwide computerized network.

Closely related to the information handling capacity, is the ability of an administrative system to integrate inputs from many disciplines and many sources into coherent policies and programs. As we have previously noted, the traditional structuring of government by function is designed for specialization and not for synthesis. But the capacity for synthesis is what is critical to the success of major efforts in national development and environmental protection. The means to attaining integration among inputs pertinent to the administration of environmental policies has not been adequately explored. The need for a more adequate understanding of the process of synthesis was forcibly stated by Paul H. Appleby, following a study of administration for the government of India:

Specialist after specialist pursues analysis; who pursues synthesis, or even pursues analysis with any sensible orientation to the larger function of synthesis? It is the synthesis which involves all the heavy burdens of practitioners, and these burdens are heaviest when the social action is most complex and most complexly environed. Synthesis becomes more and more important as one goes up the hierarchy, and more and more important as one moves from the relatively specialized fields of private administration to public administration.[24]

The task of synthesis becomes most apparent in the process of planning for the harmonious integration of efforts for development and environmental protection. Mere exhortation to harmonize developmental and environmental planning cannot accomplish the objective. Conceptual integration, a unified comprehensive view of the condition of a society, would seem to be a necessary prerequisite to synthesis at the operational level. Simply stated, to the extent that the people and government of a nation have agreed upon the goals to be pursued, policy synthesis becomes possible; where goals are contradictory or do not exist, the task of synthesis must await a reconciliation among goals or a determination of public objectives. For this reason, the Declaration of Policy (Point 1) has been placed at the head of the program of action.

7. Coordination of Environment-Related Activities

EACH OF THE TEN POINTS in this enumeration relates in some way to coordination, which is central to all other tasks of administration. But coordination is not something that the administrator does; it is a condition that his function is intended to promote. The administrative task may be assisted (or impeded) by a variety of factors of which organizational structure, adequacy and availability of information, capability of personnel, and, above all, clarity of organizational goals are especially important. These factors may outweigh whatever formal or official coordinative authority an administrative office may possess.

There appear to be limits to the ability of people to cooperate or to coordinate their efforts. These limits include psychological and personal factors unreachable through administrative processes. This circumstance has been tacitly recognized in human organizations, which are structured to cause people to behave in some ways rather than in others. Many of the rules and regulations of public (and private) organizations are intended to assist coordination through the channeling of behavior.

Coordination between independent agencies and separate

levels of responsibility poses additional difficulties. But in all cases, there can be no coordination until there is an order, which is to say, a policy, goal, or rule of procedure to provide a guideline for collaboration. The importance of a declared policy has been emphasized as a prerequisite to coordination, but a declaration is insufficient to obtain it without action-forcing provisions. But no policy can be stated so explicitly as to make its meaning evident in all conceivable cases. Provision for policy interpretation, necessarily a function of high political levels, will be considered under Point 8.

Action suggested under "coordination" would be a continuing review of how smoothly and consistently the organization machinery and administrative processes operated toward achieving a desired outcome. This supervision should be largely independent of the agencies and programs reviewed. Even when self-surveys are not self-serving, they lack the credibility of disinterested reviewers. There may be advantage in more than one coordinative review of agency activities. For example, central budget and planning agencies might play independent coordinative roles; but the chief executive or cabinet would have to assure coordination among the coordinators. Budget procedures have been among the most effective coordinative devices and have been elaborated under Programming, Planning, Budgeting (PPB) systems [25] which facilitate the examination of relationships among programs and activities involved in common areas of policy, such as natural resources management or land use, but which are located in separate administrative agencies.

8. Representation of Environmental Policy at Highest Political Levels

WITH ENVIRONMENT now becoming a major concern of national and international action, it is necessary to make visible its importance by giving it representation at the highest levels of policy making and administration. Concern for man–environment relationships in the broad sense is new to government, and it emerges in an institutional setting in which many of the forces that have contributed to the environmental problems of our times continue to exert powerful influences upon public policy and administration. National and international programs for environmental quality impinge upon nearly every other area of action in the public service, notably upon agriculture, public health, industrial development, urban and regional planning, natural resources management, outdoor recreation, transportation, and many others. In nearly every interaction, environmental policy is a restraining influence, affecting options that might otherwise be available to other programs. A newcomer to the field of public policy, environmental quality needs a prestigious and highly visible location in the administrative hierarchy, lest it be suppressed by competing interests.

For this reason, and because a high-level authority is needed for the continuing formulation and review of environmental policy, a number of governments have recently created high-level ministries, councils, or special advisers for environmental issues, among them Canada, France, Sweden, The United Kingdom, and the United States. Proposals have been made for an environmental council or committee at highest levels in the United Nations, as noted in the preceding chapter.

There are a variety of ways in which the high-level representation of environmental values might be accomplished. Environmental considerations could be added to the responsibilities of a high-level board or council for science and technology, or for development planning. In any event, environmental policies should be related to the evaluation of technoscientific applications and to development. Should a single high-level council for policy and planning encompass all three subject areas, it would be important to delineate general principles and priorities to guide trade-offs among these areas.

9. Research Facilities for Environmental Policy

IT IS READILY APPARENT that nations have very unequal resources for carrying on scientific research on the environment. But there are also great differences among them in their need for environmental research. Nevertheless, there are few, if any, nations that could not contribute in some measure to the total of knowledge concerning the human environment. As environmental monitoring stations are established throughout the world, it would be desirable for those nations in which the stations are situated to assume responsibility for their manning and administration. Yet a global environmental monitoring network, such as that proposed by the International Council of Scientific Unions and a number of United Nations specialized agencies, will require comparable levels of performance at comparable tasks in all participating countries. ICSU and UN initiatives in global environmental data gathering and research could stimulate the growth of scientific and technological capabilities in developing countries, and thereby also assist them in making more carefully considered and tested choices among alternatives in development planning, provided that their research in physical and biological aspects of the environment was related to social and behavioral factors and to questions of policy making, organization, and administration.

We have already noted proposals for a world environmental research center, and the growing possibility of such a facility being established. Regional research centers have been proposed and might be especially useful in areas such as the Caribbean and South East Asia, where the resources of individual states for the support of scientific research are limited. But even among states with advanced scientific capability, cooperative research would be sensible in the polar regions, beneath the deep sea, and in space, where the costs of research are very high.

Regional research centers would not necessarily need to consider only environmental problems, but might also deal with related aspects of development and serve as well as centers for advanced scientific education and training. With special reference to Point 6 on information systems, it is important that these centers or facilities are provided with some means for putting their findings into forms useful to policy makers. As an illustration of what might be done, the International Institute of Ecology (a nongovernmental organization with sponsors from Canada to Chile) has made social impact and policy studies an integral part of its program and will be prepared to be of service to public officials through its analysis of the implications of its scientific research findings for public policy and administration.

10. Public Understanding of Environmental Issues

THERE IS A SPECIAL ROLE for administration in the development of public awareness of environmental issues. Although many environmental problems are removed from people's daily experience and so are hard for them to understand, there are also many environmental issues that affect people in most direct and personal ways. Particularly in relation to these issues, public administrators, especially at local levels, need popular cooperation and support. But contributions to public awareness and understanding may be made at all levels. The United Nations Conference on the Human Environment has already stimulated thought and action at all levels. Public awareness of environmental problems can be increased by annual or periodic reports on the condition of the environment prepared by national agencies, such as the annual reports of the Council on Environmental Quality in the United States or the British White Paper on Protection of the Environment (1970).[26]

The most common and conventional educational role of administrative agencies is played through the dissemination of information through the communications media, especially through printed material. Merely to inform the public, however, has the disadvantage of providing no feedback, which is necessary for ascertaining the actual degree of public comprehension and consensus. This is why the device of public hearings upon action proposals, if honestly and competently managed, is an exceptionally valuable educational device, informing not only the public but also the public administrators. Thus the role of environmental administration in inducing the responsible and informed participation of citizens in public decisions may advance the practice of responsible and responsive self-government generally. It may assist the development of more adequate communication and comprehension between technical and administrative personnel in government and the general public, thus reducing social friction and encouraging a more constructive and confident relationship between people and their public officials and institutions.

8

Safeguarding the Biosphere:

STRATEGIES AND PROSPECTS

FOR TRANSFORMING

HUMAN BEHAVIOR

FOR MODERN MAN TO SURVIVE IN A FINITE WORLD, HE must restrain insatiable demands upon the natural environment and treat that environment with the respect and care that he would give his life-support system were he a passenger on a spaceship. Self-control has now become the quality essential to the individual and society alike, since man has become the greatest threat to his own survival and development.

This point was reached when human ingenuity set loose the accelerating process of technological development now called the Industrial Revolution. The explosions of human populations, of economic productivity, of information, and of technologies for exploiting resources are manifestations of a state of affairs, which Jacques Ellul describes as a technological society [1] and Zbigniew K. Brzezinski describes as the "technetronic era." [2] This course of development and growth continually accelerates through a kind of self-augmentation or positive feedback. Innovation triggers innovation, growth induces growth. The energies of peoples, of collective enterprises, and of governments are largely absorbed in maintaining the imperfectly joined components of the technoeconomic system which, at times, appears about to fly apart under the stress of unremitting accelerating change.

This preoccupation with maintaining the momentum and stability of an accelerating system, if projected indefinitely, appears to lead toward self-defeat. No phenomenon known to man, except perhaps the universe itself, seems to be capable of indefinite growth. Eventually, the technoeconomic system must slow down or drop back to a steady state, perhaps dynamic but no longer expansive. We do not know whether modern society can operate in a dynamically steady state, but it is certain that it cannot indefinitely continue to expand. A time must come when human society will either effectively manage its relationship to the planetary life-support system or see the decline and fall of the human species accompanied, perhaps, by the destruction of the planetary biosphere itself. The means to safeguard the viability of the planet are already within the reach of men, but the will to use them and a clear concept of the purposes toward which they should be directed have not yet been found.

The Institutional Context of Individual Behavior

IT MAY BE TAKEN that resolution of multiplex problems requires multiplex strategies. There are few really simple or easy solutions to the problems created by man's excessive demands upon the Earth. Few can be satisfactorily resolved by cutting Gordian knots. Although all promising forecasting techniques should be used in the development and evaluation of strategies, the large number of known variables and the many that are probably unforeseen makes it unrealistic to suppose that environmental strategies can be fully worked out in theory before being applied in practice. But the extent of analysis, testing, exploration of alternatives, and evaluation of possible outcomes would be far greater under a rational environmental administration than under the present course of environmental change. To postpone action on environmental issues until all evidence was in and all alternatives explored could result in irretrievable failure to prevent ecological disaster. Sound decision-making will take account of urgency, state of knowledge, and risks of action and inaction in attempting to assess the costs and benefits of alternative solutions.

The action now being taken on behalf of man's environment by the United Nations and by several of the technologically advanced countries appears to be in the right direction. These efforts, culminating in the United Nations Conference on the Human Environment in Stockholm in 1972, may not be sufficient to forestall major environmental disaster; but regardless of its outcome, the UN Conference on the Human Environment is already a landmark in the field of environmental problems because of the stimulation of thought and action brought about by preparations for it.

International conferences have not been notably successful catalysts of action, and whatever resolutions are taken at Stockholm will face formidable hazards before they are implemented. Most apparent among the obstacles is the resistance of many people and their political leaders to population control. But unless population growth can be halted and population levels ultimately reduced in many parts of the world, the viability of the Earth cannot indefinitely be sustained.

The widespread and indiscriminate commitment to economic growth, as distinguished from the quality of life, remains an almost equally formidable hazard. We have previously noted how the obsession with growth has distorted economic theory and practice of development. The continuing influence of growthmanship in many countries may, with little exaggeration, be called malignant. Gross national products rise—industry, agriculture, and urbanism expand—the living conditions of most people worsens and the quality of their environment deteriorates, often beyond recovery.

The major challenge to the UN Conference, however, will be to effectively mobilize action. Two traits of personality especially stand in the way of changing man's behavior toward the environment.

The first is a stubborn and often perverse unwillingness to face reality—to modify or abandon cherished concepts in the light of evidence regarding the endangered state of the Earth. The second is an intellectualized refinement of the first; it is a sophisticated skepticism about the existence or seriousness of the crisis. Unfortunately this reassuring doubt is sometimes voiced by high-ranking scientists and economists—rarely, however, among those whose work brings them closest to the evidence. But the general public and newsmen too often fail to discriminate among scientists. On a question of ecology the subjective opinion of a Nobel laureate in high energy physics may command more attention and respect than the opposing judgment of a relatively unknown ecologist. The public is then led to conclude that the scientists disagree and, therefore, there is no basis for action. The fact that the *relevant* scientists may not disagree is lost upon those who do not really understand the issues or the actors—and frequently that includes most people. Whatever strategies are adopted to move men to action in defense of the environment must find ways to remove these obstacles.

Individual human behavior in the aggregate projected over time appears as institutional inertia. It is never easy to alter the direction or momentum of a social system by voluntary and pacific means. Short of a traumatic crisis it is difficult to reform the goals or behavior of an organization or to infuse it with a sense of urgency when disaster does not appear to be immediately impending. Agencies of government and, indeed, all large organizations become so thoroughly built into their socio-economic environment that any major alteration of their form or focus may threaten disruption elsewhere in the society. Because of the interdependence of modern techno-industrial systems and the dependence of millions of people upon the continuous functioning of these systems, major changes in organizations or in society entail a high degree of risk—especially where major economic or political interests are involved.

The first step toward the transformations of behavior and institutions required for a defense of the Earth is to convince enough people that the change is necessary. This implies efforts to formulate environmental goals, for, until the destination is determined, the route to its realization cannot be laid out. Individual and institutional change must proceed together if society is to be transformed. Human behavior is at once individual and social; it is structured and reinforced through institutions. A strategy for action must, therefore, apply to individual, institutional, and social behavior simultaneously.

Making the Utopian Practical

IN A SMALL conceptualizing book entitled *Operating Manual for Spaceship Earth*,[3] Buckminster Fuller argues that managing man's relationships with his life-supporting planet will come through the development of general systems and synergies and in the proper relating of specialization to comprehensive purposeful planning. He rightly observes that it was on the oceans that men first discovered the global nature of the Earth and began to sense its unity. It may well be that in organizing and controlling man's relationship to the three-quarters of the surface of the Earth that is water, the first truly global or transnational (in contradistinction to international) institutions will be developed. Action on behalf of the biosphere can be through nothing less than a coherent system for guiding and controlling man's interactions with his environment. If this is a utopian concept, it is also practical. The needed system does not now exist, and the deterioration of the biosphere is an indirect consequence. There has been no feasible way for the many nations of the Earth at this stage in their political development to concert their efforts to protect the biosphere.

Even with the highest level of agreement and the greatest goodwill among nations, the magnitude and complexity of the task of biospheric protection would make the creation of coherent systems exceedingly difficult. Modern society has only begun to apply science and technology to the protection of the environment and to the management of man's relationships to it. There is much to be learned before we may be sure that human efforts will be successful and the results will be only those intended. But the social and psychological barriers to protection of the biosphere appear to be greater obstacles than the technical problems.

Troublesome among these are egos of political leaders, for it often seems that the personal qualities that enable men to become leaders of other men make them unfit for tasks of cooperation and peace. The mass of humanity appears to respond instinctively to leadership that was appropriate in the Stone Age or even in the era of Medieval war bands, but which is counter-productive in a society that possesses atomic bombs and persistent biocides. And closely related to the ego demands of charismatic leaders is a touchy popular pride in national self-determination. An exaggerated patriotism was once widely believed to be a civic virtue. Today, it must be modified by intelligent regard for the holistic character of the planetary life-support system and the ultimate unity of all living processes. Finally, economic temptations present barriers to international cooperation on behalf of the environment that are probably more profound and pervasive than political dogmas and ideologies.

What is required of the peoples and nations of the Earth is that they transcend their own histories. They must learn to be more farsighted and more realistic than they have ever been. There is no inexorable imperative compelling them toward this new and higher level of political development; although if they do not or cannot move in this direction, they cannot avoid the costs of failure. These costs have by now been enumerated so frequently that it is necessary only to state them here. They are:

1. Impoverishment and degradation of the human environment.
2. Adaptation to progressively lower qualities of life, accompanied by declining levels of public health and, perhaps, by increasing genetic deterioration.
3. Ultimate ecological catastrophe.

Humanity need not survive, nor even maintain or improve the present level of existence; but, if survival or improvement is wanted, then hopes and good intentions will not be enough to preserve and protect the Spaceship Earth. If the viability of the Earth were threatened by some inimical extra-terrestrial force, the peoples and nations of the world would surely make common cause to save themselves from disaster. To the extent necessary to safeguard the viability of the Earth, governments would almost certainly subordinate any nationalistic and particularistic doctrines and behaviors that would hinder defensive action. But the defense of the Earth demands no fewer sacrifices because the enemy is not from outer space but has grown out of the unecological behavior of man himself.

If modern man is asked to see himself as his own worst enemy, he is also asked to see himself as his only salvation. If, in the language of traditional religions, divine grace is the source of man's salvation, it can operate only through the acts of man himself. Man's eyes have been opened to his predicament, and human knowledge and ingenuity have equipped him with the tools and the concepts necessary to preserve the Earth from terracide or war. How modern society responds to this challenge will surely be overwhelmingly the most important event of the twentieth century. But if the unecological behavior of society changes, it can only be because human behavior, individually and collectively will, in important respects, have been transformed.

Can Human Behavior Be Transformed?

To be wisely commanded, the natural world must be understood. That world includes man, who is now its most critical factor. The purposive control of human behavior, requiring a high degree of collective self-command, cannot be accomplished while we are ignorant of the forces that influence men and human societies. Our seriously defective understanding of human behavior has resulted in a dangerous situation for humanity. At a time when *human rationality* and *responsible morality* are the only resources available to avert man's self-made threat to the biosphere and his own future, his ability to employ these attributes is inadequately developed. The conditions now confronting human society make plain the desperate need for a reliable science of mankind—a science that does not yet exist.[4]

It does not exist, because there is no general agreement that such a science is needed or even possible, and also because there have been obvious limits to the willingness of men to be scientific about themselves. Indeed, among the worst offenders against the concept of scientific universality have been scientists themselves whose artificial subdivisions of knowledge provide no unified approach either to the study of individual men or to human societies.

A successful strategy for coping with man's behavior in relation to his environment must in some measure also be a strategy for a more valid structuring of knowledge. In actual fact, sociology is a biological science, while the so-called natural sciences, at least since Heisenberg, cannot exclude cultural phenomena from their purview. There are practical reasons for the present organization of knowledge, but it carries the encumbrance of tradition and the limitations of human insight and research methodology, and it is untrue to the unity of the real world.[5]

Failure of the social and behavioral sciences to be fully accepted in the community of the sciences may be due as much to the difficulty of pursuing truth without prejudice, and the inadequacy of concerted attack upon social questions as to the inaccuracy of methods or to the lack of conceptual clarity.[6] The physical and biological sciences have been affected with conceptual biases and methodological dogmas, but their tests of truth and their ultimate willingness to consider demonstrated evidence have enabled them to be relatively reliable guides to action. In a word, they afford predictability. But among many social and behavioral scientists the tests of truth incorporate moral or political assumptions that are not submitted (nor always submissible) to dispassionate scrutiny.

Fear of research on the genetics of behavior because the findings might be socially embarrassing or politically mischievous illustrates the type of handicap that sometimes hampers science in seeking reliable prognoses of human behavior. Philosophical concepts like "human dignity" and "human rights" may be inspiring and noble but provide little practical guidance for decision makers coping with the problems of creating man–environment relationships in which these concepts might have substance. Konrad Lorenz observes, "Philosophical anthropology of a type neglecting biological fact has done its worst by imbuing humanity with a sort of pride which comes not only before, but causes, a fall."[7]

With some notable exceptions, the movement to save Earth's biosphere from death has been initiated by persons intellectually oriented toward the physical or biological sciences. For years, demographers and statistical social scientists compiled population projections, seemingly unaware of their ecological implications. With very few exceptions, it remained for environmental biologists, geographers, journalists, and other concerned individuals to translate statistical projections into news of an impending ecological crisis. And social scientists have been among the more outspokenly skeptical regarding the reality of the crisis and its importance to other social issues.[8]

If human behavior can be transformed so that men will be able to safeguard the biosphere, the social and behavioral sciences as presently oriented do not tell us how. Change in their orientation is possible—ultimately it will be necessary if society is to cope with its problems. That traditional disciplinary boundaries are ill adapted for solving complex socio-ecological problems will become increasingly apparent if the disciplines are asked to solve these problems.

Nevertheless, the means of coping with man's environmental crisis can be found only in those areas of human experience studied by the socio-behavioral sciences. Those areas include most significantly: cultural attitudes, patterns of behavior, and the dynamic structuring of social institutions. Underlying these behavioral areas is the biological foundation of phylogenetic conditioning with which civilized man must learn to deal if he is to survive. But since the stress man puts upon his environment is a phenomenon of numbers and socially created technologies, the remedies must somehow restructure social systems rather than rely wholly upon achieving changes in individual volition. As we have repeatedly emphasized, individual man, unorganized and unaided by institutions, can do little to protect the environment from the ravages of a populous society.

Our thesis assumes that human behavior *can* be transformed, but it does not assume that it *will* be transformed in a desirable way or in sufficient time. It also suggests that a major re-orientation of the sciences may be necessary if the transformation is to be realized. Effective action is dependent upon knowledge, much of which does not yet exist and much of which, while existing, has never been marshalled into applicable relationships. Science as science cannot save the world, but it can help to discover and interpret the knowledge needed to develop guidelines for social action. These guidelines can be applied only through institutions: for example, through systems of education, engineering, communication, production, distribution, public health, safety, and welfare. Institutions are instruments of social policy, and are subject to social governance; it is their behavior or performance that especially must be changed if the biosphere is to be saved.

Can institutions be changed without first changing the people whose collective behavior is reflected in them? Certainly institutional change does not occur without human agents. But how many agents of change are required? Under what circumstances are they most likely to succeed? Is there a critical mass in a population or social class that must be changed in order to transform the entire system?

Institutional changes encompass too many variables to permit simple, unqualified answers to these questions. The weakening of established institutions is one of the more plausible indications that new institutional forms may be emerging. Change is made even more probable as doctrines or ideologies emerge that predict or explain the passing of old forms and the need for new ones. The acceptance of a new way of thought has often depended upon its ability to displace prevailing concepts because it appeared to offer an interpretation of reality better adapted to the circumstances of the times. When action is required to cope with these circumstances, a philosophy that is consistent with reality and that provides a guide to action may have a powerful appeal. If the politics of ecology can forge firm links between scientific knowledge and a plan of action, it may displace prevailing political doctrines that have not proved easily adaptable to the challenge of the environmental crisis.

In a general way the sequence of events leading to behavioral change is as follows: The actual circumstances of society change more rapidly than popular beliefs or behavior patterns. Institutions progressively lose their ability to answer needs and respond effectively to events. The inadequate response to events shakes the popular faith in the validity of ideas and authority of institutions that have previously seemed beyond question. Out of an attempt to explain the malfunctioning of the established order, a new theory or ideology arises which compares what *is* to what *ought to be* and may lead to a strategy for social change. If successful the change results in new norms of behavior and is implemented by new institutions designed to succeed where the old ones failed.

Our concern has been with changing behavior in relation to the environment. The transition from an open-space to a closed-space concept of the world requires a radical restructuring of what we think is possible, of our values, and of our institutions.[9] To safeguard the biosphere the change must be worldwide, fundamental, and pervasive permeating a great diversity of classes and cultures. From now into the future men may differ but they cannot afford to differ over the necessity for changes in their collective behavior to preserve the viability of the Earth.

An Ethical Dilemma

THIS LINE OF REASONING implies the general acceptance and implementation of an ecological ethic hitherto held by no more than a small minority of people in modern society. Fortunately, for its general acceptability, the ecological viewpoint is not peculiar to any particular cultural, national, or religious system. Although in its science-based formulation it is a contemporary attitude, it implies behavior advocated in a variety of ethical systems extending through time, from the legendary Lao Tse through St. Francis to Paul Tillich. Its basic assumptions correspond to the pre-scientific assumptions of many so called "primitive" people. Thus, people may accept the ethics and political economy of Spaceship Earth without feeling that they are asked to yield to another peoples' values. Sensitivities in the less technoscientifically developed countries may be relieved if it is apparent that profound and difficult behavioral changes are also being undertaken in the highly industrialized nations.

The expression "ecological ethic" should suggest a general attitude toward the natural world rather than a single well-developed philosophical doctrine. There are, in fact, many ecological ethics, but among them there are certain propositions that may be taken as the essence of an ecologically oriented point of view. The propositions are these:

1. Man is an integral part of the natural world and, hence, inseparable from it and from its governing processes and laws.
2. Humanity has no extraordinary moral claim or rights over the natural world.
3. Through manipulation of natural forces man may in some measure control nature, but he may do so safely only within the parameters of nature's laws.
4. Natural laws cannot be violated with impunity, but punishment does not necessarily fall on the perpetrator of an offense.
5. The world continuously changes, but if it is to support life and human society, its self-renewing capabilities must be maintained.

Other propositions could be added, but few people have troubled to examine the implicit meaning and logic of ones given above. As rationale for the defense of the Earth against destruction by man, they are hardly counsels of harmony in society. Between the protectors and despoilers of the biosphere there is a basic conflict. No mere literary allusion was the title of Garrett Hardin's 1969 Brookhaven Symposium Lecture: "Not Peace, but Ecology." [10]

One change required in all countries, and now becoming especially critical in those technoscientifically less developed, is the reduction of human populations. Although there is no end to arguments regarding the numbers of people that technological improvisation might allow to subsist, the Earth is already vastly overpopulated in relation to the natural conditions in which mankind evolved and civilization arose. Optimum population is relative and when a given level of population for a given area of the Earth is described as "optimal," a set of parameters is implied. The issue cannot be rationally attacked, therefore, until these parameters are made explicit. Perhaps that can be done in 1974, which is designated by the Economic and Social Council of the United Nations as World Population Year; there will be a world conference of United Nations member states and the specialized agencies on population problems then. [11]

Two points should be made clear. First, there seem to be

no fixed or absolute numbers, except at the extremes, that, in the abstract, define an optimal population or the threshold levels of ecologically dangerous over- or underpopulation. Second, there is an approximate ceiling in human numbers and densities beyond which many human conditions and values, perhaps ultimately all values, cannot thrive, regardless of the potentialities of the available technology.[12] A rational public policy for population would require the examination of a great variety of parameters and alternatives in order to establish a range of approximate optimality. On the basis of one highly significant factor—the ability of people to live in a naturally self-renewing environment —there is substantial agreement among ecologists and population biologists that the Earth cannot indefinitely support present levels of human demand on its living space and natural systems and resources. Indeed, it could not now extend to most people anything approaching the standards of personal comfort, convenience, and mobility now enjoyed by middle and upper class inhabitants of northwestern Europe and North America.

The ecological prospects for mankind would be greatly improved were the world's population reduced to at most one-third of its present level. The distribution of this reduction could vary considerably. Some few countries could afford to gain; some, perhaps like Sweden, could remain approximately stationary; some, like the United States, would benefit ecologically and in other ways by a reduction to half of its present population; and for China, India, Mexico and many others, only reductions beyond two-thirds would overcome the present impoverishment of peoples and ecosystems.

It will doubtless be contended that nothing like these reductions may plausibly be expected within several generations. Possibly not. At any event such reductions by anything like humane means could require a century or more. In the immediate future, it is more probable that severe population imbalance and instabilities will increasingly strain the carrying capacity of nations. For large areas of the Earth, famine is now foreseen within the decade of the 1970s.[13] Other ecological disasters have been predicted, most of them relating somehow to excessive levels or densities of population. If these gloomy predictions are accurate (as present-day examples discussed in Chapter 4 indicate), a major question of public ethics arises. Are all people responsible for the ecological errors and follies of some people? Do peoples and nations, under present world conditions, have a "right" to pursue ecologically disastrous policies, and are the more prudent or fortunate morally bound to aid them in their self-caused difficulties? Just what right may peoples justifiably claim whose recklessness endangers all mankind? [14]

The efforts of the United Nations to establish human rights by declaration have not had immediate or positive success. A new declaration on the environmental responsibility of peoples and nations from the 1972 Stockholm conference will depend for its effectiveness on how largely it is accepted among the nations and whether its principles can be applied to international law and public administration.

Depending upon one's philosophical premises, there are a number of different answers to these questions. But abstract concepts of rights and morals, unrelated to actual circumstances, are not relevant to the survival of the species or of the biosphere. As the Earth becomes more populous, and as technology provides more opportunities for irremeable ecological error, the ethics of the spaceship may become more like those of a lifeboat. In circumstances of absolute crisis, in order that all may not perish, it has been necessary to restrain demented or dangerous passengers.

To each sentient individual, life is precious; yet in the aggregates of the natural world and human history individual life often has been regarded as if it were cheap—and the more abundant, the cheaper. Man's indiscriminate multiplication and reckless exploitation of the Earth cheapens his individual existence in the processes of nature, if not in all philosophies of man. In short, large numbers of men are now redundant and for the survival of the species are, unhappily, expendable.

In a world of nations, measures for the salvation of the world can be taken only by cooperative international action. If an ecologically sound and timely plan for action for the world can be drafted and implemented, there may be hope that the suffering and disaster already made inevitable by past and present human error can be mitigated and eventually survived. If it cannot be done, or is not done, will individual nations, or groups of them, be justified by the ethics of ecology and the lifeboat in taking whatever measures may be required to protect themselves from the folly of inept or willful neighbors? Whether such a denouement would be a greater or lesser tragedy than universal destruction is presently unanswerable.

Toward A More Valid Way of Thought

THERE IS, THEREFORE, need for a rapid restructuring of the hierarchy of values and institutions by which the "unecological animal" has attempted to govern his behavior. If the effects of an already inevitable world tragedy are to be contained and then reversed, a quantum leap to a new level of cooperation among peoples must occur.[15] This is to say that a new level of human organization must be achieved, one not predictable from the historical past. The new level of worldwide cooperation must have some continuity with the historical past. Man builds upon his available experience. But a new system of behavior is required that can rapidly transform itself into something without historical precedent; and this transformation implies a more valid way of thought.

The institutional elements and characteristics of this new system for guiding human behavior have been outlined in Chapters 6 and 7. Although certain of the structures and relationships proposed are unprecedented in practice, they are not without precedent in concept. Elements of experience exist for every innovation that has been suggested; only their organization into a coherent and coordinated system is novel. As often happens in human affairs, man's difficulty is not primarily with the theoretical mechanics of a new system of international cooperation; it is rather with his own nature, which is inseparable from his institutional behavior.

The secular religions of modern man, notably nationalism and socialism, overcompensated for the pessimism about human nature of traditional religious orthodoxy. A materialistic muscle-flexing optimism has characterized industrializing societies. Democratic ideologies stressed the worth of man, and seldom reckoned realistically with human inadequacies. Society itself became an object of secular worship, but this new theocrat was an abstract proposition, a philosophical concept that did not appear to be a perfect sum of its visible parts, which were obviously imperfect. More valid ways of thinking about relationships among men, societies, and their environments are required if the present challenge to man's self-direction is to be met.

An institutional system for guiding man's behavior in relation to the Earth must therefore be supported by a system of relevant thought. Whatever else they may believe, men must understand and accept their role as custodians for this unique and lonely planet if it is to survive. The conceptual basis for a new system of thought has slowly been forming, converging in the work of scientists, theologians, artists, political leaders, and many undistinguished but perceptive individuals. René Dubos epitomized its character in his phrase, "theology of the Earth." [16]

But no new thing is wholly new. Many of the elements of the system of thought required for the defense of the Earth must have been sensed intuitively by man as early as the dawn of self-consciousness. It would otherwise be difficult to explain the well-developed expression of the interrelatedness of man and nature in the earliest myths and religions. But not until the development of modern science has man had the means to test the validity of propositions about his relationships with nature, and to identify and correct those that are in error. The advent of science has not destroyed all dogmatic systems of belief, but has put all of them on the defensive.

The philosophic concept of the Chain of Being—the idea of a completely interrelated, rational, intelligible universe—could not be proved by logic. Such philosophic efforts to explain the universe and man's relationship to it ended in failure.[17] The search for understanding could not be pursued effectively without the aid of science. Unfortunately, while offering the tools, science until now has been too specialized, tentative, and incomplete to provide an adequate basis for a new cosmology that includes human society. Nevertheless, a more valid science-based philosophy has become an urgent need.

The idea of a guiding system of thought may be rejected in principle by persons who distrust dogma or who do not believe that it is possible or desirable to channel or direct human thought or behavior. But neither of these objections should apply to the kind of intellectual system that appears needed. The short-range empiricism that has rationalized political behavior during the past century not only failed to alert society to the build-up of its environmental problems, it very likely contributed to their development. The changes in the behavior of individuals and of societies implied in the "environmental revolution" [18] can be accomplished only through a massive change in human understanding, and in the concomitant assumptions as to what behavior is wise or permissible in man's relationships with the Earth.

The liberal mind may resist constraint, but man lives in a constrained world. The opportunities that the Earth affords will remain available only if the real limits of the biosphere are respected. To organize a view of life upon the basis of knowledge of the world as it really is, subject to correction as knowledge expands, is no limitation on man's spirit. It offers the best opportunity for all mankind now and in the future.

But we are in the present, and the Earth is in danger. The only skeptics are those who have not really seen the evidence. Yet, men and societies will continue along their destructive course until the force of new ideas are made operative through institutions, enabling them to move in new directions. The prospect is ominous because the threat is massive and increasingly swift. It is not clear that our defensive reactions will be adequate to meet the threat. We will now discover whether the human animal is indeed capable of guiding his own destiny. For the defense of the Earth against man's misuse is an ultimate test of man's fitness to "have dominion . . . over every living thing that moves upon the Earth." It is a test of man's collective intelligence and of his capacity for a rational shaping of his still possible futures.

NOTES AND CITATIONS

The notes contain bibliographies on many topics. The principal subjects are indicated by darker type.

Chapter 1 An Unecological Animal

1. On **the crises of our times and how society may cope with them,** see: John Black, *The Dominion of Man: The Search for Ecological Responsibility.* Edinburgh: Edinburgh University Press, 1970, vi, 169; *Blueprint for Peace: Being the Proposals of Prominent Americans to the White House Conference on International Cooperation,* Richard N. Gardner, ed. New York: McGraw-Hill, 1966, vi, 404; Richard A. Falk, *This Endangered Planet: Prospects and Proposals for Human Survival.* New York: Random House, 1971, 495; and John R. Platt, "What We Must Do," *Science,* 166 (November 28, 1969), 1115–21. Other references to the very large literature on this subject will be cited subsequently where especially pertinent.

2. On the subject of **prediction and alternative futures,** see: Daniel Bell, "Twelve Modes of Prediction—a Preliminary Sorting of Approaches in the Social Sciences," *Daedalus,* 93 (Summer, 1964), 845–80; Denis Gabor, *Inventing the Future.* New York: Knopf, 1964, 237; Robert Heilbronner, *The Future as History.* New York: Harper, 1960, 217; Erich Jantsch, *Technological Forecasting in Perspective.* Paris: Organization for Economic Cooperation and Development, 1967, 401; Bertrand de Jouvenel, *The Art of Conjecture.* New York: Basic Books, 1967, 307; Todd R. LaPorte, "Politics and 'Inventing the Future': Perspectives in Science and Government," *Public Administration Review,* 27 (June 1967), 117–27; Robert W. Prehoda, *Designing the Future: The Role of Technological Forecasting.* Philadelphia: Chilton, 1967, 310; Robert G. Sachs, "Power of Prediction—An Example," *Bulletin of the Atomic Scientists,* 20 (December 1964), 20–21; and Michael Scriven, "Explanation and Prediction in Evolutionary Theory," *Science,* 130 (August 28, 1959), 477–82. See also the journal, *Futures,* (September 1968).

3. Nicholas Tinbergen, *Social Behavior in Animals With Special*

Reference to Vertebrates. London: Methuen, 1953, xi, 150; John Paul Scott, *Animal Behavior.* Garden City, New York: Doubleday, 1963, 331; and Peter H. Klopfer and Jack P. Hailman, *An Introduction to Animal Behavior: Ethnology's First Century.* Englewood Cliffs, New Jersey: Prentice-Hall, 1967, 297. For a classic statement of niche theory, see G. E. Hutchinson, "Homage to Santa Rosalia or Why are There so Many Kinds of Animals?" *The American Naturalist,* 93 (May–June 1959), 145–59.

4. *On Aggression.* Translated from the German by Marjorie Kerr Wilson. New York: Harcourt, Brace & World, 1966, 306. For other interpretation and comment on **man's unecological behavior** see: Raymond Boulienne, "Man, the Destroying Biotype," *Science,* 135 (March 2, 1962), 706–12; Loren C. Eiseley, "Man: The Lethal Factor," *American Scientist,* 51 (March 1963), 71–83; S. Charles Kendeigh, "The Ecology of Man the Animal," *BioScience,* 15 (August 1965), 521–23; and A. M. Guhl, "Sociobiology and Man," *Bulletin of the Atomic Scientists,* 21 (October 1965), 22–24.

5. Cf. Bruce J. Cohen, "Aggressive Crimes," Chapter 2 of *Crime in America.* Itasca, Illinois: F. E. Peacock, 1970, 48, 56.

6. Paul S. Martin, "Prehistoric Overkill" in *Pleistocene Extinctions: The Search for a Cause,* Paul S. Martin and H. E. Wright, Jr., eds. New Haven: Yale University Press, 1967, 115. Note also comments of Carl O. Sauer, subtitled "Extinction of Pleistocene Mammals" in "A Geographic Sketch of Early Man in America," *Geographical Review,* 34 (October 1944), 529–73. For an interesting sidelight on prehistoric hunting, see Ludwell H. Johnson, III, "Men and Elephants in America," *Scientific Monthly,* 85 (October 1952), 215–21; and by Henry F. Osborne and H. E. Anthony, "Close of the Age of Mammals," *Journal of Mammalogy,* 3 (November 1922), 219–37.

7. Chicago: Aldine, 1968, 415. Note pp. 3–12.

8. Ibid., 3.

9. *Eden Was No Garden: An Inquiry Into the Environment of Man.* New York: Holt, Rinehart & Winston, 1967, 240.

10. *Man the Hunter,* 3.

11. A danger especially pertinent to large, complex, interdependent social systems in built-in error which is subject to amplification through the operations of the systems. For an analysis of the problem, see Theodore Morgan, "The Theory of Error in Centrally-Directed Economic Systems," *Quarterly Journal of Economics,* 77 (August 1964), 395–419. See also Zygmunt Bauman, "The Limitations of 'Perfect Planning'" in *Action Under Planning: The Guidance of Economic Development,* Betram M. Gross, ed. New York: McGraw-Hill, 1967, 109–37.

12. Arthur Koestler, *The Ghost in the Machine.* New York: Macmillan, 1968, 384.

13. Ibid., 333–36.

14. For a convenient summation of the behaviorist approach, see essay in part two of *Being, Becoming and Behavior: The Psychological Science,*

Floyd W. Matson, ed. New York: George Braziller, 1967, 288. B. F. Skinner has summarized his views recently in *Beyond Freedom and Dignity*. New York: Knopf, 1971, 225.

15. I have described some of these theories in "Health and Homeostasis as Social Concepts: An Exploratory Essay" in *Diversity and Stability in Ecological Systems—Brookhaven Symposia in Biology: No. 22*. New York: Brookhaven National Laboratory, 206–23. See also Cynthia Eagle Russett, *The Concept of Equilibrium in American Social Thought*. New Haven: Yale University Press, 1966, 203; and a review of this book by Frederic L. Holmes in *History and Theory*, 9, No. 3 (1970), 375–90.

16. Morley Roberts, *Bio-Politics: An Essay in the Physiology, Pathology and Politics of the Social and Somatic Organism*. London: J. M. Dent, 1938, xv, 240. Note also reviews in *The Quarterly Review of Biology*, 13 (September 1938), 348–49 and *Nature*, 144 (July 23, 1938), 138.

17. W. Ross Ashby, "Principles of the Self-Organizing System" in *Principles of Self-Organization: Transactions of the Illinois Symposium on Self-Organization, June 8–9, 1961*, Heinz von Foerster and George W. Zopf, Jr., eds. New York: Pergamon Press, 1962, 255–78. See also *Self-Organizing Systems: Proceedings*, Marshall C. Yovits and C. Cameron, eds. New York: Pergamon Press, 1960, ix, 322.

18. *Mankind Evolving*. New Haven: Yale University Press, 1962, 20–21. For a variety of perspectives on the relation between human behavior and evolution, see *Behavior and Evolution*, Anne Roe and George Gaylord Simpson, eds. New Haven: Yale University Press, 1958, 557. (Papers from a conference sponsored jointly by the American Psychological Association and the Society for the Study of Evolution.)

19. *The Biology of Ultimate Concern*. New York: New American Library, 1967, 98.

20. "Lesson From a 'Primitive' People," *Science*, 170 (November 20, 1970), 820.

21. See, for example, Rhoads Murphey, "The Decline of North Africa Since the Roman Occupation: Climatic or Human?", *Annals of the Association of American Geographers*, 41 (June 1951), 116–32; W. S. Rosecrans, "Land and Man in History," *American Journal of Economics and Sociology*, 17 (July 1958), 337–40; and Harry S. Ladd, "Ecology, Paleontology, and Stratigraphy," *Science*, 129 (January 9, 1959). 69–78. A classic study of human impact upon the Earth is George Perkins Marsh, *Man and Nature or, Physical Geography as Modified by Human Action*. Originally published in 1864; reprinted in the John Harvard Library Series, David Lowenthal, ed. Cambridge: Harvard University Press, 1956, 472. The principal recent collection of papers on the subject is *Man's Role in Changing the Face of the Earth*, William L. Thomas, Jr., ed., *et al.* Chicago: University of Chicago Press, 1956, 1193.

22. This statement is, of course, open to question. It cannot be proved inasmuch as the outcome of present attitudes and disorders, even if their direction were accurately ascertained, cannot be foreseen with certainty.

The degree of social consensus and of willingness to cooperate is, however, critically important to our subject. The author's reading of contemporary trends corresponds generally to those of Andrew Hacker in *The End of the American Era*. New York: Atheneum, 1970, 239; and of Bernard James, *The Death of Progress*. New York: Knopf, 1972.

23. On the **religious aspect of environment,** note, for example, discussions in the following works: Vincent Scully, *The Earth, The Temple and the Gods*. New Haven: Yale University Press, 1962, 3: "Not only were certain landscapes indeed regarded by the Greeks as holy and as expressive of specific gods, or rather as embodiments of their presence, but also that the temples and the subsidiary buildings of their sanctuaries were so formed themselves and so placed in relation to the landscape and to each other as to enhance, develop, complement, and sometimes even to contradict, the basic meaning that was felt in the land." See also Alfred Forke, *The World Conception of the Chinese: Their Astronomical, Cosmological and Physico-philosophical Speculations*. London: A. Probsthain, 1925, xiv, 300; Rhoads Murphey, "Man and Nature in China," *Modern Asian Studies*, 1 (October 1967), 313–33; and Ilza Veith, "Creation and Evolution in the Far East" in *Evolution After Darwin*, Vol. 3, Sol Tax and Charles Callender, eds. Chicago: University of Chicago Press, 1960, 1–17. For contemporary Chinese attitudes, see Leo A. Orleans and Richard A. Suttmeier, "The Mao Ethic and Environmental Quality," *Science*, 170 (December 11, 1970), 1173–76.

24. Nancy W. Ross, *Hinduism, Buddhism, Zen: An Introduction to Their Meaning and Their Arts*. London: Faber, 1968, 222; Robert C. Zaehner, *Hinduism*. New York: Oxford University Press, 1962, 272; and Henry C. Hart, "The Natural Environment in Indian Tradition" in *Public Policy*, 12. Cambridge: Harvard University, Yearbook of the Graduate School of Public Administration, 1963, 41–77. For an account of man-environment attitudes in pre-Columbian America, see Terence Grieder, "Ecology Before Columbus," *Americas*, 22 (May 1970), 21–28.

25. Clarence J. Glacken, *Traces on the Rhodian Shore: Nature and Culture in Western Thought from Ancient Times to the End of the Eighteenth Century*. Berkeley and Los Angeles: University of California Press, 1967, Chapter 4, "God, Man, and Nature in Judeo-Christian Theology," and Part 2, "The Christian Middle Ages."

26. Lynn White, Jr., "The Historical Roots of Our Ecological Crisis," *Science*, 155 (March 10, 1967), 1203–07.

27. Note, for example, Frederick Elder, *Crisis in Eden: A Religious Study of Man and Environment*. Nashville, Tennessee: Abingdon Press, 1970, 172. (List of references to theological writings on environmental problems, p. 141.) Note also: Richard L. Means, "Why Worry About Nature?" *Saturday Review*, 50 (December 2, 1967), 13–15 and "Man and Nature: The Theological Vacuum," *Christian Century*, 85 (May 1968), 579–81; Theodosius G. Dobzhansky, *The Biology of Ultimate Concern*. New York: New American Library, 1967, xvii, 152; René Dubos, "A

Theology of the Earth." *A Lecture Delivered at the Smithsonian Institution on October 2, 1969.* Washington, D.C.: Smithsonian Institution, Office of Public Affairs, 1969, 19; Leo Marx, "American Institutions and Ecological Ideals," *Science*, 170 (November 27, 1970), 945–52; and Edward B. Fiske, "The Link Between Faith and Ecology," *The New York Times*, (January 4, 1970), Sec. 4, p. 5.

28. Albert Schweitzer, *Reverence for Life*. Translated by Reginald H. Fuller. New York: Harper & Row, 1969, 153.

29. E.g., *The Future of Religions*, Jerald C. Brauer, ed. New York: Harper & Row, 1966, 94.

30. Note articles in *Zygon—Journal of Science and Religion*, 1966—. E.g., Philip Hefner, "Toward a New Doctrine of Man: The Relationship of Man and Nature," *Zygon*, 2 (June 1967), 127–51; and Joseph Sittler, "Ecological Commitment as Theological Responsibility," *Zygon*, 5 (June 1970), 172–81.

31. On the concept of the **"ecosystem" and world ecosystem** or "ecosphere," see the following references: Thomas D. Brock, "The Ecosystem in the Steady State," *BioScience*, 17 (March 1967), 166–69; LaMont C. Cole, "The Ecosphere," *Scientific American*, 148 (April 1958), 83–96 and "Man's Ecosystem," *BioScience*, 16 (April 1966), 243–48; M. B. Dale. "Systems Analysis and Ecology," *Ecology*, 51, No. 1 (Winter 1970), 2–16; F. Fraser Darling and Raymond Dasmann, "The Ecosystem View of Society," *Impact of Science on Society*, 14 (April–June 1969), 109–21; D. Otis Duncan, "From Social System to Ecosystem," *Sociological Inquiry*, 31 (Spring 1961), 146–49; Francis E. Evans, "Ecosystem as the Basic Unit in Ecology," *Science*, 123 (June 22, 1956), 1127–28; David M. Gates, "Toward Understanding Ecosystems" in *Advances in Ecological Research*, Vol. 5, J. B. Cragg, ed. New York: Academic Press, 1968, 1–35; Harlan Lewis, "Evolutionary Processes in the Ecosystem," *BioScience*, 14 (March 1969), 223–27; A. MacFayden, "The Ecosystem" in *Animal Ecology: Aims and Methods*. New York: Pitman, 1963, 267–81; Eugene P. Odum, "The Strategy of Ecosystem Development," *Science*, 144 (April 18, 1969), 262–70; D. R. Stoddart, "Geography and the Ecological Approach: The Ecosystem as a Geographical Principle and Method," *Geography*, 50 (July 1965), 242–51; Robert P. McIntosh, "Ecosystems Evolution and Relational Patterns of Living Organisms," *American Scientist*, 51 (June 1963), 246–67; and George M. Van Dyne, ed., *The Ecosystem Concept in Natural Resource Management*. New York: Academic Press, 1969, 383.

32. On the **dominant role of technology** in modern society, see the following: Jacques Ellul, *The Technological Society*. Translated from the French by John Wilkinson. New York: A. A. Knopf, 1964, xxxvi, 449; John Kenneth Galbraith, *The New Industrial State*. Boston: Houghton-Mifflin, 1967, xiv, 427; F. G. Jünger, *The Failure of Technology*. Chicago: Gateway Editions (distributed by Henry Regnery), 1956 xvii, 204; Donald Michael, "Technology and the Human Environment," *Public Administration Review*, 28 (January–February 1968), 57–60; Lewis Mumford,

Technics and Civilization. New York: Harcourt Brace, 1934, 495; and Carl F. Stover, ed., *The Technological Order.* Detroit: Wayne State University Press, 1963, xii, 280. See also Chapter 4, n. 27.

33. For a diagrammatic illustration of this flow of material goods, see Allen V. Kneese, Robert U. Ayres, and Ralph C. d'Arge, *Economics and the Environment: A Materials Balance Approach.* Baltimore: Johns Hopkins Press for Resources for the Future, 1971, 132.

34. For examples of **reinterpretation of economic processes**, see: A. A. Berle, Jr., "What GNP Doesn't Tell Us," *Saturday Review,* 51 (August 31, 1968), 10–12, 40; Kenneth Boulding, "The Economics of the Coming Spaceship Earth" in *Environmental Quality in a Growing Economy,* Henry Jarrett, ed. Baltimore: Johns Hopkins Press, 1966, 3–14 and "Fun and Games with the Gross National Product—The Role of Misleading Indicators in Social Policy" in *The Environmental Crisis,* Harold U. Helfrich, ed. New Haven and London: Yale University Press, 1970, 157–70; S. V. Ciriacy-Wantrup, "The Economics of Environmental Policy," *Land Economics,* 47 (February 1971), 36–45; Orris C. Herfindahl and Allen V. Kneese, *Quality of the Environment: An Economic Approach to Some Problems in Using Land, Water, and Air.* Baltimore: Johns Hopkins Press, 1965, 96; K. William Kapp, "Environmental Disruption and Social Costs: A Challenge to Economics," *Kyklos,* 23 (Winter 1970), 833–48; Allen V. Kneese, "Economics and the Quality of the Environment—Some Empirical Experiences" in *Social Sciences and the Environment,* Morris E. Garnsey and James R. Hibbs, eds. Boulder: University of Colorado Press, 1967, 165–93; John V. Krutilla, "An Economic Approach to Coping with Flood Damage," *Water Resources Research,* 2 (Second Quarter 1966), 183–90; Ezra J. Mishan, *The Costs of Economic Growth.* New York: Frederick A. Praeger, 1967, xxi, 190; A. Allen Schmid, "Quality of the Environment and Man: Some Thoughts on Economic Institutions," *Journal of Soil and Water Conservation,* 21 (May–June 1966), 89–91; Joseph J. Spengler, "Homosphere, Seen and Unseen; Retreat from Atomism," *Proceedings, Nineteenth Southern Water Resources and Pollution Control Conference,* April 1970, 7–16; and Nathaniel Wollman, "The New Economics of Resources," *Daedalus,* 96 (Fall 1967), 1099–1114.

35. *Oriental Despotism: A Comparative Study of Total Power.* New Haven: Yale University Press, 1957, xix, 556.

36. Gustav F. Papanek, *Pakistan's Development, Social Goals and Private Incentives.* Cambridge: Harvard University Press, 1967, 354; Aloys Arthur Michel, *The Indus Rivers: A Study of the Effects of Partition.* New Haven, Connecticut: Yale University Press, 1967, 595; and *Land and Water Development in the Indus Plain: Report by the White House—Department of Interior, Panel on Waterlogging and Salinity in Pakistan.* 1st printing, January 1964, 2nd printing, October 1964, 454.

37. Orthodox scientists have not persuaded all of the "science-oriented" as well as unsophisticated "believers" that their descriptions of the existential world are valid. For accounts of highly unorthodox and un-

scientific interpretations of the nature of the Earth, see: Harold L. Nieburg, *In the Name of Science*. Chicago: Quadrangle Books, 1966, 431; and Louis Pauwels and Jacques Bergier, *The Morning of the Magicians*. Translated from the French by Rollo Myon. New York: Stein & Day, 1964, 300.

38. For interpretations of the **environmental aspect of personality** and behavior, a different but related consideration, see the following: Gordon W. Allport, *Becoming: Basic Considerations for a Psychology of Personality*. New Haven: Yale University Press, 1955, 106. *Environmental Perception and Behavior*, David Lowenthal, ed. Chicago: University of Chicago, Department of Geography, 1967, 88 (Research Paper No. 109). For other examples of the large literature on environmental aspects of personality and behavior, see relevant writings by Kurt Lewin, Edward T. Hall, Isidor Chien, Joachim Wohlwill, Bruce L. Welch, and writers on Gestalt Psychology. Of direct pertinence, is Roger Garlock Barker, *Ecological Psychology: Concepts and Methods for Studying the Environment of Human Behavior*. Stanford, California: Stanford University Press, 1968, 242; and S. B. Sells, "Ecology and the Science of Psychology," *Multivariate Behavioral Research*, 1 (April 1966), 131–44.

39. For example, see: Clarence J. Glacken, "Man Against Nature: An Outmoded Concept" in *The Environmental Crisis*, Harold W. Helfrich, Jr., ed. New Haven and London: Yale University Press, 1970, 127–42. (Note especially p. 138, for comments on Marxist concept of domination.); Jeffrey St. John, "Environmentalists are 'Irrational,' " *The New York Times*, 59 (January 1, 1971), 23; and Eric Hoffer, "What I Have Learned: A Strategy for the War with Nature," *Saturday Review*, 49 (February 5, 1966), 27–29.

40. Hans H. Landsberg, Leonard L. Fischman, and Joseph L. Fisher, *Resources in America's Future: Patterns of Requirements and Availabilities, 1960–2000*. Baltimore: Johns Hopkins Press for Resources for the Future, 1963, 1017. (Reviewed *Science*, 140 (May 31, 1963), 971–72.)

41. C. A. Doxiadis, "The Coming Era of Ecumenopolis," *Saturday Review*, 50 (March 18, 1967), 11–14.

42. Crawford S. Holling, "Stability in Ecological and Social Systems" in *Diversity and Stability in Ecological Systems—Brookhaven Symposia in Biology: No. 22*. Upton, New York: Brookhaven National Laboratory, 1969, 128–41.

43. See *Man Adapting*. New Haven: Yale University Press, 1965, xxii, 527; "Adapting to Pollution," *Scientist and Citizen*, 10 (January–February 1968), 1–8; and "Adaptation to the Environment and Man's Future" in *The Control of Environment: Essays Presented at the Second Nobel Conference held at Gustavus Adolphus College, St. Peter, Minnesota, 1966*, John D. Roslansky, ed. Amsterdam: North-Holland Publishing Co., 1967, x, 114.

44. For more on the hypertrophic tendency, see my article "Environmental Policy in a Hypertrophic Society," *Natural Resources Journal*, 11 (July 1971). Note also, Dickinson W. Richards, "Homeostasis Versus

Hyperexis or Saint George and the Dragon," *Scientific Monthly,* 77 (December 1953), 289–94.

45. With acknowledgment to Etienne de Sénancour and Miguel d'Unamuno who eloquently advanced the moral proposition.

Chapter 2 Discovering the Biosphere

1. Roderick Seidenberg believes that all historic time is transitional. His concept of a post-historic steady-state society challenges the argument that human society can retain its vitality indefinitely after having established a condition of homeostasis equilibrium. See *Post-historic Man: An Inquiry.* Chapel Hill: University of North Carolina Press, 1950, 246; and a review by Bentley Glass, "A Biologic View of Human History," *The Scientific Monthly,* 73 (December 1951), 363–68.

2. W. (V) I. Vernadsky (Volodymyr Vernad'skĭ, 1863–1945), "The Biosphere and the Noösphere," *American Scientist,* 30 (January 1945), 8.

3. Leo Bagrow, *History of Cartography.* Translated from the German by D. L. Paisey, revised and augmented by R. A. Skelton, Cambridge, Massachusetts: Harvard University Press, 1966 edition, 312.

4. Armando Cortesao, "Nautical Science and the Geographical Revolution," *Impact of Science on Society,* 4 (Summer 1953), 111–118.

5. Ibid., 118.

6. See G. R. Crane, *Maps and Their Makers: An Introduction to the History of Cartography.* London: Hutchinson's University Library, 1964, 192. (On the International Map of the World on the scale of 1/1 million, see 163–65). On the technology of mapping, see George D. Whitmore, Morris M. Thompson, and Julius L. Speert, "Modern Instruments for Surveying and Mapping," *Science,* 130 (October 23, 1959), 1059–66. For examples of specialized types of mapping, see V. A. Kovda, "The Need for International Cooperation in Soil Science," *Nature and Resources,* 1 (September 1965), 10–16; and O. Franzle, "Geomorphological Mapping," Ibid., 2 (December 1966), 14–16. See also Dean S. Rugg, "The International Map of the World," *Scientific Monthly,* 72 (April 1951), 233–40; and Edward L. Stevenson, *Terrestrial and Celestial Globes: Their History and Construction,* Vols. 1–2. New Haven: Yale University Press for the Hispanic Society of America, 1921, 218, 291.

7. Thomas F. Gaskell, *Under the Deep Oceans: Twentieth Century Voyages of Discovery.* London: Eyre and Spottiswood, 1960, 239; and George S. Ritchie, *Challenger: The Life of a Survey Ship.* New York: Abelard-Schuman, 1958, 249.

8. Hugh Odishaw, "The International Geophysical Year and World Politics," *Journal of International Affairs,* 13 (Winter 1959), 47–56; and Walter Sullivan, *Assault on the Unknown: The International Geophysical Year.* New York: McGraw-Hill, 1966, xiv, 460.

9. David A. Davies, "Geophysics and Its Impact on International

Affairs" in *Modern Science and the Tasks of Diplomacy*, Karl Braunias and Peter Meraviglia, eds. Graz, Austria: Verlag Styria, 1965, 103–16.

10. Cited by Jack Major in "Historical Development of the Ecosystem Concept" in *The Ecosystem Concept in Natural Resource Management*, George M. Van Dyne, ed. New York: Academic Press, 1969, 11.

11. Richard Brewer, *A Brief History of Ecology: Part 1—Pre-Nineteenth Century to 1919*. Kalamazoo, Michigan: Western Michigan University, Occasional Papers of the E. C. Adams Center for Ecological Studies, November 22, 1960, 18 pp. On the growth of ecological concepts, see W. Frank Blair, "Ecology and Evolution," *The Antioch Review*, 14 (Spring 1959), 47–55.

12. "The Use and Abuse of Vegetational Concepts in Terms," *Ecology*, 16 (1935), 284–307.

13. Major, 12–14.

14. LaMont Cole, "The Ecosphere," *Scientific American*, 198 (April 1958), 83–96. Also, see reference Chapter 1, n. 31.

15. On the "where" of animal populations, see Marston Bates, *The Forest and the Sea: A Look at the Economy of Nature and the Ecology of Man*. New York: Random House, 1960, 277; V. C. Wynne-Edwards, *Animal Dispersion in Relation to Social Behavior*. London: Oliver and Boyd, 1962, xi, 653; G. Evelyn Hutchinson, "Homage to Santa Rosalia or Why are There So Many Kinds of Animals?" *The American Naturalist*, 93 (May–June 1959), 145–59; and publications on biogeography and zoogeography.

16. L. K. Frank, "Time Perspectives," *Journal of Social Philosophy*, 4 (July 1939), 293–312; J. N. Mills, "Human Circadian Rhythms," *Physiological Review*, 46 (January 1966), 128–71; Stanley R. Mohler, Robert Dille, and H. L. Gibbons, "The Time Zone and Circadian Rhythms in Relation to Aircraft Occupants Taking Long-Distance Flights," *American Journal of Public Health*, 58 (August 1968), 1404–09; and Marc Richelle, "Biological Clocks," *Psychology Today*, 3 (May 1970), 33–35, 58–60.

17. "Not Peace, but Ecology" in *Diversity and Stability in Ecological Systems—Brookhaven Symposia in Biology: No. 22*. Upton, New York: Brookhaven National Laboratory, 1969, 151–58.

18. For a historical treatment of theories of environmental influences, see the following: Franklin Thomas, *The Environmental Basis of Society: A Study in the History of Sociological Thought*. New York: Century, 1925, 336. H. B. van Loon, "Population, Space and Human Culture," *Law and Contemporary Problems*, 25 (Summer 1960), 397–405; and Paul Ward English, "Landscape, Ecosystem, and Cultural Perception: Concepts in Cultural Geography," *The Journal of Geography*, 68 (April 1968), 198–205. A standard source is Harold Sprout and Margaret Sprout, *The Ecological Perspective on Human Affairs with Special Reference to International Politics*. Princeton, New Jersey: Princeton University Press, 1965, xi, 236.

19. Robert S. Platt, "Environmentalism vs. Geography," *The American Journal of Sociology*, 52 (March 1948), 351–58; and Gordon R. Lathwaite, "Environmentalism and Determinism: A Search for Clarification," *Annals of the Association of American Geographers*, 56 (March 1966), 1–23.

20. See, for example, John B. Calhoun, "Population Density and Social Pathology," *Scientific American*, 206 (February 1962), 139–48; and "Space and the Strategy of Life," *Ekistics*, 29 (June 1970), 425–37. Note also, Frederick Sargent II and Demitri B. Shimkin, "Biology, Society, and Culture in Human Ecology," *BioScience*, 15 (August 1965), 512–15.

21. *Future Shock*. New York: Random House, 1970, xii, 505.

22. New York: Macmillan, 1913, xv, 317. Reprinted in 1958 with an introduction by George Wald. Boston: Beacon Press (Paperback No. 68).

23. Ibid., Macmillan, 1924 printing, 274–75.

24. Translated from the French by Bernard Wall with an introduction by Julian Huxley. London: William Collins, 1959; Harper Torchbook Edition, 1961, 318.

25. *Fitness of the Environment*, 312.

26. Note for instance, A. D. Voûte, "Ecology as a Teleological Science," *Acta Biotheoretica*, 18 (Series A, 1968), 143–64.

27. Note especially chapter 6, "The Fitness of the Environment," 2nd edition. Princeton, New Jersey: Princeton University Press, 1955, x, 220.

28. New York: Harper Torchbook Edition, 1962, 212A.

29. Ibid., 212.

30. Glencoe, Illinois: Free Press, 1960, 237, 270.

31. "The Meddlers" in *Voices from the Sky*. New York: Pyramid Books, 1967, 162.

32. See "The Biosphere," *Scientific American*, 223 (September 1970), whole issue. Note especially the introductory article "The Biosphere" by G. Evelyn Hutchinson, 45–53; and also by Hutchinson, "The Biosphere or Volume in which Organisms Actually Live" in *The Ecological Theater and the Evolutionary Play*. New Haven: Yale University Press, 1926, 1–26.

33. Librarie Felix Alcan. 232 pp. The volume consists of two essays. "La Biosphère dans le Cosmos," and "Le Domaine de la Vie." An appendix consists of a communication to the Society of Naturalists of Leningrad, February 5, 1928, "L'Évolution des Especes et la Matière Vivante."

34. 30 (January 1945), 1–12.

35. Ibid., 4.

36. Ibid., 9.

37. Ibid., 9–10.

38. Ibid., 9.

39. *Phenomenon of Man*, 94–95.

40. *Intergovernmental Conference of Experts on the Scientific Basis for Rational Use and Conservation of the Resources of the Biosphere, Unesco House, Paris, 4–13 September 1968; Final Report*. Paris: UNESCO (January 1969), SC/MD/9, 5.

41. "The Biosphere—A Delicate Balance Between Man and Nature," *UNESCO Courier*, 20 (January 1969), 14.

42. *Operating Manual for Spaceship Earth*. Carbondale, Illinois: Southern Illinois University Press, 1969, 143. Also included in William R. Ewald, Jr., ed. *Environment and Change*. Bloomington, Indiana: Indiana University Press, 1968, 341–89.

43. For a concise but comprehensive account of this age see Charles E. Nowell, *The Great Discoveries and the First Colonial Empires*. Ithaca, New York: Cornell University Press, 1954, vii, 150.

44. "The Energy Cycle of the Biosphere," *Scientific American*, 222 (September 1970), 74.

Chapter 3 International Conservation Efforts

1. Marston Bates, "Environment," *International Encyclopedia of Social Sciences*, 5 (1968), 91–93; Lynton K. Caldwell, "Environment—A Short Course in Semantics," *Public Administration Review* (in press); D. A. Maelzer, "Environment, Semantics and Systems Theory in Ecology," *Journal of Theoretical Biology*, 8 (May 1965), 395–402. Helpful clarification of terms is also provided in a monograph by Harold and Margaret Sprout, *Ecology and Politics in America: Some Issues and Alternatives*, New York: General Learning Press, 1971, 22.

2. Henry I. Baldwin, "The Application of Ecological Knowledge to Forestry," *Scientific Monthly*, 72 (April 1951), 225–29; Charles F. Cooper, "The Ecology of Fire," *Scientific American*, 204 (April 1961), 150–60; and Ashley L. Schiff, *Fire and Water: Scientific Heresy in the Forest Service*. Cambridge: Harvard University Press, 1962, 225. On a minor though interesting case of the modification of conservation practices by ecology, see Harold Mayfield, *The Kirtland's Warbler*. Bloomfield Hills, Michigan: Cranbrook Institute of Science, 1960, 242.

3. For example, Robert B. Platt and John F. Griffith's *Environmental Measurement and Interpretation*. New York: Reinhold, 1964, 235.

4. Charles S. Elton, *The Ecology of Invasions by Animals and Plants*. New York: Wiley, 1958, 181.

5. Alice M. Coats, *The Plant Hunters: Being a History of the Horticultural Pioneers: The Quests and the Discoveries from the Rennaissance to the Twentieth Century*. New York: McGraw-Hill, 1970, 400; Frances Louise Jewett, *Plant Hunters*. Boston: Houghton-Mifflin, 1952, 230; and Michael Sidney Tyler-Whittle, *The Plant Hunters: Being An Examination of Collecting, With An Account of the Careers and the Methods of A Number of Those Who Have Searched the World for Wild Plants*. Philadelphia: Chilton, 1970, 281.

6. Willy Ley, "The Story of the Milu" in *Dragons in Amber: Further Adventures of a Romantic Naturalist*. New York: Viking, 1951, 120–37.

7. William Bartram, *Travels Through North and South Carolina, Georgia, East and West Florida—*. Philadelphia: James & Johnson, 1791. Edited by Mark Van Doren and reprinted by Dover Publications, 1928, 369–70; and Donald Culross Peattie, "Wilderness Plantsmen: Bartram and Michaux" in *Green Laurels: The Lives and Achievements of the Great Naturalists*. New York: Literary Guild, 1936, 186–200.

8. 30 Nov. Rec. gen. 2 me, 686. The most thorough account of international conservation treaties, including their texts is, Sherman Strong Hayden, *The International Protection of Wildlife: An Examination of Treaties and Other Agreements for the Preservation of Birds and Mammals.* New York: Columbia University Press, 1942, 246 and bibliography.

9. United States Treaty Series 628. *United States Statutes at Large: 64th Congress, 1915–1917*, 39, Part 2, 1702–05.

10. Hayden, *The International Protection of Wildlife*, 77.

11. *United States Government Organization Manual*, 1970–71. Washington: U.S. Government Printing Office, 1971, 233.

12. United States Treaty Series (hereafter cited as USTS) 912. *United States Statutes at Large: 75th Congress, 1st Session, 1937*, 50, Part 2, 1311–16.

13. USTS 981. *Treaties and Other International Agreements of the United States of America, 1776–1949*. Compiled under the direction of Charles I. Bevans. Washington: U. S. Department of State, 3 (1969), Multilateral, 630–60. (Hereafter cited as Bevans.)

14. *League of Nations Treaty Series*, 172, No. 3995 (1936), 241–42.

15. "African Convention," *IUCN Bulletin*, New Series 2 (October–December 1968), 68.

16. USTS 564. Bevans, 1 (1968), 804–13.

17. TIAS 3948. Bevans, 8, Part 2 (1957), 2283–2341. Treaty signed, February 9, 1957; proclaimed, November 15, 1957.

18. Richard D. Lyons. "Mercury: No Place in the Whole World is Safe," *The New York Times* (November 1, 1970), Sec. 4, 16.

19. USTS 880. Bevans, 3 (1969), 26–33.

20. TIAS 1849. Bevans, 4 (1948), 248–58.

21. Noel Simon, "Of Whales and Whaling," *Science*, 149 (August 25, 1965), 942–46. See also *Reports of the International Whaling Commission issued from the Office of the Commission in London, Twentieth Report—1970*, and preceding issues. For the current situation, see Scott McVay, "Can Leviathan Long Endure So Wide A Chase," *Natural History*, 80 (January 1971), 36–40, 68–72.

22. *The New York Times* (November 24, 1970), "Hickel bans 8 species," 243; (November 28, 1970), "Nixon reverses Hickel order, State Department upset," 25; (November 29, 1970), "Interior Department decides to print order in Federal Register, State Department admits 'ghastly mistake,' " 40; (December 3, 1970), "Products from 8 species banned," 21: and (December 7, 1970), Editorial, 44.

23. For a concise but informative account, see William C. Herrington

and John L. Kask, "International Conservation Problems and "Solutions in Existing Conventions" in *Papers Presented at the International Technical Conference on the Conservation of the Living Resources of the Sea: Rome, 18 April to 10 May 1955.* New York: United Nations (1956), A/Conf. 10/7, 145–66.

24. "Background and Objectives of the Conference" in *Proceedings of the United Nations Scientific Conference on the Conservation and Utilization of Resources: 17 August–6 September 1949, Lake Success, New York.* Lake Success, New York: United Nations (1956), A/Conf. 10/7, 145–66. For reports following this conference, see: Francis W. Carpenter, "Conservation of World Resources: A Report on U. N. Scientific conference," *Bulletin of the Atomic Scientists,* 5 (November 1949), 313–14; and Carl N. Gibboney, "The United Nations Conference for the Conservation and Utilization of Resources," *Science,* 110 (December 23, 1949), 675–78.

25. Proceedings of the—Conference, 13.

26. Ibid.

27. Ibid., 15.

28. Ibid. The abstract of Dr. Clark's paper added the following egregious and misleading suggestion that the "real origin [of concern with unlimited population growth] appears to lie in a feeling of race superiority on the part of Europeans and Americans which the rest of the world bitterly resents." (Dr. Clark was the father of seven children.)

29. *Use and Conservation of the Biosphere: Proceedings of the Intergovernmental Conference of Experts on the Scientific Basis for Rational Use and Conservation of the Resources of the Biosphere,* Paris, 4–13 September 1968. Paris: UNESCO, Natural Resources Research, 10 (1970), 235.

30. The most complete and generally accessible account of the work and history of IUCN has been published in the following issues of the journal, *Biological Conservation:* E. J. H. Berwick, "The International Union for Conservation of Nature and Natural Resources: Current Activities and Situation," (April 1969), 191–99; and J. P. Harroy, "L'Union Internationale pour la Conservation de la Nature et de ses Resources: Origine et constitutione," 1 (January 1969), 106–10. See also: A descriptive leaflet, *This is IUCN,* published by the Union, and the *IUCN Yearbook* 1970.

31. A. Gille, "The Role of International Agencies" in *First World Conference on National Parks,* Alexander B. Adams, ed. Washington: U.S. Department of the Interior, 1962, 320 ff.

32. See ibid., *Proceedings of the Conference,* Alexander B. Adams, ed., (Note 31, 471 pp.); and also *IUCN Bulletin,* 1 (July–September 1962), 1 and supplement.

33. James Fisher, Noel Simon, and Jack Vincent, *The Red Book: Wildlife in Danger.* London: Collins, 1969, 368.

34. *United Nations List of National Parks and Equivalent Reserves,* 2nd edition. Brussels: Hayez, 1971, 601.

35. Among a large literature on international wildlife protection efforts are: Philip Kingsland Crowe, *World Wildlife: The Last Stand*. New York: Charles Scribners' Sons, 1970, 308; Richard Fitter, *Vanishing Wild Animals of the World*. London: Midland Bank & Kaye & Ward, Ltd., 1968, 144; Eric Robins, *The Ebony Ark: Black Africa's Battle to Save Its Wildlife*. New York: Taplinger, 1970, 185; *World Wildlife Yearbook: 1969*, Fritz Vollmar, ed. Morges, Switzerland: World Wildlife Fund, 343; and *The Launching of a New Ark: First Report of the World Wildlife Fund, 1961–1964* and *The Ark Underway: Second Report of the World Wildlife Fund, 1965–1967* (both now out of print). For an account of the work of WWF by two of its leading participants, see *Wildlife Crisis*, co-authored by Prince Philip, Duke of Edinburgh and James Fisher. New York: Cowles Book Co. in cooperation with The World Wildlife Fund, 1970, 256; and for a historical account of nature protection generally, see Max Nicholson, *The Environmental Revolution*. New York: McGraw-Hill, 1970, 366.

Chapter 4 Underestimating the Danger

1. Fairfield Osborn, *Our Plundered Planet*. Boston: Little, Brown, 1948, 217, and *The Limits of the Earth*. Boston: Little, Brown, 1953, 238; Paul Sears, *Deserts on the March*. Norman: University of Oklahoma Press, 1935, 231; and William Vogt, *Road to Survival*. New York: William Sloane, 1948, 335.

2. For a comprehensive statement of the danger by a thoughtful and well-informed scholar, see Richard A. Falk, *This Endangered Planet*. New York: Random House, 1971, 495. For a survey of the history of thought on resource destruction and conservation from a world point of view, see J. R. Whitaker, "World View of Destruction and Conservation of Natural Resources," *Annals of the Association of American Geographers*, 30 (September 1940), 143–62; and "Sequence and Equilibrium in Destruction and Conservation of Natural Resources," Ibid., 31 (June 1941), 129–44. A good summation of the development of worldwide ecological awareness has been provided by Henry J. Kellermann in "Ecology A World Concern," *The Great Ideas Today*, 1971, 17–39.

3. For example, The Global Atmosphere Research Program (GARP). See *An Introduction to GARP*. GARP Publication, Series No. 1. See also *WMO Bulletin*, 16 (October 1967), 212–18; 18 (July 1969), 186–88, and (October 1969), 254–55; and The Integrated Global Ocean Station System (IGOSS). *Global Ocean Research: Report of the Joint Working Party on the Advisory Committee on Marine Resources, The Scientific Committee on Oceanic Research and the World Meteorological Organization*, June 1969 (The Ponza Report).

4. Note development of this thesis by Harold F. Blum in *Time's*

Arrow and Evolution, 2nd edition, Princeton: Princeton University Press, 1955, x, 220, and especially Chapter 4, "The Fitness of the Environment."

5. Note Kenneth E. Boulding's observation: "Incoming messages are not admitted to the image gate free. At the gate of the image stands the value system demanding payment . . . we see the world the way we see it because it pays us and has paid us to see it that way." *The Image,* Ann Arbor: University of Michigan Press, 1956, 50.

6. His *Essay on the Principle of Population* was first published in 1798. Cf. Kenneth E. Boulding, "The Malthusian Model as a General System," *Social and Economic Studies,* 4 (September 1955), 195–205.

7. A. F. K. Organski, "Population and Politics in Europe," *Science,* 133 (June 1961), 1803–1807; also, Katherine Organski and A. F. K. Organski, *Population and World Power.* New York: Knopf, 1961, 263; and David V. Glass, *Population—Policies and Movements in Europe.* Oxford: Clarendon Press, 1940, vi, 490. In addition, see Harold F. Dorn, "World Population Growth: An International Dilemma," *Science,* 135 (January 26, 1962), 283–85.

8. Alva Myrdal, *Nation and Family: The Swedish Experiment in Democratic Family and Population Policy.* New York: Harper, 1941, xv, 441. See also "Sweden: A Case of Population Policies," *Population Bulletin,* 26 (November 1970), 19–27.

9. With an introduction by Julian Huxley. New York: William Sloane, 1951, viii, 380.

10. For an extreme example of this viewpoint, see Michel Cépède, Francis Houtart, and Linus Grond, *Population and Food.* New York: Sheed & Ward, 1964, xvi, 461.

11. *BioScience,* 18 (January 1968), 33.

12. November 28, 1958, 87.

13. *BioScience,* 18 (January 1968), 31. For a more recent analysis of the problem by Harrison Brown, see "After the Population Explosion," *Saturday Review* (June 26, 1971).

14. January 9, 1966, 91.

15. *Science,* 162 (December 13, 1968), 1243–48.

16. Note, for example, "A Research Panel Examines Genetic Vulnerability of Crops," *News Report,* [National Academy of Science], 21 (March 1971), 2–3. See also "Poisoning the Wells," *Environment,* 11 (January–February 1969), 16–23, 45.

17. Georg Borgstrom, *The Hungry Planet: The Modern World at the Edge of Famine.* New York: Macmillan, 1965, ix, 485. On the "Green Revolution," see Lester R. Brown, "Social Implications of the Green Revolution," *International Conciliation,* No. 581 (January 1971), 5–61; and Clifton R. Wharton, Jr., "The Green Revolution: Cornucopia or Pandora's Box? *Foreign Affairs,* 47 (April 1969), 464–76.

18. *Final Act of the International Conference on Human Rights, Teheran, 23 April to 13 May 1968.* New York: United Nations (1968), A/Conf. 32/41, 15.

19. *New York Herald Tribune Book Review* (May 27, 1951), 4. See also *International Planned Parenthood News,* 168 (February 1968), 3.

20. *The Technological Society.* Translated from the French by John Wilkinson. New York: A. A. Knopf, 1964, xxxvi, 449.

21. For discussions of the **social effects of technology,** see: *World Technology and Human Destiny,* Raymond Aron, ed. Ann Arbor: University of Michigan Press, 1963, vi, 249; Sigfried Gideon, *Mechanization Takes Command.* New York: Oxford, 1948, xiv, 743; Friedrich George Jünger, *The Failure of Technology.* Translated from the German by F. D. Wieck. Chicago: Henry Regnery, 1949, xvi, 204; and Lewis Mumford, *Technics and Civilization.* New York: Harcourt Brace, 1934, xi, 495. For a more recent critique of the social effects of technology, see Herbert J. Muller, *The Children of Frankenstein: A Primer of Modern Technology and Human Value.* Bloomington, Indiana: Indiana University Press, 1970, xiii, 431. For two contrasting views in which the evolutionary and ecological limitations on social and technological development are deemphasized or discounted, see Victor C. Ferkiss, *Technological Man: The Myth and the Reality.* New York: George Braziller, 1969, 336; and Richard L. Meier, *Science and Economic Development: New Patterns of Living,* 2nd edition. Cambridge: MIT Press, 1966, 320. See also Chapter 1, n. 32.

22. Resolution of the General Assembly 1710 (16), *United Nations Development Decade: A Programme for International Cooperation.* Official Records, 16th Session of the General Assembly, Supplement No. 17. New York: United Nations (1962), 17–18.

23. *Science and Technology for Development: Report of the United Nations Conference on the Application of Science and Technology for the Benefit of the Less-Developed Areas.* New York: United Nations, 8 (Plenary Proceedings), 1963, vii.

24. Ibid., 3 (Agriculture), 7. Resource depletion was considered at the United Nations Conference on the Conservation and Utilization of Resources held in 1949, but the menace and magnitude of a threat to the biosphere was not generally perceived at that time.

25. For a review of the experience of the *First Development Decade,* see *A Study of the Capacity of the United Nations Development System.* Geneva: United Nations, 1–2 (1969), DP/5; and Resolution of the Geneva Assembly 2626 (25). *International Development Strategy for the Second United Nations Development Decade.* New York: United Nations (November 11, 1970), A/RES/2626 (25).

26. *Address to the University of Notre Dame, 1 May 1969.* Washington, D.C.: International Bank for Reconstruction and Development (1969), 20.

27. There is a very large literature on the **social impact and assessment of technology.** For some contributions pertinent to the environmental issue, see: *The New Technology and Human Values,* John C. Burke, ed. Belmont, California: Wadsworth, 1966, 408; A. Cornelius Benjamin, *Science, Technology and Human Values.* Columbia, Missouri: University of

Missouri Press, 1965, v, 296; "Committee on Science in the Promotion of Human Welfare: The Integrity of Science," *American Scientist,* 53 (June 1965), 174–98; and Emmanuel G. Mesthene, "Our Threatened Planet: The Technological Plague," *Science,* 155 (January 27, 1967), 441, 442. Note especially papers published by the Program of Policy Studies in Science and Technology at George Washington University. E.g., Raphael G. Kasper, *Some Comments on Technology Assessment and the Environment.* Occasional Paper 8 (November 1970), 13 pp.; and Louis H. Mayo, *Social Impact Analysis.* Staff Discussion Paper 210 (March 1971), 49 pp. and *The Contextual Approach to Technology Assessment.* Monograph 9 (April 1971), 87 pp. See also Guy Black, *Technology Assessment—What Should It Be?* Staff Discussion Paper 211 (June 1971), 52 pages and selected bibliography.

28. "The modern technology, which has added much to our lives can also have a darker side." *Presidential Message to the 89th Congress, 1st Session, on the Conservation and Restoration of Natural Beauty. Congressional Record,* 3, Part 2 (February 8, 1965), H/Doc/78, 2085.

29. Dana Adams Schmidt, "Aswan Dam Alters Marine Ecology," *The New York Times* (June 7, 1970), 1,22; and Carl J. George, "The Influence of the New High Dam (UAR) on the Ecology of the Eastern Mediterranean Sea." *A Preliminary Study: Paper Prepared for the Conference on the Ecological Aspects of International Development, December 8–11, 1968, Airlie House, Warrenton, Virginia.* Published version in *The Careless Technology—Ecology and International Development,* M. T. Farvar and J. P. Milton, eds. New York: Natural History Press, 1971.

30. Mohammed Abdul-Fattah al Kassas, "Shoreline Phenomena in Dam Building and Their Impact on the Nile Delta." *Paper Prepared for the Conference on the Ecological Aspects of International Development,* ibid.

31. Henry van der Schalie, "Snail-borne Diseases in the Irrigation Projects of Egypt and the Sudan." *Paper Prepared for the Conference on the Ecological Aspects of International Development,* ibid.

32. W. H. K. Lee and C. B. Raleigh, "Fault-plane Solution of the Koyna (India) Earthquake," *Nature,* 223 (July 12, 1969), 172–73.

33. P. M. Borisov, "Can We Control the Arctic Climate? Proposed Transport of Atlantic Water Across the Arctic Basin," *Bulletin of the Atomic Scientists,* 25 (March 1969), 43–48. On the Siberian rivers, see A. Voznesenkÿ, "Do We Have Enough Water?" *Pravda* (May 13, 1971), 3.

34. "NAWPA: A Continental Water System—Symposium," *Bulletin of the Atomic Scientists,* 23 (September 1967), 8–27; and R. S. Lewis, "NAWPA: Water for the Year 2000," Ibid., 21 (May 1965), 9–11.

35. See, *The New York Times,* "Rampart Canyon Dam," (September 1, 1964), 34; *Index* (1965–1966); (June 25, 1967), 13; and (July 6, 1967), 2. See also *National Parks Magazine,* 41 (August 1967), 20; and *The Izaak Walton Magazine* (May 1966), 12–13.

36. Note reference to monitoring in, *Restoring the Quality of Our Environment: Report of the Environmental Pollution Panel of the President's Science Advisory Committee.* Washington: The White House,

12 (1965), 317; and in *Environmental Quality: The First Annual Report of the Council on Environmental Quality*. Washington: Executive Office of the President, 1970, 317. Two important reports on environmental change and monitoring are *Man's Impact on the Global Environment* (1970), and *Inadvertent Climate Modification* (1971), both published by the MIT Press.

37. Philip C. Wolf, "Carbon Monoxide: Measurement and Monitoring in Urban Air," *Environmental Science and Technology*, 5 (March 1971), 212–18.

38. *Science and Technology for Development*, 8 (Plenary Proceedings), 169–70. But in the USSR, as in other technologically advanced countries, there were sharp differences within the science community as to the nature and danger of an environmental crisis. Note, for example, the exchange between I. Sinyagin and I. Zabelin in *Literaturnaya Gazeta* (October 14, 1970), 12.

39. LaMont C. Cole, "Can the World Be Saved?" *BioScience*, 28 (July 1968), 679–84.

40. "Oceans Beginning to Die, Professor Warns," *Monterey Peninsula Herald* (March 13, 1970), 2. Gordon Rattray Taylor in "The Threat to Life in the Sea," *Saturday Review*, 52 (August 1, 1970), 40–42, summarizes the opinions of a number of scientists on this issue.

41. "The Voyage of Ra II," *National Geographic*, 139 (January 1971), 55; and Norman Baker (Navigator of Ra II), "Science, Solitude and Slime," *Industrial Ecology*, 1 (Winter 1970), 9–11.

42. "Lethal Leftovers," *Scandinavian Times*, 7 (November 1970), 16–17.

43. *Ocean Dumping—A National Policy: A Report to the President, Proposed by the Council on Environmental Quality*. Washington: U.S. Government Printing Office (October 1970), 45.

44. Sören Jensen, Arne Jernolöv, Rolf Lange, and Karsten H. Palmork, "Chlorinated By-products from Vinyl Chloride Production—A New Source of Marine Pollution." *A Paper Contributed to FAO Conference on Marine Pollution, Rome, 9–18 December 1970*, 8.

45. *Genetics of Insect Vectors of Disease*, J. W. Wright and R. Pal, eds. Amsterdam: Elsevies, 1967, 794. See summary in *WHO Chronicle*, 20 (January 1968), 20–25; and Robert van den Borch, "Pesticides: Prescribing for the Ecosystem," *Environment*, 12 (April 1970), 21–25.

46. Note, for example, "Swedes ban DDT," *Chemical Week*, 104 (April 19, 1969), 27; "Brushing off DDT," *Newsweek* (November 24, 1969), 58; "Hickel Extends Pesticide Curbs," *The New York Times* (June 18, 1970), 35.

47. For example, Wheeler McMillan, *Bugs or People*. New York: Appleton Century, 1965, 228; Edwin Diamond, "The Myths of the Pesticide Menace," *Saturday Evening Post*, 136 (September 28, 1963), 16, 18; and Thomas H. Jukes, "People and Pesticides," *American Scientist*, 51 (September 1963), 355–61 and "Pesticides Defended by Biologist," *Chicago Tribune* (November 12, 1970), Sec. 1B, 2.

48. John W. Gofman and Arthur R. Tamplin, "Radiation: The Invisible Casualties," *Environment*, 12 (April 1970), 12–19, 49; and by the same authors, *Poisoned Power: The Case Against Nuclear Power Plants*. Emmaus, Pennsylvania: Rodale Press, 1971; and *Population Control Through Nuclear Pollution*. Chicago: Nelson-Hall, 1970, 242.

49. *United Nations Treaty Series*, 480, No. 6964 (1963). "Treaty Banning Nuclear Weapons Testing in the Atmosphere, in Outer Space and under the Water." Signed at Moscow on August 5, 1963.

50. *The Hungry Planet*, vii.

51. For criticism of the GNP as an index of economic health, see: A. Berle, "What GNP Doesn't Tell Us," *Saturday Review*, 50 (August 31, 1968), 10, 12 ff; Stuart Chase, "Can We Stay Prosperous?" *Saturday Review*, 49 (February 11, 1967), 10–22; and Ezra J. Mishan, *The Costs of Economic Growth*. New York: Praeger, 1967, 190. For additional references, see Chapter 1, n. 34, *supra*.

52. For an analysis of the impact of man's artificial systems and resources, see *Man in the Living Environment: Report of the Workshop on Global Ecological Problems*, The Institute of Ecology, 1971.

53. *Economic Development in Perspective*. Cambridge: Harvard University Press, 1962, 7.

54. Ibid., 6.

55. *Research for Development in the Mediterranean Basin: A Proposal*. The Hague: Mounton, 1961, 51.

56. Boston: Houghton-Mifflin, 1971, viii.

57. *The New York Times* (January 1, 1967), Sec. 4, 7.

58. 14 (January, 1967), 93–94, 212–17. *Playboy* subsequently published a paperback collection of essays on the man–environment crisis, *Project Survival*. Chicago: HMH Publishing Co., 1971, 255.

59. *Esquire*, 68 (September 1967), 116 ff.

60. "Can the World Be Saved? *BioScience*, 28 (July 1968), n. 40.

61. *Ramparts*, 8 (September 1969), 24–28. Reprinted in *The Environmental Handbook*, Garrett DeBell, ed. New York: Ballantine, 1970, 161–76.

62. Philip Handler, "Exaggeration: The Other Pollution Peril," *Nation's Business*, 59 (April 1971), 30–33.

63. See classification of problems and crises by estimated time and intensity in, John R. Platt, "What We Must Do," *Science*, 166 (November 28, 1969), 1115–21.

64. "The Way Out of the Labyrinth," *Ceres*, 1 (May–June 1968), 20.

Chapter 5 Mobilizing International Resources

1. "On the Past, Present, and Future of Man," *Natural History*, 80 (February 1971), 52.

2. John N. Herz, "Rise and Demise of the Territorial State," *World Politics*, 9 (July 1955), 473–93; and *International Politics in the Atomic Age*. New York: Columbia University Press, 1959, 39–110.

3. James E. King, *Science and Rationalism in the Government of Louis XIV, 1661–1683*. Baltimore: Johns Hopkins University Press, 1949, 84–115.

4. Albion W. Small, *The Cameralists*. Chicago: University of Chicago Press, 1909, xxv, 606; and Louise Sommer, "Cameralism" in *Encyclopedia of the Social Sciences*, 3 (1930), 158–60.

5. Eli F. Heckscher, "Mercantilism" in the *Encyclopedia of the Social Sciences*, 10 (1933), 333–39; Jacob Viner, "Economic Thought—Mercantilist Thought," *International Encyclopedia of the Social Sciences*, 4 (1968), 435–43. See also Edgar A. J. Johnson, "The Age of Mercantilism" in *Planned Society*, Findlay Mackenzie, ed. Englewood Cliffs, New Jersey: Prentice-Hall, 1937, 79–107.

6. Bernhard E. Fernow, *Brief History of Forestry in Europe, the United States, and Other Countries*. Toronto: University of Toronto, 1910, 438; and Kurt Mantel, "History of the International Science of Forestry with Special Consideration of Central Europe" in *International Review of Forestry Research*, Vol. 1, John A. Ramberger and Peitra Mikola, eds. New York and London: Academic Press, 1964, 1–37. Includes a bibliography of historically important works in Latin, German, and French.

7. *Science*, 162 (December 13, 1968), 1243–48.

8. *The Fate of Man in the Modern World*. Translated from the Russian by Donald A. Lowrie. London: SCM Press, 1935, 78.

9. Ibid., 82.

10. "Development Theory and Evolutionist Philosophy" in *Industrial Society: Three Essays on Ideology and Development*. New York: Praeger, 1967, 49–91.

11. *Le scandale du développemènt*. Paris: Marcel Riviere, 1965, 297.

12. Egbert de Vries, "International Transfers of Knowledge and Capital" in *Natural Resources and International Development*, Marion Clawson, ed. Baltimore: Johns Hopkins Press for Resources for the Future, 1964, 415–35.

13. The structure and functions of **international development agencies** are described in the following articles and books: Persia Campbell, "United Nations Report: The UNDP Tools up for the Second Development Decade," *International Development Review*, 10 (December 1968), 35–38; William Diamond, "Development Finance Companies," *Finance and Development*, 2 (June 1965), 97–102; Jacques Ferrandi, La Communauté Économique Européan et L' Assistance Technique," *International Development Review*, 4 (September 1964), 8–10; Davil L. Gordon, "Coordinating Aid to Developing Countries," *Finance and Development*, 3 (June 1966), 129–35; Michael L. Hoffman, "The Scaffolding of Aid," *Finance and Development*, 5 (December 1968), 15–16; Ernest Parsons, "Efforts to Coordinate Western Development Aid," *OECD Observer*, 33 (April 1968), 39–42; Lewis Perinham, "The World Bank and The United Nations," *Finance and Development*, 3 (December 1966), 290–96 and "Re-

sources and Activities in Development Aid of Non-Government, Non-Profit Organizations," *OECD Observer*, 30 (October 1967), 38–41; and Arnold Rivkin, "African and the European Economic Community," *Finance and Development*, 3 (June 1966), 120–28. See also Wolfgang G. Friedmann, George Kalmanoff, and Robert F. Meagher, *International Financial Aid*. New York: Columbia University Press, 1966, 498; I. M. D. Little and J. M. Clifford, *International Aid*. Chicago: Aldine, 1966, 302; James H. Weaver, *The International Development Association: A New Approach to Foreign Aid*. New York: Praeger, 1965, ix, 268; Philip E. Jacob and Alexine L. Atherton, *The Dynamics of International Organization: The Making of World Order*. Homewood, Illinois: Dorsey, 1965, Chapter 14; Sir Robert G. A. Jackson, *The Case for an International Development Authority*. Syracuse, New York: Syracuse University Press, 1959, 70; and *The Global Partnership: International Agencies and Economic Development*, Richard N. Gardner and Max F. Millikan, eds. New York: Praeger, 1969, vii, 498. Note also the previously cited (Chapter 4, n. 25) reference to Sir Robert G. A. Jackson's review of the United Nations Development System.

14. The reasons for the lag in scientific and technological skills in underdeveloped countries are numerous and complex. Representative of a large literature on the problem are: H. S. Bhaba, "Science and the Problems of Development," *Science*, 151 (February 4, 1966), 541–48; P. M. S. Blackett, "Sensible Shopping in the Supermarket of Science," *UNESCO Courier*, 16 (July–August 1963), 30–31, "Planning for Science and Technology in Emerging Nations," *New Scientist*, 17 (February 4, 1963), 345–46, and "The Ever-Widening Gap," *Science*, 155 (February 24, 1967), 959–64; Stevan Dedijer, "Research: The Mortar of Progress," *Bulletin of the Atomic Scientists*, 18 (June 1962), 4–7 and "Underdeveloped Science in Underdeveloped Countries," *Minerva*, 2 (Autumn 1963), 61–81; N. W. Pirie, "Science and Development," *Political Quarterly*, 38 (January–March 1967), 62–71; Eugene Staley, "Research and Progress in the Developing Countries," *Research Management*, 9 (May 1966), 181–91; and Stanley White, "Status Symbol or Stimulus," *New Scientist*, 30 (May 26, 1966), 542–43.

15. See, for example, Norbert Koenig, "The Technical Assistance and Preinvestment Activities of the World Bank," *Finance and Development*, 4 (September 1967), 202–08.

16. The previously cited (Chapter 1, n. 36) mission of the White House–Interior Panel on Waterlogging and Salinity in West Pakistan is a case in point. The initial draft of its report (September 21, 1962) did not include consideration of social implications or of administrative implementation. Administrative implications were dealt with subsequently and independently in a report prepared by a consultant to the American Aid Program. Cf. Aloys A. Michel, *The Indus Rivers*. New Haven: Yale University Press, 1967, p. 481.

17. For example, see the whole issue of *Scientific American*, 209

(September 1963) on "Technology and Economic Development." Political and psychological factors are considered, but ecological factors, when present, are not treated "ecologically" but only in relation to economic or technological considerations. See also Jack Baranson, "Economic and Social Considerations in Adopting Technologies for Developing Countries," *Technology and Culture*, 4 (Winter 1963), 22–29.

Although recognizing the existence of environmental factors relevant to development, neither the first nor the second reports of the Secretary-General of the United Nations on the Development and Utilization of Human Resources actually considered ecological influences. See, *Report on Development and Utilization of Human Resources in Developing Countries, First Report*, E/4453 and E/4353, Add. 1 (May 1967); and *Second Report*, E/4483 and E/4383, Add. 1 (April 1963).

18. E.g., Peter F. M. McLoughlin, "Studying African Agriculture," *Finance and Development*, 5 (March 1968), 13–18. This article describes the World Bank's recent study of African agriculture. See also John C. deWilde, *Experiences with Agricultural Development in Tropical Africa*, Vol. 1 and 2, Baltimore: Johns Hopkins Press, 1967, 254, 466. In an interview on October 21, 1967, the Director-General of the World Health Organization emphasized the need to adapt medical education to the needs of developing countries and observed that in economic development programs too little attention was being given to predictable hazards associated with development schemes. See *Survey of International Development*, 4 (November 15, 1967), 8. Note also Freeman H. Quimby, *The Politics of Global Health*, prepared for the Subcommittee on National Security Policy and Scientific Developments of the Committee on Foreign Affairs, US House of Representatives, May 1971, vi, 79.

19. An argument for greater attention to ecological and behavioral parameters of social change was made by John D. Montgomery in "The Challenge of Change," *International Development Review*, 9 (March 1967), 2–8. In a Vice-Presidential Address, "Education for Societies in Transition," delivered at the American Association for the Advancement of Science in Dallas on December 27, 1968, Willard J. Jacobson, of Columbia University Teachers College, outlined the type of educational and institutional changes that would be necessary to cope with the changes that development programs are designed to induce. Throughout his paper there is emphasis on the importance of a "concern for consequences," and on seeing problems from many different perspectives and developing generalized approaches to what may appear, superficially, to be unique.

20. Transcript of remarks before the 1959 National Conference of the American Society for Public Administration, *ASPA Reprint Series*, 3 (December 1959), 4.

21. *Science and Technology for Development: Report of the United Nations Conference on the Application of Science and Technology for the Benefit of the Less-Developed Areas*. New York: United Nations (1963), 3 (Agriculture), 7. Note also paper by Jean-Paul Harroy, "A Strangely Unrecognized Danger of World-Wide Consequence," (C/510)

prepared for the conference. Unfortunately, the more than 2,000 technical papers submitted to the conference are not generally available as published documents.

22. Ibid., I (World of Opportunity), 9.

23. For a critique of the development concept, see Denis A. Goulet, "Development for What?" *Comparative Political Studies*, 1 (July 1968), 295–312.

24. *Development Projects Observed*. Washington: Brookings Institution, 1967, 145, 174.

25. Dennis Livingston, "Pollution Control: An International Perspective," *Scientist and Citizen*, 10 (September 1968), 172–82.

26. *The Human Environment: A Proposed International Declaration*. (Printed in five languages.) Stockholm: Svenska FN-förbundet, 1970, 16.

27. "NATO Joins the Fight to Save the Environment," *The New York Times* (November 7, 1969), 3. Dateline Brussels, November 6: Representatives of NATO member nations agreed to form a "Committee on the Challenges of Modern Society" which will hold its first meeting on December 8, 1969. See also *NATO Letter*, 18 (January 1970), 8–12; (February 1970), 1–13; (May 1970), 8–16; (July–August 1970), 7; (December 1970), 9–12; and Livingston Hartley, "Challenges to the Environment: Some International Implications," *Orbis*, 14 (Summer 1970), 490–99.

28. B. P. Uvarov, "Efforts to Control Locusts in Africa Described," *Science*, 130 (December 4, 1959), 1564–65; and Stanley Baron, "No Frontier in the Fight Against the Desert Locust," *Ceres*, 1 (September–October 1968), 32–42.

29. See *Atlas of Distribution of Diseases*. New York: American Geographical Society of New York, 1951–1955, 17 plates; *World Atlas of Epidemic Diseases*. Ernst Rodenwaldt, ed. Hamburg: Falk-verlag, 1952–1961, 3 volumes; and *The Mapping of Disease (MOD) Project: The Geographic Distribution of Infectious Diseases. Final Report, 3 August 1968*. Prepared by Howard C. Hoppes, et al. Washington: Universities Associated for Research and Education in Pathology (UAREP) and Armed Forces Institute of Pathology (AFIP), paged by sections.

30. *Man in a European Society*. Strasbourg: Council of Europe, 1966, 33–35, 58. See also issues of *Forward in Europe*, bulletin in eight languages of the Council of Europe, which has a section on environment.

31. Frantz Wendt, *The Nordic Council and Cooperation in Scandinavia*. Translated from the Danish by Aksel A. Anslev. Copenhagen: Munksgaard, 1959, 247.

32. On the activities of Nordforsk, see *Scandinavian Research Information Notes*. Published in English since 1966 as a semi-annual bulletin (Nordforsk, Grevtureg. 14, Box 5103, S-102 43 Stockholm 5, Sweden). Nordforsk also maintains a Scandinavian Documentation Center, Scandoc, in Washington, D. C.

33. For information on commissions governing **international lakes and rivers**, see: *The International River Basin: Proceedings of a Seminar . . .* , J. D. Chapman, ed. Vancouver, Canada: University of British Columbia,

1963, 53 pp., including Selected Bibliography; Albert Lepawsky, "International Development of River Resources," *International Affairs*, 39 (October 1963), 533–50; Gilbert F. White, "Vietnam: The Fourth Course," *Bulletin of the Atomic Scientists*, 20 (December 1964), 6–10, and "The Mekong Plan," *Scientific American*, 208 (April 1963), 49–59; and *Safeguarding Boundary: Water Quality*. (Place of publication not indicated), International Joint Commission, 1961, 32. A. H. Garretson, C. J. Olmstead, and R. D. Hayton, *The Law of International Drainage Basins*. Dobbs Ferry, New York: Oceana Publications, 1967, 650. Henry C. Hart, *Administrative Aspects of River Valley Development*. New York: Asia Publishing House, 1961, 112. Henri Lorgère, "The Mekong Delta Model," *Science Journal*, 4 (July 1968), 70–75.

An extensive series of studies of multi-purpose river basin development were undertaken and published by the Economic Commission for Asia and the Far East, e.g., *Multi-Purpose River Basin Development, Parts 2-A, B, and C*. New York and Bangkok, 1955–1959. These publications were a part of the United Nations Flood Control Series.

34. Wallace W. Atwood, "International Council of Scientific Unions," *Science*, 128 (December 19, 1958), 1558–61. See also *International Council of Scientific Unions and Certain Associated Unions: Hearings Before the Sub-committee on International Organizations and Movements of the Committee on Foreign Affairs*. Washington: House of Representatives, 89th Congress, 1st Session (June 7, 1965), 40. For a more general treatment, see Joseph Needham, *Science and International Relations: 50th Boyle Lecture at Oxford*. London: Blackwell Scientific Publications, 1949, 30 pp., "The International Unions," 6–12.

35. Note citations for Chapter 2, n. 8; and Sydney Chapman, "The International Geophysical Year," *Advancement of Science*, 12 (March 1957), 259–68.

36. Jean G. Baer, "The International Biological Programme," *Nature and Resources*, 3 (December 1967), 1–3; and C. H. Waddington, "Mobilizing the World's Biologists," Bulletin of the Atomic Scientists, 19 (November 1963), 39–41.

37. See "International Hydrological Decade" in *Nature and Resources*, 1 (June 1965), 6–8 and in subsequent issues; also, M. A. Kohler, "The International Hydrological Decade," *UNO Bulletin*, 12 (October 1963), 193–97; and Raymond L. Nace, "Water Resources: A Global Problem with Local Roots," *Environmental Science and Technology*, 1 (July 1967), 550–60.

38. See, Notes and Citations, Chapter 3, *supra*, n. 30.

39. Several papers from this conference have been published in *Social Information*. The collected papers are not readily available. See *Proceedings of International Symposia on Environmental Disruption: A Challenge to Social Scientists, March 1970, Tokyo*. Shigeto Tsuru, ed., Tokyo: Printed by Asahi Evening News and obtainable from the International Social Science Council in care of UNESCO in Paris, 1970, 348.

40. *The Evolution of International Technology: Science, Technology,*

and American Diplomacy. Prepared for the Subcommittee on National Security Policy and Scientific Developments by Franklin P. Huddle Washington: U. S. House of Representatives, Committee on Foreign Affairs (December 1970), 70. Note especially p. 45 ff. "Suggestions for International Institutions."

41. See listings, in *Yearbook of International Organizations,* 12 1968–69 edition. [The Encyclopedic Dictionary of International Organizations, Their Officers, Their Abbreviations. Brussels: Union of International Associations, 1969, 1220.]

42. For example, see Richard A. Falk, "Toward Equilibrium in the World Order System," *American Journal of International Law,* 64 (September 1970), 217–38; and panel discussion by Robert E. Stein, Donald McRae, and Richard N. Gardner, et al.

43. "Plan for an Institute of Studies for the Better Utilization of the Globe" in *The Population Crisis and the Use of World Resources.* Stuart Mudd, ed., Bloomington, Indiana: Indiana University Press, 1964, p. 384.

44. For a full report of recommendations, see *Blueprint for Peace: Being Proposals of Prominent Americans to the White House Conference on International Cooperation,* Richard N. Gardner, ed. New York: McGraw-Hill, 1966, 404. Several committee reports described international environmental programs and proposals in detail, e.g., Chapters 7, 11–16.

45. *Weekly Compilation of Presidential Documents: Monday, June 10, 1968,* p. 906.

46. For example, *Sea-Bed,* 1968. Indexed and annotated by Harry N. Winton, and includes 250 United Nations documents in six volumes. New York: Arno Press, 1970.

There is a very large literature on international law and organization pertaining to the oceans. Merely to list the principal contributions would require many pages. The following are a few of the works relating most directly to our subject; additional contributions are cited in subsequent notes, where especially pertinent to the text: Victor Basiuk, "Marine Resources Development, Foreign Policy, and A Spectrum of Choice," *Orbis,* 12 (Spring 1968), 39–72; William T. Burke, "Aspects of International Decision-Making Processes in Intergovernmental Fishery Commissions," 43 *Washington Law Review* (October 1967), 115–78; Daniel S. Cheever, "The Role of International Organization in Ocean Development," *International Organization,* 22 (Summer 1968), 629–48; Francis T. Christy, Jr., "Marine Resources and the Freedom of the Seas," *Natural Resources Journal,* 8 (July 1968), 432–33; J. A. Collier, "The Regime of the Seas— Exploitation and Conservation" in *Report of Conference on Law and Science held at Niblett Hall, July 1964, Under the Joint Auspices of the David Davies Memorial Institute of International Studies and the British Institute of Comparative and International Law.* London: David Davies Memorial Institute, 1964, 54–60; R. I. Currie, "Conservation and Exploitation of the Sea" in ibid., 49–53; Robert L. Friedheim, *Understanding The Debate on Ocean Resources.* Denver: University of Denver, The Social

Foundation and Graduate School of International Studies, 1969, 38; L. F. E. Goldie, "The Contents of Davy Jones' Locker—A Proposed Regime for the Seabed and Subsoil," 22 *Rutgers Law Review* (Fall 1967), 1–66; "International Law Problems of Scientific Investigation of the High Seas," translation of U.S.S.R. government document annexed to *Report of the United States Delegation to the Fifth Session of the Intergovernmental Oceanographic Commission.* Paris: UNESCO (October 19–28, 1967), 154–57; L. Larry Leonard, *International Regulation of Fisheries.* Washington: Carnegie Endowment for International Peace, 1944, 201; Myers S. McDougal and William T. Burke, *The Public Order of the Oceans.* New Haven: Yale University Press, 1962, xxv, 1226; Henry Reiff, *The United States and the Treaty Law of the Sea.* Minneapolis: University of Minnesota Press, 1959, 451; Oscar Schachter and Daniel Serwer, "Marine Pollution Problems and Remedies," *American Journal of International Law,* 65 (January 1971), 84–111; M. M. Sibthorp, *Oceanic Pollution—A Survey and Some Suggestions for Control.* London: David Davies Memorial Institute of International Studies, 1969, 53. (Includes: a table of "International Organizations Concerned With Pollution," 27–29, and an appendix, listing "Main National Bodies Concerned With Oceanography," 45–53.); *The Law of the Sea: Offshore Boundaries and Zones,* Lewis M. Alexander, ed. Columbus: The Ohio State University Press, 1967, xv, 321; and *The Sea: International Cooperation in Questions Relating to Oceans. Report of the Secretary-General to the 49th Session of the United Nations Economic and Social Council, Agenda Item 13 (a).* New York: United Nations (12 May 1970), E/4836, 19. For a collection of pertinent documents with commentaries see Norman J. Padelford, *Public Policy and the Use of the Seas,* rev. ed. Cambridge: Massachusetts Institute of Technology, Department of Naval Architecture and Marine Engineering, 1968, x, 361.

47. *United Nations Treaty Series,* 327, No. 4714, "International Convention (with annexes) for the Prevention of Pollution of the Sea by Oil, London, 12 May 1954." New York: United Nations (March 1959).

48. *United Nations Treaty Series,* 450, No. 6465, "Convention on the High Seas, Geneva, 27 April 1958." New York: United Nations (January 1963).

49. "Use of the Ocean," *Science,* 130 (October 9, 1959), editorial.

50. See, K. Langlo, "A New Look in Meteorology: The World Weather Watch," *Impact of Science on Society,* 4 (Winter 1966), 65–92; Robert L. Munteanu, "Global Assault on the Weather," *UNESCO Courier,* 19 (November 1966), 17–23; and *World Weather Watch.* Geneva: World Meteorological Organization, No. 183 TP (1966), 95. WMO has issued a number of general, and planning, reports on the World Weather Watch. See, *List of Available Publications,* January 1971. See also *WMO Bulletin* (October 1968), 172–81.

51. Daniel Behrman, "Will the Indian Ocean Yield Its Secrets?" *UNESCO Courier,* 15 (October 1962), 29–32.

52. *Official Records,* 40th Session (1966), Supplement 2, 3.

53. UN Document A/6695 (18 August 1967). See also note by Clark M. Eichelberger, "The UN and the Sea," *Saturday Review,* 50 (October 14, 1967), 22, 114. See also Persia Campbell, "United Nations Report: The Last Lawless Frontier—The Ocean Floor," *International Development Review,* 10 (June 1968), 36–40.

54. *New Dimensions for the United Nations: Seventeenth Report of the Commission to Study the Organization of Peace, Clark M. Eichelberger, Chairman.* Dobbs Ferry, New York: Oceana Publications (1966), 39–41. Resolution 15 cited in *Interim Report on the United Nations and the Issue of Deep Sea Resources,* together with *Hearings by the Subcommittee on International Organizations and Movements.* U. S. House of Representatives, Committee on Foreign Affairs, 90th Congress, 1st Session (December 7, 1967), 8.

55. *Third World Conference on World Peace Through Law, Geneva, July 9–14, 1967.* Geneva, Switzerland: World Peace Through Law Center, 1969, p. 705.

56. Elizabeth Mann Borgese, *The Ocean Regime: A Suggested Statute for the Peaceful Uses of the High Seas and the Sea-bed Beyond the Limits of National Jurisdiction, A Center Occasional Paper.* Santa Barbara, California: The Center for the Study of Democratic Institutions, October 1968, 40 p. (Contains an extensive list of references.) See also the following publications by Mrs. Borgese: *Pacem in Maribus: A Proposed International Convocation on Frontiers of the Seas to Explore Peaceful Uses of the Oceans and the Ocean Floor to be Conducted on the Island of Malta, 22 June–3 July 1970.* Santa Barbara, California: The Center for the Study of Democratic Institutions, 1970, 31 p.; and "The Prospects for Peace in the Oceans," *Saturday Review,* (September 26, 1970), 15–22. Note also an editorial by Clark M. Eichelberger, "Treading Water," Ibid., 24. (Relating to the UN Committee on the Deep Seabed.)

57. Richard D. Lyons, "Oceanic Experts Favor New Laws: Meeting Here Backs Global Curbs to Guard Resources," *The New York Times,* (December 28, 1967), 20. See also Claiborne Pell with Harold Leland Goodwin, *Challenge of the Seven Seas.* New York: William Morrow, 1966, xi, 306.

58. *National Academy of Sciences—National Research Council, Oceanography, 1966: Achievements and Opportunities.* Washington, D.C.: NAS-NRC Publication No. 1492 (1967), 183.

59. *Uses of the Seas,* Edmund A. Gullion, ed. Englewood Cliffs, New Jersey: Prentice-Hall, 1968, xv, 202.

60. The following publications on the subject have been issued by the Law of the Sea Institute: *Offshore Boundaries and Zones,* 1966 (Available from the Ohio State University Press); *The Future of the Sea Resources,* 1967; *International Rules and Organization for the Sea,* 1968; *National Policy Recommendations,* 1969; and *The United Nations and Ocean Management,* 1970.

61. *The Common Wealth in Ocean Fisheries: Some Problems of*

Growth and Economic Allocation. Baltimore: Johns Hopkins Press for Resources for the Future, 1966, 296. See also James Crutchfield and Giulio Pontecorvo, "Crisis in the Fisheries," *Bulletin of the Atomic Scientists,* 28 (November 1962), 18–20.

62. In addition to specific references cited hereafter, see also issues of the *UNESCO Chronicle* and the *UNESCO Courier.* For early years, see Walter H. C. Laves and Charles A. Thompson, *UNESCO: Purpose, Progress, Prospects.* Bloomington, Indiana: Indiana University Press, 1957, xxiii, 469.

63. Laves and Thompson, ibid., 128–29.

64. The International Council of Museums (ICOM) was established November 16, 1946, at Paris and publishes the *ICOM News.* The International Council of Monuments and Sites (ICOMOS) was established in Warsaw, June 21, 1965 and publishes *Monumentum,* 1967—. See, *Yearbook of International Organizations,* 12 (1968–69), p. 679.

65. *Records of the General Conference, 12th Session—Resolutions, Paris, 1962.* Paris: UNESCO (1963), 139–42, plus annexes. See also *UNESCO Courier,* 18 (January 1965); 20 (January 1967); and 21 (December 1968).

66. "The Race to Save Ab Abu Simbel," *Life,* 61 (December 2, 1966), 32–39. See also, issues of the *UNESCO Courier,* 13 (February 1960); 15 (October 1961); and 17 (December 1964).

67. Following the disastrous floods of November 1966, UNESCO launched a campaign for the preservation and restoration of cultural properties in Florence and Venice . . . , *UNESCO Chronicle,* 13 (June 1967), 259; and (December 1967), 486–87. UNESCO also contributed $30,000 to the Restoration Laboratory for the Florentine State Archives. The Laboratory was established to restore the thousands of documents damaged during the floods. Ibid., 15 (March 1969), 116.

68. On the Biosphere Conference, see: Michael Batisse, "Can We Keep Our Planet Habitable?" *UNESCO Courier,* 22 (January 1969), 4–5; Harold J. Coolidge, "World Biosphere Conference: A Challenge to Mankind," *IUCN Bulletin,* New Series 2 (October–December 1968), 65–66; Raymond Dasmann, "Conservation and Rational Uses of the Environment," *Nature and Resources,* 4 (June 1968), 2–5; *Inter-governmental Conference of Experts on the Scientific Basis for the Natural Use and Conservation of the Resources of the Biosphere, Unesco House, Paris, 4–13 September 1968: Final Report.* Paris: UNESCO (9 January 1969), SC/MD19, 35 p., plus annexes; and "International Conference on the Biosphere," *UNESCO Chronicle,* 14 (November 1968), 414–18.

For the ecological thinking underlying the conference, see the following report (initial draft by Raymond F. Dasmann) submitted by UNESCO and FAO to ECOSOC: *Conservation and Rational Use of the Environment.* New York: United Nations, Economic and Social Council (12 March 1968), E/4458, 131. For a discussion of the report, see the journal *Nature and Resources,* 4 (June 1968), 2–5.

69. *Final Report,* 28–29.

70. See, issues of *Nature and Resources,* 6 (June and December 1970).

Chapter 6 Inventing Transnational Structures

1. See, for example, Charles Yost, *The Insecurity of Nations: International Relations in the Twentieth Century.* New York: Praeger, 1967, x, 276. For a somewhat different view of the insecurity of national-states, see Bruce M. Russett, "The Ecology of Future International Politics," *International Studies Quarterly,* 11 (March 1967), 12–31. For analytic approaches to relations among nations, see Michael Haas, "A Functional Approach to International Organization," *The Journal of Politics,* 27 (August 1965), 498–517; and Edward Miles, "Organizations and International Systems," *International Studies Quarterly,* 12 (June 1968), 196–224.

2. *Official Record of the 39th Session, 1375th Meeting of the United Nations Economic and Social Council held in Geneva, 9 July 1965.* New York: United Nations (30 June–31 July, 1965), 90, para. 42.

3. Kenneth E. Boulding, "The Economics of the Coming Spaceship Earth" in *Environmental Quality in a Growing Economy,* Henry Jarrett, ed. Baltimore: Johns Hopkins Press, 1966, 3–14; R. Buckminster Fuller, *Operating Manual for Spaceship Earth.* Carbondale, Illinois: Southern University Press, 1969, 143; William G. Pollard, *Man on a Spaceship.* Claremont, California: The Claremont Colleges, 1967, 69; and Barbara Ward, *Spaceship Earth.* New York: Columbia University Press, 1966, viii, 152.

4. *United Nations Monthly Chronicle,* 6 (January 1969), 35–41. For the procedural steps leading to Resolution 2398 (23) of the General Assembly, see "Problems of the Human Environment," Chapter 14 of the *Yearbook of the United Nations,* 22 (1968), 473–77.

5. *Problems of the Human Environment: Report of the Secretary-General.* New York: United Nations (26 May 1969), E/4667, 39 p., plus annex summarizing activities and programs of UN bodies relative to the human environment.

6. Draft *Report of the Preparatory Committee for the United Nations Conference on the Human Environment, 1st Session, 10–20 March 1970.* New York: United Nations (20 March 1970), A/Conf. 48/PC/CRP/17, 17 p., plus reports of working groups. For more detailed information on the organization of the Conference, see *Preparatory Committee for the United Nations Conference on the Human Environment, 2nd Session, 8–19 February 1971; Report of the Secretary-General.* (9 December 1970), A/Conf. 48/PC/8, 20 p., plus annexes, and ibid., 3rd Session, 13–24 September 1971; *Report of the Secretary-General* (30 July 1971), A/Conf. 48/PC/11, 67 pp.

7. *Report of the Preparatory Committee for the United Nations*

Conference on the Human Environment, 2nd Session, Geneva, 8–19 February 1971. New York: United Nations (9 December 1970), A/Conf. 48/PC/8, 41 p., plus annexes. (Note especially, 9–15.)

8. *The Human Environment: A Proposed International Declaration.* (Printed in five languages.) Stockholm: Svenska FN-förbundet, 1970, 16.

9. "To Prevent a World Wasteland: A Proposal," *Foreign Affairs*, 47 (April 1970), 409.

10. Ibid.

11. "The Human Environment and World Order," *UN Monthly Chronicle*, 7 (June 1970), 74.

12. "For Global Initiative," *Saturday Review*, 53 (July 4, 1970), 41, 44.

13. *The Endangered Planet: Prospects and Proposals for Human Survival.* New York: Random House, 1971, 495.

14. "We Need A New Global Agency to Confront the Environment Crisis," *War/Peace Report*, 10 (May 1970), 3–5.

15. "A World View of the Environment." *Remarks Before the Second Annual International Geoscience Symposium, Washington, D.C., 16 April 1970.* Reprinted in the *Congressional Record: Proceedings and Debates of the 91st Congress, 2nd Session*, 116 (April 23, 1970), S6068–S6069.

16. *Man's Impact on the Global Environment: Report of the Study of Critical Environmental Problems (SCEP)—Assessments and Recommendations for Action.* Cambridge: MIT Press, 1971, 247. See also "The Williamstown Study of Critical Environmental Problems," *Bulletin of the Atomic Scientists*, 26 (October 1970), 24–30.

17. *Report of the President's Commission for the Observance of the Twenty-fifth Anniversary of the United Nations [Ambassador Henry Cabot Lodge, Chairman].* Washington: U. S. Government Printing Office (April 26, 1971), 67.

18. The following discussion has been largely based upon an unpublished paper prepared by Dr. Philip C. Jessup, eminent scholar in international law and former member of the International Court of Justice. The arguments and conclusions, however, are not necessarily those of Dr. Jessup.

19. "Senate Resolution 399—Resolution Submitted to Create a World Environment Institute," *Congressional Record*, 116 (April 27, 1970), S6219–S6221.

20. *Report of the Ad Hoc Committee of ICSU on Problems of the Human Environment.* (1969, undated), 30. Also printed in the *Congressional Record*, CXVI (June 3, 1970), S8309–S8315. More specialized is the proposal of Dr. John Higginson, Director of the WHO International Agency for Research on Cancer in Lyon, France, for an international research laboratory for the study of environmental biology. See "International Research: Its Role in Environmental Biology," *Science*, 170 (November 20, 1970), 935–39.

21. The concept of "monitoring" is not simple, and simple definitions beyond the very abstract may be open to many qualifications. For a discussion of the monitoring concept and its applications, see "Report of Work Group on Monitoring" in *Man's Impact on the Global Environment: Report of the Study of Critical Environmental Problems*, 168–222.

22. *National and International Environmental Monitoring: A Directory.* Cambridge: Smithsonian Institution, Center for Short-Lived Phenomena, October, 1970, 292.

23. For example, the General Assembly of the United Nations requested a comprehensive inter-agency survey of oceanic pollution. The recommendations from the resulting "Group of Experts on Scientific Aspects of Marine Pollution (GESAMP)" were expected to identify criteria for monitoring changes harmful to: (1) health, (2) food resources, (3) uses of the oceans, and (4) amenities.

24. *Report of the Ad Hoc Committee on Global Monitoring to SCIBP: Fourth General Assembly, Rome, 30 September–2 October 1970, Item 7.31.*

25. These reports were: *The Opinion of the U.S.S.R. Committee of Biologists on the Global Network of Baseline Biological Stations by the Soviet Committee of Biologists: Drs. N. N. Varontsov, A. A. Molchanov, N. N. Smirnov, A. N. Tyurynkanov, S. S. Schvartz* (July 1969), 7; *The Global Network for Environmental Monitoring (GNEM): A Report Submitted by the USEC/IBP Task Force on GNEM to the U. S. Executive Committee for Participation in the International Biological Program* (July 1970), 82; and *Global Environmental Monitoring System: Technical Report by B. Lundholm and S. Svensson—From Sweden to the IBP Committee on Global Monitoring.* Stockholm: Swedish Natural Science Research Council (1970), 64.

26. *Man's Impact on the Global Environment*, 220.

27. *Global Ocean Research: Report of Joint Working Party of the Advisory Committee on Marine Research, the Scientific Committee on Oceanic Research, and the World Meteorological Organization.* LaJolla, California: ICSU Scientific Committee on Oceanic Research (June 1, 1969), 47. See also Henry Stommel "Future Prospects for Physical Oceanography," *Science*, 168 (June 26, 1970), 1535–36. The subsequent study of marine pollution by (GESAMP) has been cited in n. 23, *supra*.

28. In *Report of Panel Five. Oceanography of Useful Applications of Earth-Oriented Satellites: Summer Study on Space Applications—Division of Engineering of the National Research Council for the National Aeronautics and Space Administration.* Washington: National Academy of Sciences, National Academy of Engineering (1969), 4.

29. For general accounts of the **World Weather Watch**, see the following publications: E. K. Federov, "World Weather Watch," *WMO Bulletin*, 15 (October 1966), 194–98; Nancy Grichow, "Weather Services: Working Toward World-Wide Forecasts," *Science*, 168 (April 1970), 352–53; and items cited under Chapter 5, n. 50. For other aspects of WMO

monitoring and research, see *A Brief Survey of the Activities of the World Meteorological Organization Relating to Human Environment.* Geneva: World Meteorological Organization (1970), 22.

30. "Future Prospects for Physical Oceanography," 1536.

31. Ibid.

32. For an account of IMCO's organization and its activities relating to oil pollution see R. I. Price, "International Activity Regarding Shipboard Oil Pollution Control," *Proceedings of Joint Conference on Prevention and Control of Oil Spills,* June 15–17, 1971, Washington, D.C.; American Oil Institute, 1971, 29–33.

33. Report of the Preparatory Committee, (26 February 1971), A/Conf. 48/PC/9, 81.

34. See Chapter 5, n. 56.

35. *First World Conference on National Parks, Seattle, Washington, 30 June–7 July 1961,* Alexander B. Adams, ed. Washington, D. C.: U. S. Department of Interior, National Park Service (1964), 471.

36. *National Citizens Commission: Report of the Committee on Natural Resources, Conservation, and Development.* New York: United Nations Associations of the United States of America (1966), 24. Quoted passages from 16 and 18. Reprinted also in *Blueprint for Peace: Bring the Proposals of Prominent Americans to the White House Conference on International Cooperation,* Richard N. Gardner, ed. New York: McGraw-Hill, 1966, vi, 404.

37. Text released by the Conservation Foundation.

38. "The President's 1971 Environmental Program . . . Message to the Congress, February 8, 1971," *Weekly Compilation of Presidential Documents,* 7 (February 15, 1971), 187–204.

39. "An Ecological Approach to International Development: Problems of Policy and Administration" in *The Careless Technology: Ecology and International Development,* John P. Milton and M. Taghi Farvar, eds. New York: Natural History Press, 1971.

40. *Public Papers of the Presidents of the United States: John F. Kennedy, 1963, 1 January–22 November 1963.* Washington: U. S. Government Printing Office (1964), p. 696.

Chapter 7 Strengthening National Capabilities

1. James McEvoy, III, *The American Public's Concern With The Environment: A Study of Public Opinion.* Davis: University of California, Institute of Governmental Affairs, 1970, 29.

2. Reported by Professor di Castri at a *Joint Senate–House Colloquium on International Environmental Science, The Old Supreme Court Chamber,* Washington, D.C., May 25–26, 1971. See *International Environmental Science Proceedings of the Joint Colloquium before the Committee on*

Commerce, US Senate, and the Committee on Science and Astronautics, House of Representatives, 92nd Congress, first Session. Serial no. 92–13, pp. 31–43.

3. Barabara Ward, "The Cities That Came Too Soon," *The Economist*, 233, No. 6589 (December 6, 1969), 56–62 and "The City May Be as Lethal as the Bomb," *The New York Times Magazine* (April 19, 1964), 22–23.

4. Leonard M. Board, "Problems and Priorities in Combating Air, Water, and Soil Pollution in Developing Countries," *Archives of Environmental Health*, 18 (February 1969), 260–64. For a commentary on attitudes in the developing countries toward pollution, see interviews with Babacar Diop, Director-General, Senegalese National Enterprise for Fisheries Equipment, *Ceres*, 3 (May–June 1970), 38–39; and A. W. H. Needler, Deputy-Minister of Fisheries and Forestry in Canada, Ibid., 34–35.

5. United Nations, Economic Commission for Europe. *Ad Hoc Meeting of Governmental Officials on the Prevention of Air Pollution, 10–14 February 1969: Report of the First Session. . . .* Geneva: ECE [E/ECE/736;E/ECE/Air Poll/2], 20 February 1969, 6 p. plus annexes, and United Nations, Economic Commission for Europe, *Body on Water Resources and Water Pollution Control Problems: Report of the First Session of the Body.* Geneva: ECE [E/ECE/Water/5], 24 September 1968, 7 p. plus annexes.

6. See *The Careless Technology: Ecology and International Development*, John P. Milton and M. Taghi Farvar, eds. New York: Natural History Press, 1971.

For abbreviated accounts of the **cases of ecological aspects of development,** see: "The Unforeseen International Ecologic Boomerang," *Natural History*, 78 (February 1969), Special Supplement, 43–72; "International Development Can Destroy the Environment," *International Development Review*, 11 (March 1969), 22–23; Luther J. Carter, "Development in the Poor Nations: How To Avoid Fouling the Nest," *Science*, 163 (March 7, 1969), 1046–48; Harmon Henkin, "Side Effects: Report of a Conference on Ecological Aspects of International Development," *Environment*, 11 (January–February 1969), 1–8; Julian McCaull, "Conference on the Ecological Aspects of International Development," *Nature and Resources*, 5 (June 1969), 5–12 and "Case Studies in Ecological Results of Development Activities," *Development Digest*, 9 (January 1971), 25–32; and John P. Milton and Kathleen McNamara, "Conference on the Ecological Aspects of International Development, held at Airlie House, Warrenton, Virginia, 8–11 December 1969," *Biological Conservation*, 2 (July 1970), 311–13.

7. "Conservationists Fear Development of Proposed Jetport in Dade and Collier Counties," The New York Times, (March 16, 1969), Sec. 5, 16; and "Dr. L. Leopold Says Jetport Would 'Inexorably Destroy South Florida's Ecosystem,'" *The New York Times* (September 18, 1969), 93.

8. William Litzinger, Albert Mravinac, and John Wagle, "The Manned Spacecraft Center in Houston: The Practice of Matrix Manage-

ment," *International Review of Administrative Sciences,* 36 (No. 1, 1970), 1–8.

9. United Kingdom. *The Reorganization of Central Government, October 1970 (Cmnd. 4506).* London: Her Majesty's Stationery Office (1970), 16.

10. *France.* New York: Ambassade de France, Service de Presse et d' Information, March 1971, 10.

11. "The President's Message to the Congress . . . March 29, 1971," *Weekly Compilation of Presidential Documents,* 7 (March 25, 1971), 545–60.

12. For an application of this principle at the project level, see Arthur T. Masker, "Administrative Experimentation as a Way of Life for Development Projects," *International Development Review,* 9 (June 1967), 38–41.

13. Chapter 5, n. 14. See also J. A. Berberet, *The Measurement of the Scientific and Technological Capabilities of Nations.* Santa Barbara, California: TEMPO Independent Research Program, General Electric Company, August, 1968, 57.

14. Claire Nader and A. B. Zahlan, *Science and Technology in Developing Countries: Proceedings of an International Conference, held at the American University of Beirut:* Cambridge, England: Cambridge University Press, 1969, xx, 588.

15. Walter Sullivan, "8 East–West Nations to Set Up Center on Technology Problems," New York Times (October 14, 1971), 1. [Reports establishment of two centers in Europe, the International Institute of Applied Systems Analysis, and the International Institute for the Management of Technology.]

16. Chapter 3, n. 23.

17. Chapter 5, n. 28.

18. Richard A. Johnson, Fremont E. Kast, and James E. Rosenzweig, *The Theory and Management of Systems,* 2nd edition. New York: McGraw-Hill, 1967, xiv, 513; and David I. Cleland and William R. King, *Systems Analysis and Project Management.* New York: McGraw-Hill, 1968, xvi, 315.

19. American Association for the Advancement of Science, Committee on Science in the Promotion of Human Welfare. "The Integrity of Science," *American Scientist,* 53 (June 1965), 174–98.

20. United States Council on Environmental Quality. *Environmental Quality: The First Annual Report of the Council. . . .* Washington: U. S. Government Printing Office, 1970, 326.

21. United Nations. *Public Administration in the Second United Nations Development Decade: Report of the Second Meeting of Experts.* New York: United Nations Department of Economic and Social Affairs, Public Administration Division, [ST/TAO/M/57], 1971, v, 163.

22. Wu Ci-Yuen, "Operational Research for Developing Countries," *International Review of Administrative Sciences,* 36 (No. 2, 1970), 99–108.

23. J. K. Gerdel, "The Skill File," *Personnel Journal*, 26 (October 1947), 150–56.

24. Letter to Lynton K. Caldwell, May 6, 1953.

25. Bertram M. Gross, "The New Systems Budgeting," *Public Administration Review*, 29 (March–April 1969), 113–37; and John Haldi, "Applications of Program Budgeting to Environmental Problems" in *Social Science and the Environment: Conference on the Present and Potential Contribution of the Social Sciences to Research and Policy Formulation in the Quality of the Physical Environment*, Morris E. Garnsey and James R. Hibbs, eds. Boulder: University of Colorado Press, 1967, 195–217. See also *The Analysis and Evaluation of Public Expenditures: The PPB System, A Compendium of Papers. . .* , Vols. 1–3. U. S. Congress, Subcommittee on Economy in Government of the Joint Economic Committee, 91st Congress, 1st Session (1969), 1241.

26. United Kingdom. *Protection of the Environment, The Fight Against Pollution, Presented to the Parliament by the Secretary of State for Local Government and Regional Planning*, The Secretary of State for Scotland, and the Secretary of State for Wales by Command of Her Majesty, May 1970 (Cmnd. 4373). London: Her Majesty's Stationery Office, 1970, 29.

Chapter 8 Safeguarding the Biosphere

1. *The Technological Society*. Translated from the French by John Wilkinson with an introduction by Robert K. Merton. New York: Alfred A. Knopf, 1964, xxxvi, 449.

2. *Between Two Ages: America's Role in the Technetronic Era*. New York: Viking Press, 1970, 330.

3. Carbondale: Southern Illinois University Press, 1969, 143. Reprinted by Simon and Schuster.

4. See Laura Thompson, *Toward A Science of Mankind*. New York: McGraw-Hill, 1961, 276; Ernest Van den Haag, "Man as an Object of Science," *Science*, 129 (January 30, 1959), 243–47; and *Toward A Unified Theory of Human Behavior*, Roy R. Grinker, ed. New York: Basic Books, 1959, 375.

5. Problems of the organization of knowledge are lucidly discussed by Kenneth E. Boulding in *The Image: Knowledge in Life and Society*. Ann Arbor: University of Michigan Press, 1956, 175 and *The Meaning of the Twentieth Century*. New York: Harper & Row, 1964, 199 (especially, 54–74.

6. There is a large literature of criticism. Especially relevant to our discussion is John Rader Platt, *The Step to Man*. New York: John Wiley, 1966, 216. For more systematic examination of the state of the social and behavioral sciences, see President's Science Advisory Committee,

"Strengthening the Behavioral Sciences," *Science*, 136 (April 10, 1962), 233–41, and especially *The Behavioral and Social Sciences: Outlook and Needs. A Report by the Behavioral and Social Sciences Survey Committee Under the Auspices of the Committee on Science and Public Policy, National Academy of Science* [and] *the Committee on Problems and Policy, Social Science Research Council*, Englewood Cliffs, New Jersey: Prentice-Hall, 1969, xv, 320.

7. *On Aggression.* Translated from the German by Marjorie Kerr Wilson. New York: Harcourt, Brace & World, 1966, 306 (especially p. 298).

8. Note for example, Amitai Etzioni, "The Wrong Top Priority," *Science*, 148 (May 22, 1970), 921.

9. Note the relationship between historical experience, perception, and political attitudes analyzed by Jean Labasse in *L'organisation de l'espace: éléments de géographie volontaire.* Paris: Hermann, 1966, 604 (especially Chapters 10–11).

10. In *Diversity and Stability in Ecological Systems—Brookhaven Symposia in Biology: No. 22.* Upton, New York: Brookhaven National Laboratory, 1969, 151–58.

11. Resolution of the Economic and Social Council 1484 (48), *Third World Population Conference.* Official Records, 25th Session of the General Assembly, Supplement No. 3 (A/8003). New York: United Nations (1970), 43.

12. Paul R. Ehrlich and Anne H. Ehrlich, *Population, Resources, Environment: Issues in Human Ecology.* San Francisco: W. H. Freeman, 1970, 383 (Note especially Chapter 8, *Optimum Population and Human Biology.*) See also Paul R. Ehrlich, *The Population Bomb.* New York: Ballantine Books, 1968, 223.

13. William Paddock and Paul Paddock, *Famine, 1975!* Boston: Little Brown, 1967, 276.

14. Note discussions in Chapters 5 and 6 on international declarations of environmental rights.

15. John R. Platt, whose work has been cited on several points previously in this chapter, has conceptualized this process in *Hierarchal Restructuring: Sudden Jumps to New Levels of Organization Occur in Personality Changes and Social Revolutions Like the Present*, Communication 269. Ann Arbor: University of Michigan Mental Health Research Institute, 27 pp., multilith. Also printed in *Bulletin of the Atomic Scientists*, 26 (November 1970), 2–4 and *General Systems*, 15 (1970), 49–54.

16. *A Theology of the Earth. A Lecture Delivered on 2 October 1969 at the Smithsonian Institution in Washington, D.C.* . . . Washington: U.S. Government Printing Office, 1969, 19.

17. Arthur O. Lovejoy, *The Great Chain of Being: A Study in the History of an Idea.* Cambridge: Harvard University Press, 1936, 382.

18. Max Nicholson, *The Environmental Revolution: A Guide for the New Masters of the World.* New York: McGraw-Hill, 1970, 366.

APPENDIX A
INTERNATIONAL ORGANIZATIONS
AND PROGRAMS CONCERNED
WITH ENVIRONMENTAL ISSUES
A REPRESENTATIVE LISTING

AGENCIES	ABBREVIATIONS

United Nations System

General Assembly	
Secretariat	
International Court of Justice (World Court)	
Economic and Social Council	ECOSOC
United Nations Development Program	UNDP
United Nations Industrial Development Organization	UNIDO
United Nations Institute for Training and Research	UNITAR
United Nations Conference on Trade and Development	UNCTAD
United Nations Fund for Population Activities	UNFPA
Inter-Agency Consultative Board of the U.N. Development Programme	IACB
United Nations Scientific Committee on Effects of Radiation	UNSCEAR
Advisory Committee on Application of Science and Technology to Development	ACASTD
Administrative Committee on Coordination	ACC

U.N. Regional Commissions

Economic Commission for Europe	ECE
Economic Commission for Latin America	ECLA
Economic Commission for Asia and the Far East	ECAFE
Economic Commission for Africa	ECA

Specialized and Affiliated Agencies

United Nations Educational, Scientific and Cultural Organization	UNESCO
International Labor Organization	ILO
Food and Agriculture Organization	FAO
World Health Organization	WHO
International Civil Aviation Organization	ICAO
International Telecommunications Union	ITU
World Meteorological Organization	WMO
International Maritime Consultative Organization	IMCO
International Oceanographic Commission (UNESCO)	ICO
International Atomic Energy Agency (Affiliated)	IAEA
General Agreement on Tariffs and Trade	GATT

International Funding Agencies

International Bank for Reconstruction and Development (World Bank)	IBRD
International Development Association	IDA
International Finance Corporation	IFC
Inter-American Development Bank	IDB
Asian Development Bank	ASDB
African Development Bank	ADB

Non-U.N. Intergovernmental

Organization for Economic Cooperation and Development	OECD
North Atlantic Treaty Organization	NATO
Committee on Challenges to Modern Society	CCMS
European Communities	EC
Council of Europe	CE
Organization of American States	OAS
Organization of African Unity	OAU
Council for Mutual Economic Assistance	CMEA
International Council for the Exploration of the Sea	ICES

Non-Governmental Scientific

International Union of Scientific Unions	ICSU
Scientific Committees:	
on Oceanic Research	SCOR
on Antarctic Research	SCAR
on Space Research	COSPAR
on Problems of the Environment	SCOPE

Special Committee on the International
Biological Program   SCIBP
International Center for the Environment
(projected)   ICE
International Social Science Council   ISSC
International Union for Conservation of Nature
and Natural Resources   IUCN
International Association for Ecology   INTECOL
The Institute of Ecology   TIE

Non-Governmental Quasi-Scientific and Professional

Council for International Organization of Medical
Sciences   CIOMS
International Union of Forest Research Organizations   IUFRO
International Federation of Landscape Architects   IFLA
International Council of Museums   ICOM
International Council of Monuments and Sites   ICOMOS
World Peace through Law   WPL
International Council for Environmental Law   ICEL
International Union of Local Authorities   IULA
International Federation for Housing and Planning   IFHP
World Wildlife Fund   WWF

International Scientific Programs

Global Atmospheric Research Program   GARP
International Decade of Ocean Exploration   IDOE
International Hydrological Decade   IHD
International Biological Program   IBP
Group of Experts on Problems of Marine Pollution   GESAMP
Study of Critical Environmental Problems   SCEP
Study of Man's Impact on Climate   SMIC
World Weather Watch   WWW
Integrated Global Ocean Station System   IGOSS
Man and the Biosphere Program (UNESCO)   MAB

APPENDIX B
INTERNATIONAL CONFERENCES, AGREEMENTS, OF PARTICULAR SIGNIFICANCE FOR PROTECTION OF THE BIOSPHERE 1945-1972

1931 International Council of Scientific Unions (ICSU), established in 1919 as the International Research Council, reconstituted under new name and organization.

1945 Establishment of the United Nations Organization, UNESCO, and FAO.

1946 Establishment of the World Health Organization.

1948 Establishment of the International Union for the Conservation of Nature and Natural Resources following an international conference sponsored by UNESCO and the Government of France.

1949 United Nations Scientific Conference on the Conservation and Utilization of Resources. Lake Success, New York, 17 August–6 September.

1951 International Meteorological Organization, established in 1878, reconstituted as the World Meteorological Organization.

1954 World Conference on Population. Sponsored by the Economic and Social Affairs Department of the United Nations. Rome, 31 August–10 September.

1955 International Technical Conference on the Conservation of the Living Resources of the Sea. Rome, 18 April–16 May.

1955　United Nations Scientific Committee on Effects of Atomic Radiation established.

1956　Establishment of the International Atomic Energy Agency.

1957–1958　International Geophysical Year.

1958　Adoption of the Geneva Convention (Treaty) on Fishing and Conservation of the Living Resources of the High Seas.

1959　Antarctic Treaty signed December 1 establishing the South Polar region as an international scientific reserve.

1959　Intergovernmental Maritime Consultative Organization activated after delay of ten years.

1959–1966　International Indian Ocean Expedition.

1961　United Nations Conference on New Sources of Energy. Rome, 21–31 August.

1963　Conference on Application of Science and Technology for the Benefit of Less Developed Areas. Geneva, 4–20 February.

1963　International Treaty Banning Nuclear Weapons Tests in the Atmosphere, in Outer Space and Under Water promulgated.

1964　Inauguration of the International Biological Program.

1966　International Treaty on the Peaceful Use of Outer Space promulgated.

1967　Implementation of World Weather Watch, under sponsorship of the World Meteorological Organization.

1968　Treaty for the Protection of African Wildlife. Sponsored by the Organization for African Unity signed.

1968　UNESCO Intergovernmental Conference of Experts on the Scientific Basis for Rational Use and Conservation of the Resources of the Biosphere. Paris, 4–13 September.

1968　United Nations General Assembly Resolution 2398 (December 3) on the Problems of Human Environment.

1970　European Conservation Year. Sponsored by the Council of Europe.

1970　FAO Technical Conference on Marine Pollution and Its Effects on Living Resources and Fishing. Rome, 9–18 December.

1970　Scientific Committee on Problems of the Environment

(SCOPE) established by the International Council of Scientific Unions.

1971 Symposium on Problems Relating to Environment, Economic Commission for Europe. Prague, 2–5 May.

1971 International Conference on Environmental Future. Helsinki and Jyväskylä, Finland, 27 June–3 July.

1972 United Nations Conference on the Human Environment. Stockholm, 5–16 June.

INDEX

academies of science, 109, 129
Ad Hoc Committee of ICSU, 161, 169–73
"ad hocracy," 203
administration of environmental protection, 191–224
African Conventions on conservation, 60–61
agencies dealing with the environment: multipurpose international, 205–7; nongovernmental international, 206–8; proposed Agency for Prevention and Settlement of International Disputes, 166–69; regional, 207–8; within United Nations, 120, 122
Alaskan Fur Seal Convention, 69
Alfonso X of Spain, 34
Amber Data Book, 77, 179
Antarctic Treaty, 36, 135
anti-ecologists, 27–28
Apollo program, 200
Appleby, Paul H., 219
arbitration, international, 167–68
Ardrey, Robert, 39
Arid Zone Research, 141
Aristotle, 33
Aron, Raymond, 89, 113
assessment of environmental action, 213–24
Aswan High Dam, 92–93, 142
Auger, Pierre, 133
Austruy, Jacques, 112, 113

awareness of environmental issues, 146–48, 224

Bacon, Sir Francis, 108
Baker, Howard H. Jr., 152
Bartram, John, 57
Bartram, William B., 57–58
Behaim, Martin, 33
behavior. *See* human behavior
behavioral sciences, 231–35
Berdyaev, Nicholas, 6, 113
biological evolution, human, 13–16
biological monitoring, 179
BioPolitics, 14–15
Biosfera, 45
biosphere: concept of, 4; development of term, 45; discovery of, 31–52; evolution towards noösphere, 46–47; and interdependencies of living world, 37–40; international conferences on protection of, 282–84; international protection of, 107–44; and limitations of the living world, 40–44; public policy towards, 44–50; safeguarding by transforming human behavior, 225–41; underestimating danger to, 80–106; Vernadsky's concept of, 45–47; *see also* environment
Biosphere Conference of 1968, 7, 48–50, 78, 143–44
Biosphere Conference of 1972 in

wildlife: international protection of, 58–61, 78; monitoring of, 178
Wittfogel, Karl A., 23
WMO, 122, 136, 178, 180, 181
Woodwell, George, 52
Working Party on Environmental Problems . . . , 192
World Conferences on National Parks, 185
World Environment Fund, 184–88
World Geophysical Organization, 180–83, 278
World Health Organization, 112, 122, 124, 137, 174
World Heritage, 183, 184–88

World Meteorological Organization, 122, 136, 178, 180, 181
World Peace Through Law, 138–39, 153
World Population Year, 236
world structure. *See* transnational structure
World Wildlife Fund, 78
World Weather Watch, 136, 174, 176, 178
Wright, Edward, 34
WWF, 78
WWW, 136, 174, 176, 178

Yellowstone National Park, 185